ORAL
COMMUNICATION

FOURTH EDITION

ORAL COMMUNICATION

A Short Course in Speaking

DONALD C. BRYANT
University of Iowa

KARL R. WALLACE

PRENTICE-HALL, INC., Englewood Cliffs, New Jersey

Library of Congress Cataloging in Publication Data

Bryant, Donald Cross. (date)
   Oral communication.

   Includes bibliographies and index.
   1. Public speaking. I. Wallace, Karl Richards. (date),
joint author. II. Title.
PN4121.B776   1976   808.5'1   75-33792
ISBN 0-13-638429-3

© 1976, 1962, 1954, 1948 by Prentice-Hall, Inc., Englewood Cliffs, New Jersey

Printed in the United States of America

10 9 8 7 6 5 4 3 2

PRENTICE-HALL INTERNATIONAL, INC., London
PRENTICE-HALL OF AUSTRALIA, PTY. LTD., Sydney
PRENTICE-HALL OF CANADA, LTD., Toronto
PRENTICE-HALL OF INDIA PRIVATE LIMITED, New Delhi
PRENTICE-HALL OF JAPAN, INC., Tokyo
PRENTICE-HALL OF SOUTHEAST ASIA (PTE.) LTD., Singapore

Contents

Preface

Like the three preceding editions, this fourth edition of *Oral Communication* is intended primarily as a textbook for those courses in public speaking which require ample coverage of essential precept and operational instruction but do not permit time for extended study of philosophy, theory, and critical principles. Like its predecessors, therefore, it is an abridged and adapted counterpart of the corresonding revised edition (the fifth) of our *Fundamentals of Public Speaking* (1976). We have retained, essentially, our earlier plan of presenting extended treatment of such essential operations as getting started properly, finding and selecting subjects and materials, analyzing audiences, developing and organizing ideas, fostering good style and delivery. Of the two major purposes for speaking—the informative and the persuasive—we give most attention to the informative as involving almost all the basic principles and skills of speech-making and as being fundamental to sound persuasion. Our chapter (8) on Materials and Methods of Persuasion, however, provides a sound foundation for further study and practice of that kind of speaking. We reduce to a minimum, though we do not eliminate, treatment of the theoretical background in rhetoric and the science and psychology of communication and the philosophical discussion of speech in the social and political fabric, which figure substantially in our *Fundamentals of Public Speaking*. Thus we offer a relatively brief book—a "short course in speaking"—but without the expository inadequacies of handbook or manual.

Our plan, we think, follows progressively the needs of students in a beginning college course in public speaking, where prepared speeches are required almost from the outset, before there has been time for much study of the textbook. Therefore, after introducing the study and its implications briefly, we present and explain some mimimum operating principles and methods for fashioning short speeches. Hence the student may begin his systematic preparation and presentation of speeches on bases which will be extended and deepened later but will not have to be unlearned or essentially modified. We then proceed to extended treatment of the chief investigative and rhetorical undertakings which are basic to all sound public speaking.

In the years since the previous editions of our two books, we are aware of no change in our underlying view of public address and in our pedagogical stance, though we accept the likelihood that they have matured and have become more sophisticated. Our purpose is still to provide college students and other mature learners with a secure foundation and sound principles for the study and practice of public speaking. More explicitly, no doubt, than in our former editions, we ground our instruction in the idea of responsibility in the speaker—responsibility to his society, to his public—for the ends he pursues and the means he employs toward those ends. Hence we give special treatment to the ethical problems of communication. We assume that young adults in collegiate settings are capable of improving their speaking and writing through instruction and guided practice. Modern society, we may well agree, does not necessarily need more public speaking, but it certainly needs and deserves better public address and discussion from its most able and responsible members.

Our pedagogical purpose has led us to write primarily for the student. We have attempted, wherever possible, to supply how-to-do-it directions. Nevertheless, we have steadily endeavored to foster some understanding of the principles necessary to intelligent practice. Even the novice should *understand* as well as *do.*

We assume that the student who makes the most profitable use of this book, or of any textbook in public speaking, is a learner and will read to understand and to apply its teachings. Some of those teachings, perhaps many of them, will seem obvious, even commonplace—what every sensible person knows. We know, however—what the student will realize upon consideration—that many such principles are too often accepted in theory but ignored in practice. They seem like the essence of common sense; but as with common sense in other areas, they seldom work unless the learner tries consciously to make them work.

Some of the methods and procedures we present may seem at times unduly thorough for the modest speeches being undertaken. The student must realize, however, that he should be gaining knowledge and developing reliable methods and habits of work and thought which will be adequate to large occasions as well as small, to difficult problems as well as easy ones. In the establishing of habits of orderly procedure—for example, in organizing ideas into a workable pattern for easy recall during delivery—the student must go through the whole process, no matter how obvious much of it may seem, and the instructor who would serve him best should see that he does. He must be required to think in detail about the way to go about thinking. We intend *Oral Communication* as a fitting textbook for an introductory course in speechmaking—speechmaking as a part of the essentially humanistic tradition of the liberal arts. The student or teacher who is inclined to pursue that tradition further or to deepen instruction in a more advanced course may find profit in turning to our longer book, *Fundamentals of Public Speaking*, and to its most direct lineal ancestor, James A. Winans' *Public Speaking* (1915, 1923).

In the suggestions for further reading at the end of most of our chapters, we take into account some of the other important points of view and textbooks in the field. To them we refer students and teachers who seek varied approaches to teaching and learning in public communication and in specialized forms and vehicles of oral performance, such as voice and pronunciation, oral interpretation of literature and reading aloud, speech science, interpersonal communication, and group discussion. Our chapter on group discussion is intended to provide only a brief introduction to the process of small-group problem solving, which is closely related in procedures and techniques to public address and debate.

Improvement in speaking, we know, may be stimulated and in a sense guided by the study of good speeches. We include again, therefore, in the Appendix, a brief selection of examples for study and analysis. Some, such as Bruce Barton's *Which Knew Not Joseph* and President John F. Kennedy's *Inaugural Address*, we retain from the previous edition; and others, such as Dora Damrin's *The James Scholars and the University*, are new to this edition.

To the many students and colleagues over the years who have assisted, advised, and cautioned us we are grateful—and to the editorial staffs of Appleton-Century-Crofts and Prentice-Hall.

D.C.B.
K.R.W.

ORAL
COMMUNICATION

CHAPTER 1

The Study of Public Speaking

Speechmaking as a collegiate study participates in the tradition of the liberal and practical arts. Founded in theoretical principles derived and inferred from practice and experience over many centuries to the present time, public speaking exhibits characteristics of both art and technology. Like technology it is improvable—it is learnable—through study and understanding; like art, which is in a measure also improvable through study and understanding, public speaking depends for its best achievements on critically guided practice. Even as early as the fifth century B.C. the ancient Greeks found public speaking both so essential to the working of their society and so obviously teachable to their young citizens that they began organizing instruction in its principles, which they called *rhetoric,* into courses and textbooks.

Thus the study of speechmaking is perhaps the oldest and most continuous systematic academic study we know of. Unless generation after generation of people has been grossly deceived, therefore, history provides little basis for the naive (though to some people comparatively comforting) notion that skill in speechmaking is unteachable and unlearnable in the strict sense; that it is a "gift"—like grace we either have it or we don't—or that it is a "knack," as Socrates ironically observed, which we catch onto from others without knowing how. It will be well, therefore, if the student of public speaking who would get the most profit from his time and effort cast aside that hoary misconception. He should reject also that other false notion that somehow, somewhere there is a "secret" to successful speaking which someone can let him in on (perhaps for a fancy price); or that skill in speaking is presumptive evidence of dishonesty, that there is some special virtue in a kind of bumbling public inarticulateness. Let the student accept the assumption—for otherwise he would not have been advised to study public speaking as part of the regular college program—that he is to be involved with principle and practice, with study and performance, with knowledge and experience. His business will be to understand speechmaking as art and technology and as one of the most characteristic and persistent activities of man in society, and to enhance his ability to speak effectively and responsibly.

Probably it is that sense of public responsibility in speaking, responsibility for the substance and the normal consequences of the message, which makes the difference between the commendable speaker and the facile fraud whom we all deplore. Of course, over the centuries the teachers of public speaking and their textbooks' doctrines have varied in kind and quality. The theory and the practice have been good and they have been bad, socially valuable and socially questionable—as have the theory and practice of politics, medicine, morals, and poetry. In ancient Athens, however, the philosopher-scholar Aristotle established the principle, still valid in today's complex and sophisticated world, that good public discourse is not founded in glibness of tongue and emotional appeals to ignorance, of which his contemporary, Plato, accused speakers of the time. It was and is founded on knowledge, human sympathy, and sound thinking vitalized by imagination.

Some people today, in both the academic and the larger society, seem to think of speechmaking, of "public speaking," as something from a former time, as something irrelevant in our electronic age, our "global village." One is excusably puzzled by such an idea, considering the barrage of public talk for which we are the perpetual audience. True enough, the terms *oratory* and *oration*, with which public speaking is often associated, have dropped from our working vocabularies except for the names of certain traditional events in scholastic contests, or for the performances of celebrated ancients such as Cicero, Edmund Burke, Gladstone, and William Jennings Bryan. Oral discourse with "public" dimensions, however, spoken by individual men and women in groups and to groups of their fellows, is surely as plentiful and as various in function, form, and quality as it ever was, though the idiom and the trappings of "formality" in speaking are forever changing.

Students of public address should not be overly concerned with fine distinctions between public utterances and private ones. The word *public*, of course, is ambiguous. Two persons make a public whenever they are in each other's presence, or are talking to one another or are otherwise in communication, whatever the medium. A group of persons, whether engaged in conversation or occupied in a common task, as in small-group discussions, is manifestly a public. The customary combinations of speaker-audience and writer-reader are public rather than private situations. Perhaps there is a mass public. But whatever the size and kind of "public," everyone discovers, sometime or other, that he takes on a public role. In this book we are concerned that the speaker recognize his public character, in whatever communicative situation he chooses to regard as public, and that he fulfill that character skillfully and responsibly.

Oral communication is a term and concept which may include a wide variety of linguistic activities, and we would not exclude any of them from some consideration in this book. Our major concern, however, is with the principles and practice of popular discourse directed toward adjusting ideas to people and people to ideas in a public situation through spoken words and accompanying nonverbal cues.

VALUES OF PUBLIC SPEAKING

As the study of public speaking has enjoyed dignity and importance in all the ages of Western civilization, so it thrives today when the demands upon the spoken word and the facilities for transmitting it are much greater than they ever were before. Today, of course, to aid in the running of our complicated society, we have as well tremendous quantities of all sorts of visual matter. But because of the extent and the increased complexity of our social, economic, and political life, there is not less but more demand for oral communication.

The student will recognize for himself the values which modern society associates with public speaking. Some are personal; some are social. Some are self-evident, because they are linked to such motives as self-improvement, personal success, and confidence. Others are less evident, because they are connected with such values as social responsibility, the welfare of others, and the health of democratic society. Perhaps these values are obvious and are generally accepted. At any rate, the student who is enrolled in a course in public speaking is convinced that there are significant advantages to be gained. In Chapter 1 of our *Fundamentals of Public Speaking* (5th edition, 1976), we discuss the personal and social values at some length. In this chapter, however, we wish to point especially to one of those values which is, perhaps, more likely to be overlooked than the rest—the ability to listen critically.

The Habit of Critical Listening

Training in public speaking should not only help one become a better speaker; it should also make one a better *listener* and should facilitate a more critical and intelligent understanding of those social processes in which public speaking plays a prominent role. In former times the art of listening was widespread and necessary. In the earlier stages of our society, public speaking was practically the only means available for the large-scale dissemination of news, information, ideas, and opinions. But with the invention of printing, the rise of literacy, the appearance of the newspaper, and the simultaneous growth in the size and complexity of social and political organization, the printed word became the chief means of reaching great masses of people. As a result, skill in listening seemed less essential than skill in reading. Since the rise of radio and the development of television, however, the spoken word has regained much of its lost stature and now competes with the press in reaching great audiences. We get our news now as much by radio and TV as by newspaper; our political leaders address us as much by radio and TV as by newspaper; our advertisers sell us goods by radio and TV in greater quantities than they ever did through the press or mail solicitation.

Under this barrage of words, we have not as a people acquired the attitude of the judicious critic. We do not *habitually* weigh and consider; rather, we tend to respond according to our likes and dislikes. If a speaker can interest and entertain us, we are likely to listen with approval; if we like a speaker because of his reputation or his political allegiance, we approve of what he says without much resistance; if we dislike a speaker, we may well condemn his message. Extremely valuable in modern society, then, is the ability to listen with discrimination. The more accomplished a speaker becomes, the more critical he will be as listener—less gullible, more stable, wiser, and clearer-minded, better able to distinguish the solid from the hollow, the forthright from the dishonest, the real from the fake. The audience is as vital a part of public speaking as the speaker. The analytical and critical study of public speaking, such as that undertaken in this book and conducted in public speaking classrooms, will usually result in an individual's becoming a better listener, a better member of an audience.

Substance and Use

Among the values of public communication, it should go without saying, substance and social usefulness will always be primary. As we have hinted, public speaking is sometimes a fine art, creating artifacts to be contemplated in part for themselves. But first it is a useful art, a practical art, whose products are to be valued more for what they do than for what they are. The principles of good speaking, therefore, are never entirely separate from the materials and purposes to which they are to be applied. Accordingly, both speakers in public situations and students of speaking must have something of consequence to say—must have messages worth preparing and hearing. The person who knows most about most things and most people—has thought most, has read most, has experienced most, has observed most, has become familiar with the minds and hearts and manners and values of his fellow men—this person, if he has also learned the principles of rhetoric and has cultivated the will to communicate, will be the best speaker. Of course, most good speakers fall somewhat short of these ideals. Nevertheless, no matter how restricted the area of subject matter, speakers must know their subjects well. They must also know human beings well, and have available a store of ideas by which they can make their subjects clear, interesting, and convincing to the various kinds of audiences they wish to inform and influence.

AUDIENCE IS CENTRAL

Of the four chief elements in a communicative situation—speaker, message, audience, and circumstances—audience-in-circumstances is central. All that goes on is conditioned by audience responses. Arousing desirable responses, and being careful not to arouse undesirable ones, is the speaker's whole business. He will always be making choices—of purposes, of subjects, of materials, of means—which he thinks correspond to the probable responses in the audience he is to influence.

The Classroom Audience

The student of public speaking will gradually discover a good example of a specific audience—an audience whose interests, abilities, and opinions he will learn much about. It is, of course, the classroom audience, ever present and ever real. In spite of appearance, the class situation is neither solely, nor primarily, artificial. It is a contrived situation only in part. Both listener and speaker are studying and practicing the art of oral communication and are self-consciously aware that they are. And in the classroom, as a rule, listeners don't invite their fellows to speak to them—the instructor does that. But in all other respects, they are in a real communicative environment. They face real persons. They face the same audience often enough to know much about its "personality." (Indeed, unless one becomes a clergyman or a trial lawyer, one may never again as a speaker know an audience so well.) By accepting his classmates as they are, by speaking to them rather than to some remote, imaginary group, by trying to make them understand, to interest them, or otherwise to influence them, a student can help himself acquire a lively sense of *direct* communication.

Audience Response

The different responses to a speech correspond to three kinds of effects. (1) The effect may be that of knowledge and understanding. The listener is able to say "I see," "I know," or "I understand." His knowledge has gained breadth or depth. (2) The effect may be some change (including strengthening or weakening) in the listeners' opinions or attitudes, and the shift may be in different directions. This response is well illustrated in a classroom audience that hears a speech contending that alimony in divorce cases is justified only when the wife or the children need support. Some listeners who already hold this view find their beliefs reinforced and intensified. Some who hold no opinion on the subject accept the speaker's belief. Still others, in disagreement with the speaker, seem less strongly opposed than previously, even uncertain. (3) The effect may be some type of action, ranging from polite hand-clapping to enthusiastic applause to doing what the speaker suggests or directs.

These are the main types of responses to speeches (and to any practical discourse), although on rare occasions there are speeches to which we respond only with interest, pleasure, or amusement. It is important only to recognize that there is always some kind of response to a speech and that the response consists in whatever the audience thinks and does in consequence. Sometimes the response is immediate and observable, as when someone buys insurance after a sales talk. More often the response is remote and unrecognized, as when one day we find that we have a new attitude toward Orientals and are unaware that past information and argument, absorbed through forgotten speeches, articles, and discussions about Far Eastern problems, have brought about the change. Such gradual changes illustrate the observation that talk, anybody's talk, anywhere and anytime, may be responsible for creating or changing belief.

KINDS OF SPEECHES

The responses to speechmaking and to practical discourse in general furnish the basis for classifying speeches into kinds. There are two broad kinds, the informative and the persuasive.

Informative

The informative speech is intended primarily to impart knowledge or to illuminate a subject. Its materials consist of facts and data, on the one hand, and the principles, laws, and standard explanations of facts, on the other. The informative speaker uses the basic materials of the various fields of study—engineering, home economics, physics, accounting, medicine. The listener is a learner and the result of his learning is knowledge and understanding.

Persuasive

The persuasive speech is intended to influence the opinion and behavior of an audience. Its materials are drawn from problems about which people hold differing beliefs and opinions—controversial matters that call for decision and action. The problems may be very general: In what ways can public school education be improved? They may be quite specific: Should the high school graduate be able to speak a foreign language? Very broadly considered, the persuasive speaker is an adviser. Technically, the materials of persuasion are the facts, data, laws, principles, and explanations that furnish the informative speech, plus the opinions, arguments, and circumstances bearing on a problem that calls for decision. The speaker says or implies that the audience should accept this view or act in ways consistent with it. The listener is the judge. He accepts, rejects, or doubts the view. He may or may not act on the view when he has the chance.

The persuasive speaker is always telling hearers what they ought to believe or do. We ought, for example, to give to the United Way. An informative speaker, by contrast, does not ask his audience to accept one belief rather than another, or to act one way rather than another. He always says, "Here are the facts and ideas as seen and understood by persons in a position to know them; these are the ways the facts are interpreted and explained by such persons." Accordingly, an informative speaker would not argue whether his hearers should contribute to the United Way, but he might explain how the United Way is organized and run and how it handles its funds. The informative speech is descriptive, explanatory, and diagnostic; the persuasive speech is prescriptive, instigative, directive, and advisory.

SPEAKER AND AUDIENCE

The character, the personality, and the physical person of the speaker as perceived by the audience compose important dimensions of the message of the speech. Some qualities of personality and character that are critically important in communication are revealed through our language. Our words reflect such values as truthfulness, humor, knowledge and competence, accuracy of statement, sincerity and consistency of belief, respect and sympathy for others, or their contraries. Personal qualities are evident whenever we use language, particularly in writing and speaking. Some, however, are signaled most directly by the inflections, intonations, and qualities of the voice. Our ears, for example, instantly recognize notes of friendliness, sympathy, humor, modesty, and respect, or the reverse. They at once sense the ring of conviction and truth and detect as readily tones of insecurity, sarcasm, and falsity. Our eyes, observing the gestures of face and body, take in at a glance the signs of friendliness, liveliness, and directness; and they also derive impressions from appearance and dress. Thus the speaker, like any of us in our everyday conversations, draws his own portrait swiftly and surely. The novelist's personality and character are usually in the background and must be searched for; the person of the speaker is in the foreground and is revealed in everything he says and does.

ETHICS AND COMMUNICATION

The ethics of communications is perhaps of greater national concern than at any time in this century. Many people have lost confidence in the communications coming from the Federal government and its bureaus and from many politicians, whether local or national. Many persons know they cannot take commercial advertising literally, whether they are bombarded by it through radio, TV, or the print media. Even in private discourse, each individual makes the most plausible explanation, the most effective argument, he can for himself. In short, human beings are the makers and users of verbal and gestural language and they use it for their own purposes and motives; they are bound to be biased. In every instance of communication, then, the basic problem is this: Is the speaker or writer using his communicative resources as he *ought* to? In better ways rather than worse, in right ways rather than wrong?

THE MEANING OF ETHICAL

What makes a problem ethical? There are two infallible signs. Whenever an individual finds himself thinking about what he *ought* to do, or *should* do, his problem is ethical. Or when he advises or persuades another person that that person ought to do something, or believe something, he is thinking ethically. Such thinking is set off or triggered by *the need to choose among alternative actions or beliefs*. The choice one confronts may be two-pronged and may appear simple. A question is asked: "Should I reply?" or "Should I cut classes today?" "Should I pick up a hitchhiker?" "Should I accept a job rather than finish school?" The choice may be many-pronged and complex: "What should I believe about U.S. involvement in Indochina?" "What kind of career should I undertake?" "What should my community do about pollution?" "Should I change my job?"

The second infallible sign of an ethical situation is that there are standards or criteria governing one's choice. "Do unto others as you would be done by." "Respect the truth." "Respect promises." "Kindliness is preferable to cruelty." "Slavery is wrong." Such standards of conduct and belief function as *rules*, which in turn reflect the practices, values, and ideals of a society or culture. Usually they are embedded in law, and hence are punishable in the breach. In any event, ethical rules are accepted widely enough in a society to carry the force of public opinion.

In responding to situations that present choices, one acts by habit or by deliberation. If by habit, he reacts almost automatically. He finds a purse and takes immediate steps to find the owner. He has learned to respect honesty through his family upbringing, and he makes the choice without thought, without reasoning and debating whether or not to keep the purse. The kind and number of such responses seen as a whole constitute one's *character*, or ethos. The other kind of response to the choice situation is deliberative. The rules and their values are applied consciously. One uses them as reasons because he feels he has to justify his choice either to himself if he values his integrity, or to others if he values his public image. It is the choice situation and the deliberative reasoning it evokes that establish common interests among the fields of ethics, political science, and rhetoric. Through these studies one becomes a moralist in the highest sense.

Purposes and Means

The rules of ethical discourse reflect the ideals and best practices of political life. For most of us, political life is considered democratic; that is, we assume we live in a free society ordered and governed by the people and for the people. It is a society, moreover, whose supreme value assumes the dignity and worth of the individual. In a free society, furthermore, it is assumed that people are capable of learning and, given the opportunity, of reading, listening, and reasoning. Consequently, we are led to the great principle of discourse: Communications should be for the welfare of the audiences for whom they are intended and for audiences who want them. The credo for any speaker says: A speech should serve the basic values and interests of human beings. This is not to say that a speaker in choosing the purpose of his speech should not respect his own private motivations. He may, of course, want to promote his own prestige, power, and influence, or to secure office and position, or simply to make a good speech and earn a good grade. He should satisfy himself, however, that his own motives are not inconsistent with the welfare of others.

As for the means of achieving one's purpose or goal, communicators should ever remember one of the oldest and soundest of ethical rules: A justifiable purpose does not justify the use of any and all means. What means, then, are justifiable? The answers are to be found by observing the practitioners of an art or science, by discovering the methods and techniques and skills of a vocation or profession. One looks not only at current methods and means but at their history. Physicians and lawyers, builders, advertisers, and realtors, have codes of ethics. And for the most part the codes concentrate on the doing of good work and the producing of good products rather than bad. They forbid unethical practices. The codes require that the practitioner have the knowledge to do his task, that he understand the nature of his task, and that he select appropriate materials and use approved methods and techniques in accomplishing his task. The codes are based on the study of thousands of cases; hence there is the assumption that a practitioner who respects his code will not only achieve his purpose but will produce work of good quality, work he can justify if challenged.

Rules

The ethical rules of rhetorical discourse are very general. They have to be, because they should apply wherever speech and language are understood by all people within the boundaries of a nation-state. In a free society rhetoric touches all men, not merely the few who are privy to a specialized language—the language of chemistry or of calculus, for example. The first rule, which we have already stated, concerns the purpose or goal of the communicator:

1. The communicator's purpose should be consistent with the best interests of the audience.

Other rules concern the means to be chosen in accomplishing the purpose.

2. The communicator should aim to know the subject matter of his discourse as thoroughly as he can; that is, he should possess more or better information than his audience.
3. The communicator should know the principles, precepts, and practices of his art, that is, the art of rhetoric.
4. The persuader should not suppress material so as to prevent the audience from judging fairly what is said.
5. The persuader should neither manufacture information nor distort materials in ways that are self-serving.
6. The audience should be the final judge of what is said, of accepting or rejecting what is presented to it.

The rationale of these basic rules is probably self-evident. If we live in a reasonably free society and if the ultimate power in that society can be exercised by the electorate, it is essential that information be readily and widely available and that a variety of points of view be made known. This state of affairs lays an obligation on speakers to be fair with their audiences. The speaker has been in a position to know more about his subject than have his listeners; he has had a special opportunity to prepare his own arguments and appeals and to become aware of opposing arguments. He can in part offset his audience's lack of opportunity by dealing fairly with them—by producing the important, critical facts and testimony on the situation or case, instead of suppressing them or of warping them to his advantage.

A glance at the rules will show that the primary responsibility for ethical communication rests with the communicator. His is the burden, for he has most of the advantages. He selects the materials he wants to use and rejects others; he knows what his private motives are and whether in order to keep the record straight he ought to reveal them; and his is the absolute power over suppression and distortion of materials. Nevertheless, members of an audience hold the power of final decision. They are free to believe or not; they can choose to act or not, and in what way. Adults, furthermore, are sophisticated enough to know when they are being subjected to persuasive situations and influences. Few people do not know what advertisers are up to, whether their methods are subtle or blatant, and whether they are selling toothpaste or building up the good will of a public utility. When an individual chooses to become party to the persuasive process he accepts some responsibility for its effects on him. If there is a completely naive audience, it would seem to consist of children, too young in experience and knowledge to recognize persuasion and its methods. Hence, parents and teachers have a special responsibility for their communications to the young.

In considering the ethics of rhetorical discourse, one must see clearly that its media are speech and language and must understand whay they imply. Speech and language are symbols and signs, and in these are embedded our thoughts and meanings. All these we have learned so thoroughly that they have become part of our being and behavior. So in communicative situations that invite or impel us to make choices and decision, we are thinking with the very materials we communicate with. Ordinary language, then, is of the nature of human beings. It is their substance. In systematic education this kind of substance is added to and refined. Language, therefore, is not merely a matter of form, syntax, and style. Nor is it a specialized vocabulary, like that of logic or of the sciences, to be used or not used as particular circumstances require. It is used everywhere, and wherever it is used it presents choices of what to say and how to say it. Such choices involve our morality. If we have to justify them, we must do so on ethical grounds.

CONCLUSION

A student of speaking can begin at once to develop or confirm evidences of those qualities of character and personality which will themselves speak to audiences on his behalf. He can undertake to master those fundamental processes, to which this book is devoted, which underlie good oral communication. He can learn, moreover, to handle them methodically, for he can look ahead to his scheduled speech, take early stock of resources, add to them as soon as possible, set aside time for organizing and outlining materials, and reserve definite periods for oral rehearsal. Intelligent planning and work bring gratifying results; it doesn't take a genius to fashion a good speech. Recognizing these facts, a student can rapidly develop a great deal of confidence in his own abilities. Furthermore, through speeches he can win respect and influence as a person. He can offer useful knowledge and information to classroom listeners. He can present opinions that are well reasoned and well grounded on evidence. He can prepare thoroughly and speak clearly and accurately. He can respect the interests of hearers and treat them in a direct and friendly manner. By having their welfare at heart, he creates the right impression.

We now turn at once to the methodical business of constructing and presenting speeches.

INQUIRIES

1. When a communicative situation calls on you to respond, what choices do you have? When you choose to speak, why do you? When you choose not to speak, why that decision? Moments of choice and decision are dominated by our purposes and motives. In considering occasions when you have spoken and not spoken, what purposes were operating? Do you think your set of purposes corresponds with that of your classmates? Have you discovered some personal values in communication?

2. People have always argued about the value to the state of skill in speaking. Plato, in his dialogue *Gorgias*, represented rhetoric as specializing in trickery and flattery, as concerned with impressions and appearances rather than with knowledge. Modern editorialists are fond of demanding "more performance and less rhetoric" from our leaders.

Would society be better off with less, or no, emphasis on skill in speech? Cite some examples of what you consider misuse of communication by, for instance, candidates for public office. Which of these abuses are the result of rhetoric? Which are only made possible by rhetoric but not caused by it? Would you blame the skill of the speaker or his character? Is there an adequate alternative to rhetoric?

3. Ghostwriting presents problems in ethics. Consider the ghostwriter and the person, or institution, he writes for. Is the ethical responsibility shared? Equally?

4. Is the public relations expert or the writer of advertising copy in the same ethical position as the ghostwriter?

5. Both Plato and Quintilian would allow leaders to lie to the people for their own good. If you, too, think so, what rules or limits would you apply?

FURTHER READING

Baier, Kurt. *The Moral Point of View.* 1958.
Baird, A. Craig, Franklin H. Knower, and Samuel L. Becker. *General Speech Communication.* 4th ed. 1971. Chapters 1 and 2.

Bryant, Donald C. "Rhetoric: Its Functions and Its Scope." *Quarterly Journal of Speech*, 39 (1953), 401-24.

Bryant, Donald C., and Karl R. Wallace. *Fundamentals of Public Speaking.* 5th ed. 1976. Chapters 1-2, 4-5.

Bryson, Lyman, ed. *The Communication of Ideas.* 1949.

Hayakawa, S. J. *Language in Action.* Rev. ed., 1949.

Johannesen, Richard L., ed. *Ethics and Persuasion: Selected Readings.* 1967. See especially Sidney Hook, "The Ethics of Controversy."

Minnick, Wayne C. *The Art of Persuasion.* 2nd ed. 1968. See especially Chapter 11, "Ethics."

Monroe, Alan H., and Douglas Ehninger. *Principles and Types of Speech Communication.* 7th ed. 1974.

Stevens, Leonard A. *The Ill-Spoken Word: The Decline of Speech in America.* 1966.

Wallace, Karl R. "The Substance of Rhetoric: Good Reasons." *Quarterly Journal of Speech,* 49 (1963), 239-249.

CHAPTER 2

The First Speeches

At the beginning of the first course in speechmaking the learner's principal problem may appear to be breaking the ice and getting adjusted to talking on his feet. It is evident, however, from teaching experience that the student may overcome much of his initial hesitancy and timidity and may gain some confidence before an audience at the same time that he is learning to crystallize, clarify, and develop ideas on sound and systematic principles. The person who feels he has something of value to say and who is concerned with communicating it intelligibly and vividly to his listeners usually does not have much time to focus on himself and his apprehensions about how he is doing.

In this chapter we assume that a secure grasp of some simple, fundamental patterns for the first speeches, that the conscious application of sound principles, patterns, and procedures, will help establish in the student speaker useful *habitual* ways of thinking. Then many of the problems that plague beginning speakers will disappear.

At times, of course, when one is obliged to speak, he feels little sense of message. Then the first problem is finding a subject and material. Most students, however, after very little reflection will find their accumulated resources quite equal to the demands of their initial short speeches. In their previous schooling they have had considerable experience finding subjects and materials for writing papers in English classes and therefore in utilizing their reading and taking stock of their own knowledge and experience. The problem of finding subjects and materials, therefore, we will defer for the time being.

MANAGING SUBSTANCE

The problems of advantageously managing the substance of speeches—the problem of making statements and filling them out—may properly occupy attention at this point. Most college students and educated adults are more experienced and better prepared in this phase of speechmaking than at first they may be aware. The ways of careful, thoughtful conversation are also the ways of good public speaking. Consider the following responses to conversational situations.

I think I understand what you mean, but say it another way so I can be sure.

That sounds like a sensible statement. Can you back it up with facts and information?

What do you mean by saying people seldom do anything much better than they have to? Who, for example? In what circumstances?

I would not be surprised if you have something which may be useful in your new method of determining public opinion, but I don't really understand. What is it like?

I believe you mean what you say, and I respect your opinion, but it is only your opinion. Who else says so?

The Basic Pattern

Each of the preceding requests points up the prime principle of systematic, orderly discourse. Each involves crystallizing an idea, an opinion, a judgment, or an inquiry into a statement and enriching, supporting, reinforcing, and developing it.

Each situation illustrats the basic operating pattern of thinking for speaking and of organizing speeches—an arrangement of *statement* and *development* for the statement. The concept of *topic sentence* in the student's written composition somewhat resembles the pattern underlying good speeches. Anyone who has considered the various methods of developing a topic sentence into an effective paragraph has begun his initiation into the methods of giving form and development to the substance of his first speeches. Theme writing and speechmaking are by no means the same undertakings, but the methods of giving order and movement to materials in each are certainly comparable.

As Aristotle asserted long ago and as practice still demonstrates, a good speech and each of the basic units which together make up a good speech consist essentially of two elements: (1) a *statement* and (2) a *development* which explains or reinforces the statement.

Subject Statement

For our present purpose a subject statement is a declarative sentence formulating an idea, a feeling, a judgment, an opinion, or a matter of inquiry that needs *development* through particularization, illustration, concretion, interpretation, reinforcement, or support of some sort if it is to convey its intended meaning and force to its audience. Each of the demands and queries on page 15 occurs because some declarative statement has been made or implied, the meaning of which is not clear enough or full enough for the listener. The speaker, in replying to the query, would probably make the subject statement again and then would satisfy his listener with the kind of developing material asked for.

Development

By *development* we mean the sum of such methods, materials, and language as should serve, with the particular listeners involved, to make intelligible, to make concrete, to reinforce, to enliven, to support, or otherwise to fill out the meaning and significance of the *statement*. Anything a speaker says, then, which tends to prove his point, explain his idea, or make his statement clear, vivid, or attractive to his audience is considered development.

There are many possible sources and methods of development, most of which we will discuss in later chapters. First speeches, however, should reveal perhaps four or five obvious means of development. These means are indicated by the queries on page 15. In answer to query (1) what is needed is a *restatement* of the same thing that has been said; in answer to (2) the speaker will give *factual information*; in replying to (3) example should clear up the uncertainty; in order to satisfy the inquirer in (4) the speaker will have to make *comparisons*; and for (5) the speaker will offer *testimony*.

Developing material

The most common and most useful kinds of development may be identified in the following ways.

Restatement.   Restatement is largely a matter of language. By recasting a statement in other language or other form or both, a speaker not only adds emphasis but often hits upon terminology and phrasing which will strike his listeners as clearer, fuller, more familiar, or in some way more understandable or forceful than the language of the original statement.

Factual Information.   When we say that a speaker knows what he is talking about and has the facts on his subject, we usually mean that he has filled out and supported his contentions with plenty of verifiable information, factual data, figures and statistical material, and firsthand evidence.

Example. Whether as the short, undeveloped specific instance or as the longer, fully developed illustration, example is the detailing, sketching, narrating, describing, or otherwise setting before the audience of typical circumstances, characteristic cases, or particular objects or events which help to make clear, vivid, or credible the statement that the speaker wants his audience to accept.

Comparison and Contrast. Comparison and contrast are closely related to example. They are concerned with showing likenesses and differences among objects, ideas, and situations; with associating the new with the familiar. The former puts stress upon illuminating similarities; the latter on dissimilarities.

Testimony. Simply described, testimony is the say-so of someone other than the speaker, in support of a point or in explanation of an idea. One very common form of testimony is quotation, including quotations from men and books of the past.

Such, in brief, are the five most common and useful methods and materials of development. We will discuss each more fully under the general topic of amplification in the informative speech in Chapter 5, and under the topic of support in the persuasive speech in Chapter 8. Now we will proceed to illustrate the use of these materials of development in characteristic patterns of the short speech.

PUTTING THE SPEECH TOGETHER: PATTERN

Arrangement of statement and development of statement, as we have said, constitute the basic operating pattern for a speaker's thinking for organizing speeches. That is, when one thinks most efficiently for speaking, one habitually thinks of truths or opinions one wishes to communicate, and one thinks of them in connection with material that might develop them. These elements may come to mind as idea first, followed by developing matter; or as some of the potential material first, then a version of the idea, followed by more developing matter. The order is largely dependent on habit and circumstances and will vary with the speaker and the occasion. But for all speakers the habit of joining the two basic elements into regular patterns of movement is important. The formulation of an idea should result immediately in the movement toward material with which to develop it; and the apprehension of facts, events, similarities, and so forth, should lead to an idea of what they signify—to a relevant *statement.* These patterns in the speaker's own thinking serve him as patterns for organizing his material into speeches, or units of speeches. The three common patterns may be represented schematically as follows:

<table>
<tr><td align="center">Pattern 1
Statement to be developed
developing material</td><td align="center">Pattern 2
developing material
Statement to which it leads</td></tr>
</table>

Pattern 3
developing material
Statement being developed
further developing material

The diagrammatic arrangements above are intended to illustrate two principles: (1) Development materials may precede the statement they support, or they may succeed the statement, or they may both precede and follow. (2) No matter what the time order of the statement and its developing ideas, the development is always logically subordinate to the statement, and the statement is always logically superior to the development. In the diagrams this relationship is suggested by beginning the statement to the left of its developing materials and distinguishing it by a capital letter.

We observe in passing that these patterns also illustrate possible nuclei for the speech outline, which is the plan, or blueprint, for the construction of the speech. Like the blueprint for a house or a machine, it is most useful if it is prepared before final construction is begun. Full consideration of the speech outline will be given in Chapter 7. For the present we will concern ourselves only with the basic patterns in their simplest forms.

Patterns of the Short Speech

1. The most usual pattern of the short speech on a simple, expository theme may be illustrated by the following scheme. The governing *statement* is made at the beginning and is developed through information, example, testimony, contrast, and restatement.

STATEMENT

Fluorescent lighting increases office efficiency and saves money.

DEVELOPMENT

The spectrum of the light emitted from the fluorescent tube is much closer to that of natural light than is the spectrum from the incandescent bulb. (*Information, contrast*)

A natural spectrum causes less eye fatigue in employees than does an artificial spectrum. (*Information, contrast*)

In hot weather, employees are more comfortable under fluorescent than incandescent light because it gives off less heat. (*Information, contrast*)

A local plant manager testified that his electric bill dropped 30% after the installation of fluorescent fixtures. (*Testimony*)

The more natural spectrum of light and the reduced heat have prompted the use of fluorescent lighting in animal cages (zoos) and in acquaria. (*Example*)

The positive attributes of fluorescent lighting have made it a necessary piece of equipment in a well-run establishment. (*Restatement*)

Observe that in the brief speech of this sort, restatement may serve as conclusion as well as additional development.

2.   A simple speech can be developed almost entirely through the use of information. This sort of pattern and development might be more likely to appear as one of the basic units of a complex speech, but it is sometimes effective as well for the short and simple informative speech.

STATEMENT

The cost of national political campaigning has reached staggering figures.

DEVELOPMENT

Half-hour TV programs cost from $10,000 to $15,000 for air time alone. (*Information*)

These are priced by the networks at one-half to one-fourth of the cost of regular, prime-time advertising time. (*Information*)

The cost of producing such programs may go as high as $300,000. One of McGovern's in the 1972 campaign did. (*Information*)

By October 26 the major presidential contenders in 1972 reported spending $54,500.00 The Nixon committees reported $36,050.00. The McGovern committees reported $18,470,000. (*Information*)

These are the highest costs ever. The previous high came in 1968, when the total cost reported by the presidential candidates was about $44,200,000. (*Information*)

It is hardly remarkable that in 1972 Senator Harris of Oklahoma withdrew from presidential competition for lack of money. (*Restatement*)

3.   The pattern for the short speech in which the development precedes and leads to the statement is illustrated in the scheme below for a speech

employing example exclusively. The speaker plans to cite briefly several specific instances, then to clinch his idea with extended illustration. With this speech the audience would probably get a special satisfaction out of the explicit appearance of the statement at the end, where the statement would serve as a neat conclusion as well.

As sketched below, this speech would be intended principally for entertainment through a kind of ironic humor. If the speaker's purpose were more serious, if he were addressing the university administration and advocating improvement at registration time, he would probably want to use additional kinds of materials for development, especially information and comparison. He might give figures, perhaps collected by the campus newspaper, showing just how long the average student spends in getting registered, at which department's station he has to wait the longest, and at what hours the congestion is worst. The speaker might also wish to offer comparison with registration in other universities, and testimony from individual students and faculty.

DEVELOPMENT

As we begin our academic year, we have to stand in line (*Specific instances*)

at the registrar's to get our cards,
at each department's station to register for our courses,
at the bursar's to pay our fees,
at the health center for our physical examinations,
at the bookstore to buy our supplies,
at the cafeteria counter to get our dinner.

Let us follow a friend of ours from 6:00 a.m. to 7:00 p.m. of registration day of his freshman year. (*Illustration*)

STATEMENT

Obviously, getting into the university and staying in are largely matters of standing in line.

4. A special kind of short speech developing an idea (stated or implied) by offering one extended example, or *illustration*, usually of the narrative sort, may be most interesting and effective in pointing a moral or enlivening an idea. Such for example, is Jesus's parable of the Good Samaritan (*Luke* 10:30-37).

STATEMENT

(*Your neighbor is he who needs your help.*)

DEVELOPMENT

The story of the man who went down from Jerusalem to Jericho illustrates what it is to be a neighbor.

Observe that the *statement* in this little speech is not the question which was asked of Jesus, "Who is my neighbor?" It is the *answer* to that question. That answer never appears as a formulated statement in the speech. Hence it appears in parentheses in the scheme above. Nevertheless it is the governing proposition, implicit in the story, and must be included in the scheme.

All the details of examples need not be included in the scheme or outline, but there should be a separate descriptive heading for each example. Consider how one would phrase the statement for the parable of the Prodigal Son (*Luke* 15:11-32), and for the parable of the Talents (*Matthew* 25:14-30).

In a speech about registration, like the one already sketched, the speaker might well limit himself to one narrative example of his own experience, including all the appalling (or amusing) episodes, and either formulating the statement explicitly at the end or suggesting to the listeners that they reach their own conclusions. This also would be a speech of one extended *illustration*.

5. *Testimony* alone seldom provides adequate development when a proposition of any consequence is to be explained or supported (though some tournament debaters seem to think that quoting authorities is all that is needed to win). Even the writers of advertising, who are the most flagrant users of testimony, do not regularly rely on it exclusively, except for very brief, quick impact. "Buy Kleen Kine Milk. Babe Ruth approved of milk; the Bible associates milk with honey; and we all know the phrase, 'the milk of human kindness.' " Advertisers usually couple testimony with something which is intended to seem like information: "Kleen Kine Milk is up to three times more nourishing for up to 15 percent less." (More and less than *what* is seldom indicated.) Though easily abused, testimony may be very well and effectively used in conjunction with other kinds of supporting material, especially example and information.

The following scheme illustrates development by testimony which enlivens the information it carries. It also serves as an example of the pattern in which the statement is both preceded and followed by development.

DEVELOPMENT

"A man's a man for a' that," said Robert Burns. (*Testimony*) Edmund Burke said that he did not know how to draw up an indictment against a whole people. (*Testimony*)

STATEMENT

A man is best judged for himself, not for his race, class, nationality, or religion.

DEVELOPMENT

The Constitution of the United States recognizes no qualitative categories for judging men. (*Information*) Records of crime show that native-born Americans commit as serious crimes as do immigrants. (*Information*) There is no reliable evidence of the inherent intellectual or moral superiority of the white man over the black. (*Information*)

"The fault, dear Brutus, is not in our stars but in ourselves...."
(*Testimony, serving as conclusion*)

6. The following scheme suggests the development of a statement through the use of comparison and analogy.

STATEMENT

The government of the U.S.S.R. is based on an ascending concentration of power, from the local soviets to the Supreme Soviet.

DEVELOPMENT

It may be called a pyramid of power. (*Metaphor*) It is like a large business organization, where each of the minor executives has several supervisors reporting to him, and he in turn reports to a superior who reports to a superior, and so on. (*Comparison*) It is like the English system of privy councils under Elizabeth I. (*Analogy—to be extended*)

Every flea has little fleas
Upon his back to bite 'im,
And little fleas have lesser fleas—
So on *ad infinitum.*

(*Testimony, as illustrative comparison*)

The schemes just given illustrate the speeches simplest in form and plan: speeches in which only a single statement requires development. Most speeches are not so simple. Nevertheless, the best speeches, however long and complex, consist of basic units of statement-and-development combined into larger patterns. The structure and outlines of such speeches, as we have said, will be the business of Chapter 7.

Introductions and Conclusions

Little or nothing has been said about introductions, conclusions, connective and transitional material, and the sort of filling in with words and sentences that transforms the bare structure into the neat, shapely speech. These elements deserve full consideration. Later chapters will be devoted to them. The important reminder at this point is to keep introductions and conclusions in the first speeches brief and simple. An introduction need consist only of a statement or two which will get the attention of listeners and at the same time lead into the ideas that follow it. The conclusion of a short speech, as we have suggested in the scheme on page 19, often consists simply of *restating* the idea expressed in the statement.

STAGE FRIGHT

That form of emotional distraction often associated with learning public speaking and called stage fright probably deserves some attention in connection with the first speeches. When a speaker yields to it, he is possessed by a kind of fear which inhibits his thinking and chills his responsiveness to ideas. Stage fright as real, persisting fear, however, is rare among students. Much of what is *called* stage fright is only a kind of apprehensiveness as normal as roses in June. It is the sort of feeling evoked by any new situation to which a person wants to respond appropriately and successfully. Furthermore, because people are only human beings and not machines, they know that they can never be certain that they will behave as they would like to. For example, if a student applies for a scholarship and is asked to an interview with the dean, he may be quite rightly concerned over saying what needs to be said and making a favorable impression. The delivery of a speech presents the same kind of situation. We want to do well; we care about making a good speech, but we are not sure we will be completely successful. So we feel worry and concern, just as one does over any task one really cares about. Such feelings are quite different from true fear.

Nervousness and worry are often accompanied by tension. Unless tension is so extreme as to freeze one into a state of immobility, however, it is desirable and useful. Just as a runner does his best when set, spring-like, to be off, so a speaker is at his physical and mental best when keyed up to his task. In fact, no one does his best at a task unless he regards it as a challenge, a challenge sufficient to cause some concern. The man who takes public speaking in his stride as a routine job will make a routine speech.

True stage fright, on the other hand, is a special kind of fear response. First, it is a withdrawal or retreat. Although the everyday fear experience may result in running away or otherwise avoiding the object of fright, stage fright is often marked by trembling, knee shaking rigidity and ·immobility, and fast irregular breathing prior to the speech or during delivery. Furthermore, the suffering speaker finds himself in a situation where he cannot run away without publicly admitting failure and thus damaging his pride. Consequently, his response on the platform is not ordinary avoidance behavior, such as running away or simply avoiding speaking, but tautness, rigidity, and immobility of both body and mind. Second, the basis of such behavior, as in any case of fear, is twofold: (1) the situation means harm and danger, and (2) this danger can be avoided by flight and withdrawal. To the speaker, danger means failure—failure to remember, to do well, to say the acceptable thing, to behave acceptably.

It should be clear, therefore, that if stage fright is this kind of experience it can be attacked in three ways: (1) by minimizing the appearance of danger in the situation, (2) by dispelling the idea that danger can be met only by withdrawing and running away; and (3) by not running away. A speaker may be able to attack at all these points, but if he can attack at only one point he will experience less fear and apprehension. What he should do is to analyze the experience as frankly and completely as he can (here his instructor may be of great help) and try to discover what point to assault and what tactics to employ.

Minimizing the Hazard

The novice speaker has effective ways of coping with emotional problems rationally and objectively. First, he can recognize that speaking to an audience does not differ greatly from speaking in private; public speaking is but enlarged conversation. Thus public speaking may become less formidable and be associated with what he may already do well.

Second, he should rapidly build up a feeling of familiarity about public speaking. This he does through experience, an unsurpassed teacher, and through the study of principles and through listening to speeches and reading them. Knowledge of what makes a good speech and of what is expected of speakers in the way of information and interest, composition and organization, presentation and behavior, in both informative and persuasive speeches, does much to minimize feelings of risk. It is the new and strange, we think, that may cause harm, and once the situation is experienced and understood one possible cause of harm is removed.

Third, the classroom speaker should realize that his fellows are with him. Since all are engaged in the same enterprise, the classroom audience is not so critical of his endeavors as he may think; it is as sympathetic and as helpful an audience as exists anywhere. It is quick to praise and admire good work because it appreciates, much better than does the casual, outside audience, the sweat and labor behind a good speech.

Finally, he can capitalize upon the advantages of beginning preparation early and of preparing thoroughly. Thorough preparation brings with it four psychological aids: (1) a speaker knows that he is ready to meet the situation; (2) he knows that he is better equipped to cope with any last-minute adjustments to his audience than if he were not well prepared; (3) he knows that good preparation means less chance of forgetting; and (4) he gains confidence.

Confronting the Hazard

The starting point of fear, as we have seen, is perceiving that a situation is harmful and that harm can be escaped by retreating. It is possible to perceive danger and still not judge it something to run from. Indeed, we do this when we get angry, for the source of anger is danger plus awareness that there is something to be attacked and destroyed. It should be evident, then, that what we see or think of as dangerous need not cause fear. This fact has important application for the anxious speaker. He can deliberately interpret the hazardous situation as something to be confronted squarely, to be faced positively and directly—like a foe to be conquered, not to be fled from. Thus, he induces or adopts the attitude of determination toward his task. In effect, he says to himself, "I will speak; I will continue to speak; I will welcome every opportunity to speak; I will keep at it." He knows full well, moreover, that if he quits even once and runs, he has let fear get the better of him and the job is much harder.

Emotional Conditioning

In a few unusual instances, stage fright may be traced not to apprehension over the new and unknown, but to unfortunate experiences in the past. It is learned behavior and may represent emotional conditioning and emotional conflict.

An individual may have made three or four speeches, each inducing real fright. As a result, the fear experience becomes closely and intensely conditioned to speechmaking. Then the mere prospect of having to make another speech and face another audience evokes fear.

When stage fright is thus learned, the individual employs two direct approaches. The first makes use of this idea: No two speaking situations, even in the classroom, are, strictly speaking, precisely the same. If Situation 1 was accompanied by fright, then Situation 2, different in some respects from Situation 1, need not evoke fright. Consequently, one seeks comfort by clearly recognizing in what ways his next speech will differ from his last. Is the *occasion* different? the *subject* different? the *treatment of the subject* different? the *audience* different in some respects? the *speaker* himself changed? The second approach is to recognize and to emphasize the pleasant and successful aspects of one's speaking experience, and thus build up positive, attractive associations. Has the speaker been commended for being clear? Informative? Interesting? Direct and communicative? For effective platform behavior? Usually a speech deserves praise in some respect, and praise stimulates the feeling of pride. Accordingly, as one faces successive speeches, one should take inventory of successes; the pleasant associations thus secured will soon counterbalance, then overbalance, unpleasant associations.

Emotional Conflict

Some psychologists hold that stage fright is a symptom of two conflicting desires: craving for an audience and for the approval of others, and fear of an audience and of the disapproval of others. The speaker wants an audience and he doesn't want an audience, and the resulting conflict knots him up physically and mentally.

Where such conflict is evident, the general method of reducing it consists of making one desire dominant so that the other desire loses much, if not all, of its power to compete. The speaker strengthens his desire for an audience by making himself keenly aware of any favorable associations with it. He finds good reasons for speaking to the particular audience, at the particular time, and on the particular subject. He makes an inventory of his past successes as a speaker. He isolates the special reasons why his audience may be, or should be, kindly, sympathetic, and respectful toward him. Then he sets about to *make* his speech interesting to his hearers. In brief, he does everything he can to strengthen his connection with an audience and to make prominent all favorable associations with it.

Much has been written about stage fright, its causes and remedies. Some of the most useful readings are listed at the end of the chapter. In fact, however, we possess little exact knowledge about the phenomenon, and there appears to be no general medicine good for every case. Perhaps, after all, the wisest advice comes from a veteran teacher: "One can't be abnormally self-conscious if he gives first place to the welfare of others. So put your audience first. Plan everything you do for your hearers. Interest them. Their welfare is the thing, not your ego."

CONCLUSION

The attentive student will find himself prepared to proceed to fuller study of the several principal aspects of public speaking at the same time that, following the guidance of this chapter, he begins to get profitable experience in speaking. He will be establishing the habit (1) of stating and developing ideas according to a few basic patterns, (2) of bringing to bear on his main ideas the force of factual information, examples, comparisons and contrasts, and testimony, and (3) of concentrating on his audience and his message rather than on himself as he is talking. In his subsequent study he will find elaboration, refinement, and reinforcement of the habits he has begun to establish in this first speeches.

The following is the text of an excellent first speech.

Howard E. Schmitz

The Old Crank Next Door

This speech was delivered by a young college graduate, a chemist, in an adult evening class in public speaking. His audience was composed of a variety of men and women from many businesses and professions, having in common chiefly their desire to improve their speaking. The speech was intended to fulfill a regular assignment of a 3-to-4-minute speech of simple structure.

All of us have a conscience and each of us has a pretty good idea of what a conscience is. I am not concerned, therefore, either with proving that you have a conscience or with explaining what I think a conscience is. What I want to do this evening is to point out three things which I think are important to keep in mind if we are to understand and get along with our consciences.

In the first place, the only thing that conscience does is to punish us. Its nature is clearly shown by the words used to describe it: "strict," "stern," "harsh," "pricking," "scolding," "nagging." Even "guilty," when used in this connection, refers not to the conscience itself, but to the way that it makes us feel. On the other hand, who ever heard of a "kind," "generous," or "forgiving" conscience?

Secondly, we can subdue our conscience but never escape from it, as evidenced by the story about Mr.— which we all read in the papers two weeks ago. Here was a man who in a period of fifteen years embezzled something over $200,000 from the bank for which he worked. To me, the amazing thing about the story is not that he was able to embezzle so much money successfully, without even his wife's knowledge, but that he was caught by his own word. Not only did he admit his guilt without being accused, but he continued to volunteer a great deal of information about what he had done—information which might not have been found out even by close cross-questioning. I think it is plain that although his conscience had been by-passed for fifteen years, it finally caught up with him.

The last important thing to remember is that the punishments handed out by conscience are often much too severe for the crime committed. For example, think of the normally moderate drinker who goes to an especially good party one evening and has three or four too many drinks. He soon begins to feel pretty good and does and says things that he ordinarily would not, much to everyone's delight. But he finally goes home and goes to sleep, and by morning his drugged conscience will have regained full strength. You can rest assured that no one who was at the party will feel as ashamed of his behavior as he himself will, and it will probably be some time before he will be able to square himself with this precious conscience.

Thus we can see that although the conscience is often called "a little voice inside," it acts more like "the old crank next door." It never has a good word for us, is always looking for trouble and when it finds it, often makes the punishment outweigh the crime. As with the crank next door, the best we can do is to understand its nasty disposition and try to give it few things to complain about.

INQUIRIES

1. What would be the most effective kind of developing material with which to support or enlarge upon the following statements before such kinds of audiences as you specify? Specify the audience as precisely as you can, indicate the kind of developing material you think would get the best results, and explain why you think so? Would you open with the statement? or lead into it? or conclude with it?

   a. Women's libbers are on the right track.
   b. Television commercials are their own burlesques.
   c. Many modern Americans hurry to save time in order to waste more of it.
   d. College education is not in as high repute as it was in our parents' youth.
   e. The demand for "relevance" has materially changed college education.

Compose one or more two-to-three-minute speeches illustrating your decision.

2. Compose a comparatively restricted *statement* for a single-unit speech of about three minutes in one of the following areas, and show how you might develop it using exclusively any one of the kinds of development discussed in the chapter: "rated" films, attending church, soap operas, dormitory living, the theater today, campaign oratory, bargain shopping, bicycling, and health.

3. Examine some expository and argumentative articles in such popular magazines as *Readers Digest* or the *New Yorker* and on the editorial page of your favority newspaper to determine their characteristic use of developing materials. Find paragraphs developed primarily with each of the kinds of materials we have discussed. Report on what seems to you the effectiveness of the materials as used.

4. A proper test of a speaker's ability to present his ideas clearly is a listener's ability to report him clearly. For your next speech, therefore, designate someone to report you back. Have a classmate or friend try to report your subject statement, your main supporting statements, and the kinds of development you used.

FURTHER READING

Baird, A. Craig, Franklin H. Knower, and Samuel L. Becker. *General Speech Communication.* 4th ed. 1971. Chapter 4.

Clevenger, Theodore, Jr. "A Synthesis of Experimental Research in Stage Fright." *Quarterly Journal of Speech,* 40 (1959), 134-45.

Monroe, Alan H., and Douglas Ehninger. *Principles and Types of Speech Communication.* 7th ed. 1974. Chapter 4.

CHAPTER 3

Subjects and Basic Materials

Student speakers in the classroom, and some other speakers as well, sometimes must speak in public without benefit of a need arising from particularly lively matters of immediate concern to themselves or to their intended audiences. For persons in such situations the present chapter is intended to be helpful; but there can be no adequate substitute for an active interest in the world of people and events. Faced with making a speech, an individual should not say to himself or herself, "I have to speak, but what *shall* I talk about?" but rather, "I have an opportunity to do business with an audience; how can I achieve something useful to them and me?"

SUBJECTS

Subjects and subject matter for speeches rise out of audience's needs and a speaker's resources, particularly where those needs and resources overlap. It usually is helpful to consider them with respect to their appropriateness to the communicative situation.

Specific Time and Occasion

Is the occasion the regular weekly meeting of a service club, such as Rotary, Lions, or Kiwanis, where a twenty-minute speech is the usual after-luncheon fare? The audience is used to great variety in subjects, speakers, and talent, and it has probably developed considerable tolerance in all three. A speaker, therefore, will be listened to appreciatively on almost anything he will make interesting. He will not want to waste the occasion, however, or to miss some special opportunity it may offer. There are many subjects which could fit almost any season of the year or any date—public service, civic pride, business prospects, and the like. If, however, the speaker is to address such a club in mid-January, say, and the community has suffered a bad fire during the Christmas holidays, or if a vote on a new School Board bond issue is a week or two away, he has a special opportunity to focus interest on his choice and treatment of subject. In brief, an audience meeting at a particular time has ideas and feelings about recent or coming events; a speaker should be aware of these when he chooses his subject and general purpose.

The Classroom Occasion and Audience

Most readers of this book should give special consideration to circumstances of place and time in the classroom. True, student speakers confront the same audience session after session; they speak under the same general conditions; the general purpose—to inform, to amuse, to persuade—may be prescribed by the instructor, but the circumstances of the classroom, fortunately, are not always the same from day to day. It is true that in a public speaking class students have the impression that practice in speaking is the main thing, and the audience merely furnishes a chance for practice, and that the set-up, in short, is an artificial learning situation. Although circumstances are somewhat artificial, the speaker should not make the situation even more artificial. For example, it is a mistake to suppose that by imagining the class to be the Young Men's Business Club and selecting a subject appropriate to that group one can make his speech more genuine. The speaker who fancies the class to be something other than what it really is virtually ignores his listeners. They quickly realize the neglect and rightly conclude that if they are to be interested at all they must be concerned with skill, technique, and presentation. If in selecting a subject a student sidesteps his audience in the classroom he cannot expect to secure attention for his ideas. Classroom audiences *often* become interested in what is said. After all, both students and instructors are human beings to be dealt with as an audience or as a series of audiences. They have their interests, their feelings, their experiences, their enthusiasms, their share of ignorance, their prejudices, and their wrong ideas. They can stay awake or go to sleep. They can be interested or bored. Their ignorance can be removed, their opinions changed. And they are probably as sympathetic an audience as a speaker will ever address. The good student speaker will speak in his own person to his classmates in their own persons. Their natures are various enough so that his problems will be sufficiently real as long as he stays with them. "Interest *us*, inform *us*, persuade *us*," they say, "Never try just to make a speech; it can't be done." The student speaker should consider his audience in the classroom as he would anywhere else.

Influence of Time Limit on Subject and Purpose

In the occasion and circumstances of any speech, the time allotted to the speaker must greatly influence the choice of specific subject and purpose. The time factor is especially important in the short speech. Once the proper subject is chosen, the problem becomes how to limit and restrict it so as to leave a single impression with the audience.

A *personage,* asked to speak before the East End Kiwanis Club or the students of Central High School because they want to hear him, regardless of what he speaks about, has the whole responsibility of choosing the subject—both the general subject, "Education," for example, and the particular delimitation of that subject, for instance, courses in safety on the highway. An authority on South America, asked to speak before the St. Andrew's Men's Club but not given a subject, will, no doubt, choose to speak on South America, but he will have to decide what limited aspect of the subject to explore in his twenty-minute speech. Perhaps he will choose some new evidences of the success or lack of success of the Alliance for Progress in Brazil, as most proper for audience, occasion, and time available. Even if one is asked to speak to the chapter of Sigma Beta on the founders of the fraternity, he still has the problem of defining just what part of that subject he will try to cover.

Delimiting the general subject into a specific subject of such size and simplicity that it can be handled fully enough in the time available is not always easy, but it must be done in order to avoid the skimming speech, the speech of too-little-about-too-much. It is what the audience remembers that matters, not what the speaker thinks he has presented; and listening audiences, even more than reading audiences, remember a few ideas that have been vividly and fully amplified, whereas they retain almost nothing from a large collection of undeveloped statements—a rapid sequence of pellets of information or ideas.

In deciding how to limit his ideas and supporting material, the speaker might construct a potential test of the knowledge or behavior which he would expect from his audience as a result of the speech. If his objective were to impart an understanding of the value-added tax, for example, he might expect his listeners to answer correctly a question concerning the difference between it and a sales tax. To answer any question, the listener must have received the information in a form interesting enough to listen to and clear enough to understand. Formulating such a test will help the speaker focus on the essential aspects of his topic—the ones that he hopes the audience will retain.

Limiting the subject must be a process of *cutting down,* not *thinning out.* Strange as the advice may seem, experience shows that most student speakers need to say *more about less,* not less about more. They need to say *enough about something* rather than too little about everything. Therefore we suggest two helpful expedients in choosing a limited view of a subject and of making a single impression upon hearers. We shall assume a brief speech of from four to seven minutes. We shall assume, too, an audience interested in collective bargaining and pretty well informed about it.

1. *Determining and phrasing concisely the specific purpose will often limit the subject satisfactorily.* Is the audience to be firm in its support of collective bargaining? But for whom? Public employees? A particular class of public employees such as firemen? Or teachers? Or policemen, if the right to strike is not included? In particular kinds of situations? The speaker should phrase his specific purpose accordingly: To show that people are right to support collective bargaining for industrial workers; or to show that it is right to exclude domestic help from collective bargaining. To state the purpose in a general way is not enough: "To explain why collective bargaining exists"; "to argue against collective bargaining"—these are far too broad in scope, even for a ten-minute speech.

2. In developing the ideas that will accomplish the purpose, it would be well to *plan to use at least two one-minute illustrations.* If there isn't time for two detailed illustrations, the purpose and subject are probably still too broad to make a single vivid impression on the hearers.

APPROPRIATENESS TO THE SPEAKER

In looking for a subject that arises out of the occasion and is also fitting for him, a sensible speaker will consider his own immediate resources:

His life and experience.

His vocation, business, or profession.

The work of persons he knows.

Information he has gained from reading, watching television, listening to public speeches.

His reactions to movies, plays, exhibitions, sporting events.

The current affairs, events, and problems of his locality, his city, his state, his nation, and the world.

Knowledge and Experience

The notion is much too common (and particularly in public speaking classes) that nothing that one knows, believes, wants, or has done can be of interest to other people. We all, to be sure, have many of the same experiences and the same thoughts. We also have many of the same interests, and we often enjoy nothing more than proving to each other that we have common experiences. Witness any gathering where people talk about their ailments and operations. One's own mind and one's own experience are the first good sources of subjects; and no subject is really good until, in the broadest sense, it has become one's own. One doesn't have to be a real estate operator or a builder to have just gone through the experience of buying property and building a house. The information gathered and the problems faced are fresh in the speaker's mind and will prove interesting to his audience, whose experiences and information are likely to be either nonexistent or more re-mote than his. What an individual knows more about, what he understands more fully, what he has thought through more completely than most people—therein lie subjects for speeches. If he doesn't know enough, though he knows more than most people, he can learn more.

Taking note of conversations should prove useful in finding subjects for speeches. What do we and our friends talk about? What questions do we ask? What do other people talk and ask about? Answers to these questions give fairly good notions of what people are interested in and curious about.

Occupation and Profession

Everyone is to some extent a specialist. He knows his own job more inti-mately than other people know it, and he is better acquainted with the jobs that go on about him—in his shop, in his department, in his plant, in his in-dustry, in his neighborhood, or in his home town—than are strangers. We all, of course, know a little something about the work of a secretary, a book-keeper, a file clerk, a salesman, a crane operator, a head usher, a filling-station attendant; and if a speaker tells us, in general terms, only what everyone knows, he will not interest us. If, however, from his own experience, he distinguishes his job as a secretary to the vice-president of the Chow-Chow Mills, or as file clerk in the U.S. Inspector's Office, from other such jobs, we will be interested. What does it take to be editor of the campus newspaper, manager of the basketball team, server of hot foods in the cafe-teria, assistant telephone operator, laboratory assistant in zoology? What does one do? What does one have to know?

Reading and Listening Habits

Let the speaker searching for a subject ask: "Have I read a book, an article, a piece in the paper lately that seemed informative, interesting, provocative? Have I thus run across a fresher or newer or better approach to something that stirs my interest anew? Perhaps it is worth explanation or interpretation. Perhaps I can recommend that my hearers read it." Of course the speaker's job will be to explain the book or article to the audience, not merely to indicate that he has read it; to show his audience that they will enjoy the book, not merely to tell them so. This means the use of much vivid, specific detail.

"What have I heard on the radio or television that provoked ideas or gave me interesting or valuable information my audience may have missed?" If a speaker listens for subjects he will find many possibilities.

Courses of Study

For students in school or college, reading and listening are likely to be largely connected with courses of study, from which may come many good subjects for classroom speeches.

The aspects of ideas that people find attractive and interesting are the new, the familiar, and the systematic. Consider the student who explained what a chemical solution is. He drew his subject from his chemistry course in quantitative analysis. One-third of his listeners were taking the same course with the same instructor, yet the speaker did not bore them; nor did he speak over the heads of the rest of his audience. All found the speech interesting. Why? Because he was wise enough (1) to take a subject that everyone knew something about and that was to a greater or lesser degree familiar; (2) to amplify the information he had heard in class and had read in the textbook by consulting other books on the nature of chemical solutions and by asking his instructor for further information on one matter that was not clear to him, thus gaining and presenting information that was new to his audience; and (3) to present the results of his thinking so clearly and systematically that the order and structure of his ideas made listening easy and pleasant.

What this student speaker did, others can do—if they have the wisdom, the imagination, and the energy to add new information to the old, to find a new "slant," or point of view, and to work over their ideas until they can deliver them clearly. There are great potentialities for subjects in courses in science, the social sciences, English literature and language, engineering, law, and medicine. One of the most practical steps to take toward finding subjects is to thumb through notes and textbooks, with these questions in mind: What topics need further clarification and illustration? Which may be especially interesting and timely? Perhaps this is a neat formula for a short speech: Add new information to old, include new illustrations for old information, and present everything so clearly that it cannot be misunderstood.

Current Affairs

Current affairs constitute a source of subjects that is most often, and rightly, turned to by students of public speaking. The danger, however, is that students will turn to it too frequently and conceive of it too generally. There are many small subjects as well as large ones in these areas. It is not necessary to discuss a public question in all its aspects in order to speak on it. One does not have to tackle the whole subject of economic discrimination in order to expose the inequities of pay for women in a particular business, industry, or profession. Nor does one need to be a national authority on state governments in order to make himself well enough informed on the legislative article of the proposed new state constitution to talk profitably about it to a general audience.

People are often scantily or vaguely informed on current affairs and problems, except those few that strike them immediately, personally, and deeply. However, we are all eager to be told. Otherwise there would be far fewer analysts and commentators on radio and TV and in the press. Any speaker who will inform himself with reasonable thoroughness on a public question, or even on any phase of such a question, will have several good subjects for speeches. People with technical specialties, too, may find subjects adapted to their special knowledge in current events. For example, one engineering student noticed in the newspaper an account of the collapse of a new river bridge in a high wind. The event prompted him to look into the history of similar accidents, and his investigations resulted in a very good speech on the current collapse, others like it, and the probable cause.

Current problems and questions are often only the immediate versions of problems and questions that are always with us, the discussion of which is always pertinent and potentially interesting. Religion, love and marriage, divorce, health, education, taxation, war and peace, race relations, good government—all these are subjects that are unlikely to be exhausted for many years to come. Though they are old subjects, phases of them may be made new by a speaker who will restate them in a new way, give them fresh illustration, and adapt them to current conditions.

The speaker as learner

Students have made excellent speeches simply by following up subjects about which they were curious and wanted to learn more. They frequently find that their public speaking class provides the opportunity, which their full schedules would not otherwise permit, of reading (for credit!) materials outside their specialties. They often pick subjects on which they have little knowledge but strong curiosity. A young woman who spoke on the plight of the American Indian won a university-wide speech contest. Her curiosity had first been piqued by a chance conversation with a lawyer who represented an Indian reservation. Later she made her speech class the occasion for informing herself fully.

APPROPRIATENESS TO THE AUDIENCE

What are audiences interested in? First, more often than not, they can be interested in what others know about and are interested in. Especially is this true of the classroom audience, and many of these possibilities we have pointed to already.

Second, they are interested in what all human beings are fundamentally interested in. They are attracted by new light on what is already familiar to them, that is, "news"—news about the current campus notable or some public figure, about the latest thing in airplanes, automobiles, medical techniques, engineering procedures, clothing styles, accident insurance, computers. Or, the old and familiar presented in a new and unusual way. Or, a fresh point of view or a new interpretation. Not only do new facts and data claim attention; new ways of looking at the established, familiar facts also are often effective. Detective stories almost always illustrate this truth. The facts are put before the district attorney, the slow-witted police sergeant, the sharp detective, and the reader, and each supplies his own interpretation. Each interpretation usually produces a different suspect, and each is interesting, although eventually there is but one correct solution.

Third, people are interested in familiar ideas and facts presented systematically and clearly. We often enjoy seeing familiar facts brought together and given structure and continuity, so that we recognize the whole and its parts all in neat order. A student might discover, for example, that after the class had read this chapter he could hold their interest on the topic "How to Find Speech Subjects" if he did nothing more than present an orderly and concise review.

Subjects Too Difficult for Oral Presentation

Though many more kinds of subjects are available than some student speakers realize, it is true that certain subjects are unadaptable to successful oral presentation and that others require the use of facilities usually not available. In one phase of the instruction intended to improve the effectiveness of employees in an industrial plant, the leader of a group of foremen first described fully and carefully how to tie the fire underwriters' knot. He then asked members of the audience to tie the knot—but no one could. Next he explained and demonstrated, but still no one could tie the knot. Until he guided an individual several times through the actual performance, the instruction proved ineffective. Here was a subject unadapted to effective oral presentation. The audience learned from the speaker's words that there was a knot to be tied. He might also successfully have informed them of the uses of the knot, and possibly why the knot was better than others for certain purposes. He could not make them understand the knot itself.

Subjects of the following kinds are likely to be very difficult or impossible for unaided oral presentation:

Subtle or complicated processes, the explanation of which requires the accurate visualization by the listener of a long series of actions and the correct remembering of them.

Technical subjects requiring the mastery of specialized concepts and vocabulary, and the pursuit of close reasoning which demands reviewing and slow working out through study. Many papers read at scientific and learned gatherings, even before specialists, result only in the audience's realizing that some investigation has been done and some conclusions reached by the speaker, the account of which it will be necessary to read over and study carefully later on.

Subjects requiring the detailed understanding of large quantities of figures and statistics. (If, of course, only the conclusions and the fact that statistics have been used to derive the conclusions are important, then these subjects are quite usable.)

Subjects which involve the discussion of intimate or personal material which people would read alone without embarrassment or discomfort, but which they would be reluctant to listen to in a group.

The Value of a Good Subject

A speaker who is satisfied with his subject, whether in the classroom or elsewhere, enjoys important initial advantages, for a good subject both increases his desire to "do business" with his audience and enlivens his manner of presentation.

When a speaker senses that his subject fits the occasion, the audience, and himself—that it is important for his audience and for him—his delivery benefits markedly. A good subject sharpens the speaker's sense of immediacy and enhances his sense of direct communication with his audience. If the subject really fits the audience and matters to the speaker, and if he thinks that he knows more about it than the audience does, or that he has a new slant on it, he will be eager to address his listeners. Both his voice and manner will reveal those intangible clues that indicate to an audience "This speaker has real business with us." The speaker's inflection has greater variety, force and energy, and directly commands attention. Words come more easily, and his rate of utterance shows greater flexibility.

The speaker who likes his subject invariably puts the stamp of his own personality on his speech. Although he may have picked up ideas from a number of sources, *he* reacts to them in *his* own way; he turns them to *his* use and for *his* purposes; he combines them in *his* manner and gives them *his* emphasis and *his* own peculiar coloring. As a result, his speech is a new combination of ideas, a compound that bears the impress of his own judgment, imagination, and personality. It becomes a speech that only *he* can produce. Although his speech may reflect in part old and familiar notion, it is a new, *individual* product.

Important as a good subject is, however, searching or waiting for the perfect subject is a waste of time. There is no such thing. If the student speaker can persuade himself that what he values his fellow students ought also to value, if he understands his subject and attempts to make his audience understand or accept it, he will go a long way toward making a good speech.

To conclude: Good subjects for speeches arise from the right occasions and from a sense of what speakers and audiences consider significant, worthwhile, and valuable. The intrinsic worth of a subject may be less important than what the speaker does with it—what he makes of it for his classroom audience. An adequate subject chosen early is much better than an excellent subject chosen too late to be developed fully.

MATERIALS

When a speaker has chosen his subject, or at least has a possible range of subject matter in mind, he can proceed to work efficiently. Conscious of his subject and beginning to live with it, he finds it attracting ideas from many sources and often at unexpected times.

What is a speaker looking for? He wants to find two kinds of materials: (1) reliable facts, and (2) authoritative interpretations and opinions. These constitute the basic material for both informative and persuasive discourse. Sometimes these spring readily out of the memory and experience of the speaker; more often they have to be searched for.

Kinds of Materials

Facts

In the communicative situation, facts consist of verifiable data that are held to be true, independent of the speaker's use of them. When these data appear in informative communications, they can well be called *information*. When they occur in persuasive communications and in argument, they are properly thought of as *evidence*.

The difference between fact and interpretation can be illustrated in this way. Suppose some persons are playing bridge when they hear a piercing scream in the street. They rush to the window and behold a woman yelling in the road, a car passing by, a man running in one direction, and a dog running in another direction. These events are facts observed by each person. Now suppose one observer says, "The man hit her"; another, "The car hit her"; another, "The dog bit her." These statements are interpretations of the data by three different persons. Suppose it becomes important to decide which interpretation is to be accepted. Each statement, each interpretation, is open to question. An undemonstrable statement is known technically as an opinion. If one is looking for information, then, facts should not be confused with interpretations, nor interpretations with opinions.

The first type of fact is the single, isolated fact or event, historical or present. The X Corporation will spend a quarter of a billion dollars on new machinery in 1975. James's grade last semester in History 777 was "B." Franklin was present at the Constitutional Convention in Philadelphia in 1787.

The second kind of fact is statistical data. We need to recognize simply that one function of statistics is classification of a number of facts for whatever purpose the investigator has in mind. The Acting Director of the University Honors Program was interested in knowing how well the James Scholars, academically superior high school students, had performed in the University. These bright students had been grouped according to their rank in their high school class and according to their achievement in the honors program. In the speech printed on page 243, Professor Dora E. Damrin reported:

> In 1959 we admitted 137 students [into the James Scholar Program]. This group had a mean high school rank of 93.8. By the end of their freshman year 36 percent—or one out of every three students—had been dropped. Last year, September 1963, we admitted 289 students. The mean high school rank for the group hit an all-time high of 94.7. By the end of their freshman year 49 percent —or one out of every two students—had been dropped.

In reading newspapers and magazines we almost always encounter statistics. To get some idea of the many ways data are classified statistically, inspect *Information Please Almanac* and the *Statistical Abstract of the United States*. (See these and other bibliographic resources in Chapter 4.)

A third kind of fact is represented by scientific laws and principles. Like statistics, they are ways of describing and classifying a large number of related events. From our study of elementary economics, we have all learned that in a free market the greater the supply of a commodity, the lower the price; in other words, the more oranges, the lower their price. This is the old law of supply and demand. From our first encounter with electrical phenomena, we learned that like charges of electricity repel, that unlike attract, and that electricity flows from the negative pole to the positive pole. From psychology we know that every stimulus has its response, every response its stimulus. Indeed, all our sciences and disciplines have established principles and laws. They may be considered general statements of fact, because they describe the behavior of many individual events under conditions of controlled observation. The events have been noted and verified time and again. Hence, the principle derived from the events is considered to be true, until someone makes an observation that calls it into question. Our textbooks on any subject contain scores of up-to-date examples of such principles and laws.

Opinions

In making their explanations and enforcing their arguments, speakers, like all of us, often have to rely on the opinion of others. This is certainly the case when facts are unobtainable. We seek opinions in which we can have confidence. We tend to honor the opinions of scientists and technologists on technical matters. The courts of law make much of "expert" opinion and testimony. We may find ourselves believing that municipal bonds of small cities in our state are sound investments because our banker says they have yielded well for years. He should know, and unless we have other grounds for belief or disbelief, his statement carries weight.

Reliability of facts and opinions

In gathering materials, a speaker must, of course, evaluate what he reads and hears, for other facts, evidence, and opinions are checks on the reliability and trustworthiness of his sources.

Are the Sources of Evidence Reliable? Who observed the fact or compiled the statistics? Is there any reason to suspect that the observer was influenced by more than ordinary bias? The "facts" about lung cancer and cigarette smoking are many and various. One puts more trust in those reported by an independent laboratory than in those given out by the laboratory of a tobacco company.

The reliability of authoritative opinion must be weighed with special care. Is the person expressing the opinion in a special position to know the facts on which his opinion is based? A local banker is presumably in a position to know about the behavior of municipal bonds in his state or region. But would he be as acceptable an authority on bonds of other sorts across the country as the investment department of the Chase Manhattan Bank?

Furthermore, does the person expressing the opinion have a reputation for good judgment, that is, for making conservative and valid inferences from the facts behind his opinions? Is he free of prejudice? A practical way of deciding these questions is to discover whether the authority enjoys the respect and confidence of others who know of him and his work. Has the book from which the speaker has drawn the opinion been favorably received by those qualified to pass upon its worth? (A convenient source of evaluation is the *Book Review Digest*, where many reviews of recent books are brought together.)

Finally, does the opinion run counter to the author's natural interest and bias? If so, it can be given great weight. When Wendell Willkie, a Republican campaigning for the presidency against Franklin Roosevelt, a Democrat, publicly endorsed Roosevelt's foreign policy and his treatment of the Second World War, the endorsement was especially significant because it was contrary to Mr. Willkie's interests to express an opinion that would help the Democrats.

Is the Evidence Sufficiently Inclusive in Scope? Are there other witnesses to the same fact, and do they make the same report? Agreement among a number of witnesses is an excellent check on accuracy. The single evidential fact seldom carries much weight. The law usually insists on more than one witness to a fact.

If a speaker relies on the opinions and judgements of others, he must be sure that a number of authorities hold similar opinions on the same matter. This gives a check on the *consistency* of opinion, as well as on its scope.

If the evidence is statistical, what do the statistics really mean? Does the observer or reporter indicate for what purpose they were gathered? Does he state the method of investigation used? Do the statistics cover a large number of cases? If statistics are valuable in influencing his and other persons' decisions, the speaker should be able to explain the data clearly in his speech.

Is the Evidence Recent? In using the opinions of authorities, the speaker should become date-conscious and should prefer the reliable opinion that is most up-to-date. Authorities, like any of us, do change their minds. And the speaker should check whether or not the witness who is reporting an event cites a specific date.

In short, evidence may be used to support almost any statement. In truth, most of our arguments find their sources in facts and opinions. We discover an argument in the first place when some experience, condition, or opinion is interpreted. One person will see the significance of grades in one way, another in another way. When the meanings clash, argument is created. In this way argument springs from evidential fact and opinion. It leads us away from evidence into the methodical and systematic exploration of its controversial significance. If argument becomes idle and futile, it is in part because its basis—facts, evidence, and opinions—has been lost.

EXPLORING FOR SUBJECT MATTER AND MATERIALS

Anyone who want to prepare speeches efficiently should write down ideas when he gets them. If he merely resolves to record the idea later, or tells himself he couldn't possibly forget *that*, the chances are that he will not have the idea when he wants it. We no longer cultivate the art of remembering, as our ancestors did in a more oral society. We rely on what we record outside our heads.

Economy of effort in speech preparation is the result of working methodically. Because no two minds work exactly alike, there is, of course, no single method of working that is equally effective for everyone. And because there is no universal formula, the young speaker in particular should develop an individual method.

Recognizing the following general conditions of creative activity should help one work out procedures for creating a speech that is clearly one's own and nobody else's.

Much Out of Much

The mind is like a storehouse. If much is in it, much can come out; if little is in it, little can come out. Ten items of information can be grouped in thousands of different ways; three items can be grouped in only six. "Inspiration" seems to be directly proportional to abundance of information and to extent and depth of experience. The preparation of a speech is basically a matter of rapidly increasing materials on a subject—of working them over and stirring them around until a satisfying product is created.

Like Attracts Like

Unlike the elementary law of electricity that holds that like charges repel, an idea supported by a motive attracts similar ideas and repels dissimilar ones. We see what we want to see and do not see what we do not want to see—unless someone forces us to. To stack the cards intelligently in his favor, the speaker should keep subject and motive in the forefront of his consciousness. Then, without deliberate effort, he will find himself picking up related ideas out of his past experience and his current studies and conversation with others.

Listening and Talking

Listening and talking, together with observation and investigation, are the most direct methods of extending knowledge and gaining experience about a subject. We may acquire some new ideas and information through casual discussion with friends; but we cannot depend solely on casual contacts. It is profitable to talk with others on the subject, to plan interviews with informed persons, and to steer the conversation in the right direction. Especially in college circles can we find such persons—both students and instructors. The great virtue of conversation is that it not only shows us what we do not know and what we need to verify and clarify but it also strengthens and intensifies what we do know and gives us practice in talking about it. Furthermore, the questions other people ask, as well as the information they disclose, tell us what they do not know and would find interesting.

Observing and Investigating

If his subject makes it possible, the speaker should look as well as discuss. If he plans to speak on the functions or the problems of the local school board, he could well observe a session of the board. If he intends to condemn the tactics of the justice of the peace, he could easily go look at the local justice in action.

The special boon of observation is that it makes experience vivid and intense. Because it registers sharp impressions, it lengthens memory—and it yields firsthand examples for speeches.

Reading

Conversation, observation, and direct investigation are the preferred ways of knowing what one is talking about, but for most speakers at most times, these methods are extremely limited and uneconomical. Students especially do not always have the time and opportunity to travel, and being young they have limited experience. So reading remains the fastest and most practicable avenue for the extension of their knowledge.

The student can read up on a subject for a speech efficiently if he will distinguish between focus and perspective. Remembering for a speech that the focus is the specific subject, the student can go directly to the relevant source materials in the library or elsewhere. Indeed, he may have acquired a number of foci for his subject—through conversation and in other ways—that he needs to extend or verify. At any rate, he can read as a hound hunts, with nose on the trail.

Gaining the perspective on a subject entails reading not only on the subject but around it. The more we can learn about the history and background of the subject, the better. Any special subject is closely related to more general ones. For example, if he plans to talk on the best method of reviewing for examinations, a student would soon be led to the principles of learning and memory. He should be especially sure to read anything on his subject that his audience is very likely to have read or to know about. Otherwise the listeners may well react "Doesn't he know we know so-and-so and are thinking about this and that?" Finally, in working on a controversial subject, it is best not to take sides firmly until after one has read widely and considered fairly the best arguments on all sides. The speaker in controversy needs as much perspective as possible.

How much reading? No one can say for sure. But a few trusted rules of thumb may help to decide. In general, read as much as time will permit—and then a little more. The extra article adds to confidence. For an informative speech, reading should be extensive enough to enable the speaker to answer a relevant question from anyone in the audience. For a persuasive speech, we can be reasonably sure we have not missed the important arguments if we read until the arguments begin being repeated.

Read critically

The person who is determined to disbelieve everything he reads is usually as badly off as the person who swallows everything whole. One should read to learn and to understand, or as Bacon said, "to weigh and consider," not to approve or disapprove. The speaker should decide on approval or disapproval, if either is involved, only after he knows the subject. He should also read with skepticism about the source and authority of the material. When reading opinion and argument, and even when reading primarily informative, factual material, he should determine, if possible, who wrote it and why it was written, being careful, also, to notice when and where it was published. Who a writer is, what his basic beliefs and assumptions are, and the purpose for which he is presenting his explanation or his argument may tell much about the value of the material for present purposes. One can learn a good deal about an author by consulting the sources of biographical information listed in Chapter 4.

Read accurately

Enough misunderstanding, misinformation, and misrepresentation already exist. A careful investigator and an accurate communicator guards against creating more. He understands not only what the source says but what it means. One's first reading of a book or article may be swift to get the general drift. But thereafter one should read only as fast as he can do so with understanding. Moreover, it is essential to consider statements, ideas, and information in the contexts in which they occur. A statement often means one thing in its context and something different out of it.

Conclusion

The substance of this chapter lies at the center, or composes the foundation, of good speech-making. A good speech grows out of: (1) a good subject appropriate to audience, to circumstances of time and occasion, and to speaker; (2) sound and plentiful facts (information and evidence) and tested, verified, relevant opinion (testimony); and the fullest possible investigation, experience, and thought by the speaker. Otherwise the speech is not likely to be worth the making or the hearing.

INQUIRIES

1. Within each of the following broad areas of public concern, list a number of specific, delimited subjects for speeches which would be appropriate for making to your class at the present time: *good government, vocational education, public morality, environmental protection, public health, birth control and abortion, entertainment, recreation, war and peace, youth and age.*

2. After adequate study of this chapter and consultation with your instructor and selected classmates, draw up a list of subjects you would be interested in using for speeches during the rest of the course. What would be, say, two general *subjects* in which you are, or think you could become, genuinely interested? Turn them over in your mind, make a preliminary survey of available materials, and select some special or restricted aspects of each with a view to speaking on them in the future. Be prepared to explain or defend your choices on the basis of audience, circumstances, and available materials.

3. What seem to be the subjects of immediate and perennial interest and concern to people in your social-political context? In order to extend your notions, read two successive issues of *Time* and *Newsweek* and follow for at least one week the editorial pages and the syndicated columnists in a daily paper in your area. Look also at the columns of letters to the editor. What *are* people interested in—or what should they be?

4. On the basis of sound criteria, criticize the subjects, or the particular aspects of prescribed subjects, chosen by speakers whom you have heard recently, in class and outside it. Explain your favorable or unfavorable judgments. Suggest alternatives or modifications for those you found inappropriate.

5. What are facts? As distinguished from what? Guesses? Falsehoods? Imaginings? Poetry? Observe the use among your associates and in other public and private talk of the expressions "In view of the fact that," "The fact of the matter is," "The facts speak for themselves" or "Let the facts speak for themselves." Do you find people generally meaning *fact* as we use the word in this chapter? Or are they, perhaps, using the word to suggest strength when what they are talking about is really some vague notion, some feeling, some doubtful opinion?

6. People often seem to use the term *testimony* to mean what we in this chapter refer to as *opinion evidence.* Account for that "fact." What do those concepts have in common? How are they to be discriminated, if they are?

7. On the use of documentary evidence, two major factors need to be investigated—or at least confirmed—*authenticity* and *reliability*. What do these terms mean? Why are both important in testing evidence?

FURTHER READING

Baird, A. Craig, Franklin H. Knower, and Samuel L. Becker. *General Speech Communication*. 4th ed. 1971. Chapters 6 and 8.

Monroe, Alan H., and Douglas Ehninger. *Principles and Types of Speech Communication*. 7th ed. 1974. Chapter 7.

Reid, Loren. *Speaking Well*. 2nd ed. 1972. Chapter 5.

CHAPTER 4

Finding Materials and Library Resources

FINDING INFORMATION IN PRINT

The library is to the speechmaker what the laboratory is to the scientist. It is the speaker's place of search and research. A full discussion of sources for reading material is ordinarily found in any good book on composition and rhetoric. Furthermore, the reference librarians in any school or public library will gladly introduce a student to the many guides to reading matter. For the convenience of the student whose memory needs jogging, we include a brief mention of some of the most important bibliographical aids.

The Card Catalogue

As most students doubtless know, the card catalogue in a library lists all the books in that library alphabetically. For each book there are usually cards in three places in the catalogue, one filed under author, another by title, and a third by subject matter. Either of the first two will make it possible to locate a specific book. If one has only a subject in mind, say *plastics, advertising,* or *vitamins,* he may start with it, and after the card bearing the subject name, he will find the books related to it.

Each catalogue card for a book not only lists the book's publication date and its contents but notes whether the book contains a bibliography, which can be helpful in spotting related books. At the bottom of the card appear two or three subjects under which to look for related books.

In general, the latest book on the subject is preferable. To discover it consult the *Cumulative Book Index*. This work lists all books printed in the United States since 1928 and is kept up to the month.

Encyclopedias: Encyclopaedia Britannica,
Encyclopedia Americana, Collier's Encyclopedia

These sources try to keep their materials up to date by regularly publishing supplements, some of which appear annually. See *Britannica Book of the Year*, 1938 to date. Encyclopedias are valuable not only for their general articles on a variety of subjects but for the short reference lists usually given at the ends of the principal articles.

Most of the more specialized encyclopedias are out of date, but in two of them, at least, students still find the short historical articles helpful: the *Encyclopedia of the Social Sciences* (1930-1935), and the *Encyclopaedia of Religion and Ethics* (1908-1927). The *International Encyclopedia of the Social Sciences*, edited by David Sills, is current to 1968.

Articles and Pamphlets

Indexes general in scope

The *Readers' Guide to Periodical Literature*, subscribed to by most libraries, is an up-to-date listing of articles in many popular and general magazines in America which are largely nontechnical. Articles are listed alphabetically by author, title, and subject, as books are listed in the card catalogue. In looking for articles on a subject, a searcher should not limit himself to looking only under the name that he happens to have in mind for that subject, for example, *taxes*. He should look also under other possible names for the same general subject, such as *taxation, revenue, finance*. (See figures 1 and 2.) The *Readers' Guide* is published monthly and the monthly installments are assembled into quarterly and yearly volumes. *Poole's Index to Periodical Literature* is useful similarly, especially for articles published before the *Readers' Guide* was begun (1900). The *Nineteenth Century Readers' Guide*, 1890-1899, published in 1944, covers some of the same material within *Poole's Index* but arranges the entries according to the same system used in the current *Readers' Guide*.

The *Social Sciences and Human Index*, formerly the *International Index to Periodicals*, covers periodicals not usually indexed in the *Readers' Guide*, including scholarly journals in the humanities and social sciences.

The *Public Affairs Information Service*, similar to the *Readers' Guide* in form and method of listing, includes not only periodical articles but books, pamphlets, and documents related to all subjects connected with public affairs.

PROPAGANDA

Dilemma of cultural propaganda: let it be; American propaganda, A. Goodfriend. Ann Am Acad 398: 101-12 N '71

Promotion of chaos: the three major catalysts; address, July 17, 1971. R.E.L. Eaton. Vital Speeches 37:687-20 S 1 '71

Propaganda: morally questionable and morally unquestionable techniques. R. K. White. bibliog f Ann Am Acad 398:26-25 N '71

Selling Uncle Sam in the seventies. K.R. Sparks. bibliog f Ann Am Acad 398:113-23 N '71

Six 'big lies' about America. A. Beechman. 11 NY *Times* Mag p 32-3 + Je 6 '71

See also
Moving pictures—Propaganda films
Propaganda, International
Vietnamese war, 1957—Propaganda

PROUST, Marcel

Lunch: excerpt from On reading: tr by W.S. Burford, Vogue 158: 118-9 + N 1 '71

Proust's prefaces to Ruskin; excerpts, ed. by J. Autret and W. Burford, Nation 212: 565-9 My 3 '71

about
A la recherche de Marcel Proust. il por Time 98:30 + Jl 5 '71*
Eat. M. Cantwell, Mlle 74:9 + N '71*
Letter from Paris. Genêt. New York 47:53 Jl 3 '71*
Marcel Proust: a centennial volume, ed. by P. Quennell. Review
Time il por 98:106 0 11 '71.
M. Maddocks*
One Hundred Years of Proust. H. Moss. New Yorker 47:124 + D 18 '71*
Proust: a prophet remembered. M. Maddocks, Atlan 228:02-5 Jl '71*
Unfinished cathedrals, P. Schneider il Vogue 158:90-101 + D '71*
Woman in Proust's life. S. de Gramont. por Harp Baz 104:54-5 Je '71*

FIGURE 1. Sample Index Entries
Specific headings and reference to specific articles

The *New York Times Index* lists by subject (and author, if any) all articles that have appeared in the *New York Times*. The *Index* will also help to locate material in other newspapers to which there is no index. In the *Times Index* the date of an event or material is a guide for finding things in other newspapers.

The *Vertical File Index* is especially useful for locating valuable pamphlet material published by a variety of organizations. It is issued monthly. Users should realize that most libraries cannot acquire all the pamphlets listed in this catalogue. The general reference room in a library usually keeps the current pamphlets on hand, and the quickest way to find out what may be available on a subject is to ask the reference room attendant. Large colleges maintain departmental libraries housed in special rooms in the main library or elsewhere on the campus; these include collections of materials devoted to journalism, engineering, social sciences, education, and the like. Inquire at such places for pamphlet material. Consult also the Card Catalogue, for libraries keep the most important pamphlets permanently.

The *Monthly Catalog of United States Government Publications* lists all publications issued by the various departments and agencies of the government. The entries are arranged by subject and title. The *Catalog* is extensive and rather complicated, but it is probably the best single source of authoritative government information. When one uses it for the first time, he may need to ask the librarian for guidance.

CIS (*Congressional Information Service*) *Index* (monthly) provides abstracts of almost all documents issued by the U.S. Congress in the previous month. It also provides a main index of data according to subject, of names of witnesses, of names of authors, affiliations of witnesses and authors, names of subcommittees, popular names of bills, reports, or laws. Although cross references are numerous, *CIS Index* is not so complicated as the *Monthly Catalog*.

Indexes restricted in scope

The range of the specialized indexes is indicated fairly accurately by their titles. They concentrate on materials appearing in publications dealing with particular fields. Each aims to cover everything in its field. Hence one discovers more articles related to farming in the *Biological and Agricultural Index* than he does in the *Readers' Guide*. Similarly, the *Readers' Guide* lists

PHYSICS

See also

American institute of physics
Cyclotron
Diffusion
Dimensional analysis
Dynamics
Elasticity
Electrons
Evaporation
Fluids
Fluorescence
Force and energy
Free energy
Friction
Gravitation
Gravity
Heat transmission
Ionization, Gaseous
Ions
Light
Liquids
Magnetism
Meteorology
Molecules
Nuclear physics
Particles, Elementary
Photoelasticity
Plasma (physics)
Plasticity
Porosity

Pressure
Quantum theory
Radiation
Reflection (optics)
Relaxation time (physics)
Sound
Space and time
Statistical mechanics
Steam
Temperature
Thermodynamics
Turbulence
Uncertainty principle
Velocity
Vibration
Viscosity
Vortex motion
Wave mechanics

Bibliography

Publications of the National bureau of standards. Phys & Chem 70A:447-52, 557-63 S-N '66
Resource letter PP-2 on plasma physics; waves and radiation processes in plasmas. G. Bekefi and S.C. Brown, bibliog Am J Phys 34:1001-5 N '66
Your child's physics books. M. Freeman. il Phys Today 19:67-70 + D '66

FIGURE 2.   Sample Index Entries
Topics related to a specific subject

fewer articles on education than the *Education Index* does. The more specialized the subject, the more useful the appropriate special index.

> *Applied Science and Technology Index*
> *Art Index*
> *Biological and Agricultural Index*
> *Business Periodicals Index*
> *Cumulative Dramatic Index*
> *Education Index*
> *Engineering Index*
> *Speech Index*

The last-named source is an index to collections of speeches, by subject and speaker.

Statistical Information

The sources below collect a vast amount of miscellaneous information concerning business, labor, industry, and social welfare. They are mines of facts.

> *World Almanac, and Book of Facts* (1868 to date)
> *Information Please Almanac* (1947 to date)
> *Statistical Abstract of the United States* (1878 to date)
> *Statesman's Yearbook: Statistical and Historical Annual of the States of the World* (1864 to date)
> *Monthly Labor Review* (Reports on employment, payrolls, industrial disputes, retail prices, cost of living, etc.)
> *Survey of Current Business* (Statistics on domestic and foreign trade, exports and imports, etc.)

Biographical Information

> *Who's Who* (British)
> *Who's Who in America*
> *International Who's Who*
> *Current Biography*
> *Webster's Biographical Dictionary* (includes pronunciation)
> *Twentieth Century Authors* (See also its *First Supplement*)
> *Directory of American Scholars*
> *American Men of Science: Physical and Biological Sciences; Social and Behavioral Sciences*

National Crime, Rate, and Percent Change

Crime Index Offenses	Estimated crime 1970		Percent change over 1969		Percent change over 1965		Percent change over 1960	
	Number	Rate per 100,000 Inhabitants	Number	Rate	Number	Rate	Number	Rate
Total	5,568,200	2,740.5	+11.3	+10.6	+90.0	+81.3	+176.4	+143.9
Violent	731,400	360.0	+11.7	+11.0	+90.9	+82.2	+150.5	+126.4
Property	4,836,800	2,380.5	+11.3	+10.6	+89.9	+81.1	+179.7	+146.8
Murder	15,810	7.8	+8.4	+8.3	+60.5	+52.9	+75.7	+56.0
Forcible rape	37,270	18.3	+2.2	+1.1	62.3	+53.8	+121.1	+94.7
Robbery	348,380	171.5	+17.1	+16.4	+152.3	+140.5	+224.4	+186.3
Aggravated assault	329,940	162.4	+7.7	+7.0	+55.6	+48.3	+117.1	+91.7
Burglary	2,169,300	1,067.7	+11.3	+10.6	+71.9	+64.9	+141.7	+113.3
Larceny $50 and over	1,746,100	859.4	+14.5	+13.8	+120.4	+110.2	+224.9	+204.4
Auto Theft	921,400	453.5	+5.7	+5.0	+86.9	+78.3	+182.9	+149.7

FIGURE 3. Typical Reference Table

Source: Table is taken from *Uniform Crime Reports for the United States for 1970* (U.S. Govt. Printing Office).

For the most part, the sources above contain information about living persons, although *Webster's* lists famous persons of all time. The two publications below contain only the noteworthy dead. They are highly authoritative.

> *Dictionary of American Biography* (America)
> *Dictionary of National Biography* (United Kingdom)

Both works have supplements which bring them up to date.

Collections of Noteworthy Quotations

Probably the best is John Bartlett's *Familiar Quotations*, the latest revised edition of which is the fourteenth. Here the speechmaker can often find some of his ideas superbly and tellingly expressed. Even the novice should be conversant with it.

GATHERING AND RECORDING MATERIAL

To save time in searching for material in print, the student should first consult the experts and specialists available to him. If he wants a modern biologist's view on evolution, for example, he may ask a teacher of biology to recommend a book or article. The instructor will be delighted to have him show interest. If the speaker has had a college course related to his subject, he should consult his notes and reference lists. Then when he enters the library he can look directly for the material and can use the sources mentioned above to amplify his information.

Taking Notes

Perhaps workable techniques of note taking are as numerous as readers. Yet in developing his own methods, a student should be aware of the standard timesavers and conventions.

Index cards, $3''$ x $5''$ or $4''$ x $6''$, or half-sheets of paper are better than full pages for taking notes. Cards and half-sheets are faster to handle and sort when one gets to the stage of grouping one's ideas.

In general it is best to restrict each card to a single idea or topic, whether the idea be general or highly specific. Card 1 records one authoritative statement on a complex subject. Card 2 cites a single word needing clarification. Other cards might have as their headings other related concepts.

When one starts reading, often he does not know what specific ideas, facts, examples, or quotations he will eventually use in his speech. He obtains

THE BACKGROUND OF STUDENT PROTEST

Student discontent in America did not begin at Berkeley
in 1964, or with the civil rights movement in the early
1960's. The President's Commission on Campus Unrest observes:
"The history of American colleges during the early 19th
century is filled with incidents of disorder, turmoil, and
riot. These disturbances generally arose over poor food,
primitive living conditions, and harsh regulations. But
though 19th century campus turbulence occasionally reflected
a rebellion against the dominant Puritan religious ethic of
the colleges of the time, student discontent . . . was largely
apolitical."

The Report of The President's Commission on Campus
Unrest (New York: Avon Books, 1971), p. 20.

CARD 1

BASIC BUDDHIST CONCEPTS (Nirvana)

The concept of "nirvana" is one of the most misunderstood
elements of Buddhism. Huston Smith says, "Nirvana is the
highest destiny of the human spirit. Negatively nirvana
is the state in which the faggots of desire have been completely consumed and everything that restricts boundless
life has died. Affirmatively it is boundless life itself."

The Religious Man (New York: Harper and Row Publishers,
1958), p. 125.

CARD 2

likely looking books and articles and explores them. He proceeds to summarize, as briefly as he can, each article, book, or important section thereof, on a single card. Card 3 is an example of such a summary. In shaping the ideas of his speech at a later date, he may suddenly realize that a certain source is relevant. He can then use its card to help him recall its content and decide whether it contained usable facts and illustrations. A summary card, then, guides one back to a source and to pointed research for special items. Summary cards are valuable in another way. Reviewing several cards together may suggest to the speaker the central idea of the speech or some of its leading ideas.

Card 4 refers to a person of note. The speaker records only the infor-

Gregory Mowe, and W. Scott Nobles, "James Baldwin's Message for White America," Quarterly Journal of Speech, 58 (April 1972), 142-51.

Theme: James Baldwin has contributed significantly to the understanding and solution of racial problems in our country. His major themes should not be forgotten.

1. Baldwin redefines racial inequality not as a "black problem," but instead as a problem of White America.

2. Present solutions for racial unrest are doomed unless they take into account the black man's need for identity.

3. White America will be called to account for her sins.

4. White American can be redeemed if it will honestly reassess its past and reinterpret reality in accordance with the reality of the black man.

CARD 3

```
Golda Meir                          (Women Leaders of the World)

   Mrs. Meir has been Premier of Israel since March

1969. Prior to gaining that position, she was

Israel's ambassador to Russia and the United Nations.

   Mrs. Meir, now 75 years of age, was an influential

leader in Israel's fight for recognition and indepen-

dence following WWII. Prior to Israeli independence,

she occupied the highest post in the community of

Palestine. She stepped down, however, and assumed

a cabinet post under David Ben Gurion, who described

her as "the only man in my cabinet."

   Being a former U.S. citizen, Mrs. Meir has worked

closely with the U.S. to end hostilities in the

Middle East and promote the acceptance of Israel

by her Arab neighbors.

   In 1969, Golda Meir ranked fourth on the list of

women most admired by the American public.

                              Current Biography
                                 (Dec. 1970)
```

CARD 4

mation he needs to identify the person for his audience and to show the connection with his subject. The words in parentheses may reflect the speaker's
idea of a possible main head or topic within his speech. If so, another card,
or cards, would bear the same heading, "Women Leaders of the World,"
and would record information on, for example, Indira Gandhi.

Reference cards should always show the source, the date, and the page of
the material—accurately. To have to go back for these facts is a woeful, but
very common, waste of time.

How many note cards? A good rule is, many more than at the moment
seem necessary. Later on in building the speech, it is a lot easier to eliminate
superfluous cards than to make additional trips to the library for further
reading. It is better to have too much material at hand than too little.

HANDLING MATERIALS

After substantial progress in finding and gathering materials, a speaker needs time to contemplate what he has been putting into his mind. So an efficient and productive workman begins his speech preparation early and spaces it at planned intervals. In these intervals he thinks consciously about his subject, reads, takes notes, converses, reviews his materials, groups and classifies his ideas, adjusts his subject to meet the time limits of his speech, and anticipates the actual building of the outline. These are his moments and hours of deliberate thinking. But much of our most productive, creative thinking goes on subconsciously between periods of deliberation. Our minds cook, stew, boil, and mix the ingredients of our experience when we are entirely unaware of the process. That process may properly be called "incubation" of thought, and out of it springs the unexpectedly bright idea whose appearance seems so mysterious and inexplicable. In his preparation, an intelligent speaker provides for intervals of incubation between his periods of deliberate thought and effort. He "rests," and when the bright idea flashes out, he jots it down to consider later. After some intervals of deliberation and incubation, it is time to build the outline.

ORIGINALITY

The speaker who saturates himself with a subject, who goes through such an experience as we have described, will create an original speech though he probably will not be the first person in the world to speak or write on the specific subject. He will produce an original speech because, first, his product will differ from any one of his sources. It will be a compound formed from diverse ideas and materials. It will not be a copy of somebody else's product, nor will it be a weak imitation in the shape of a digest or summary. Second, as his peculiar reaction to the many sources consulted, the speech will reveal his individuality.

Whatever is original contains elements of new experience. Suppose a student hears a lecture or reads an article about the frontier and plans to make a speech on that subject. Will his speech be significantly different from the lecture he heard? Will he make his speech "new" by adding materials and ideas to those of the lecture or by presenting the lecture's ideas in an appreciably different order and style? An original speech, from the speaker's point of view, is a product that differs significantly from the impulses and sources that occasioned it. The report, the summary, the digest, and the précis do not differ appreciably either in substance or in treatment from their originals; they are reduced copies. Indeed, in making a report—an activity valuable as intellectual training—a speaker does not intend to make his product significantly different from the original; rather, he tries to adhere closely to the thought and structure of the original. The reporter merely wishes to act as transmitter of another's ideas, which he endeavors to transmit as faithfully as circumstances will allow.

An original speech reveals something of the speaker's individuality; it is the form in which only he can react to the impulses that gave birth to his speech. Three persons may be asked to read a certain article, "In Defense of Politicians," and to make a speech based on it. Each will react differently to the article and the three will give three different speeches—different in point of view, type, and treatment of ideas, according to past experience and present outlook. That is, they will be original.

Acknowledging Sources

Although a person knows his speech is original, he must not sidestep explicit acknowledgment of his sources. Reference to his sources, of course, enhances the speaker's image; it gives him personal authority and prestige, for his hearers realize that he has paid them the compliment of preparing carefully and that he is more widely informed than they. The speaker also has a moral obligation to acknowledge his indebtedness. A person who has exerted effort to make information available or who has expressed an idea with striking effectiveness has some right to be recognized. It is not only right but courteous to recognize another's labor and inventiveness.

Although it is not easy to know when to acknowledge sources, the following general suggestions should be observed scrupulously. (1) A speaker should cite the source of any quotation or close paraphrase he uses. To use the ideas and phraseology of another without acknowledgment is plagiarism—literary theft. (2) An unusual idea or an exceptional fact that has increased a speaker's knowledge or has set him thinking, or an effective and unusual expression that he knows he has derived from a definite source, he should acknowledge. He should try to cultivate some awareness of the difference between out-of-the-ordinary ideas and those that are the common stock of everyday conversation or those that he has assimilated so thoroughly that their original source is beyond his recall. Obviously one cannot pay his respects to a forgotten source; and common ideas and expressions on a situation or a problem need not be acknowledged, for such materials belong to everyone.

Phrasing acknowledgment

With a little oral practice in referring to sources, a speaker can learn to make swift and smooth acknowledgments. Some common ways of managing references follow.

Early in the speech, in the introduction wherever convenient and relevant,

refer to the principal source or sources. Then, no additional acknowledge-
ment is necessary. For example:

> In discussing the influences that made Robert E. Lee a kind and honorable
> man, I have been greatly helped by Douglas S. Freeman's four-volume biog-
> raphy of Lee, and by the same author's first volume on *Lee's Lieutenants*. Pro-
> fessor Wilkes suggested in history class last week that Lee's sense of honor was
> not derived merely from tradition. The remark set me thinking.

Work in acknowledgements wherever they can be put conveniently and
logically. Usually the "spot" acknowledgment concerns a fact, a particular
idea, a quotation, or a striking phrase or figure of speech.
It may precede the reference:

> Goethe expressed his advice on the acknowledgment of source materials in this
> way: "The most foolish error of all is made by clever young men in thinking
> that they forfeit their originality if they recognize a truth which has already
> been recognized by others."
>
> Goethe said that "the most foolish error. . . ."
> According to Goethe, "the most foolish error. . . ."

The reference may be dropped neatly into the middle of the quotation or
the idea being expressed:

> "The most foolish error of all," said Goethe, "is made by clever young
> men. . . ."
>
> "This machine," so the American Match Company states in a recent pamphlet,
> "turns out 5,000 matches every minute."

Acknowledgment may follow the reference:

> "An idea is his who best expresses it," Bacon said.
>
> "The most foolish error . . . recognized by others." In those words Goethe ex-
> pressed his conviction.

Where the trustworthiness or the recency of information is important,
make the reference explicit and as complex as necessary to be accurate. For
example:

> As to the proper method of pronouncing foreign place names, W. Cabell Greer,
> in his 1948 edition of *World Words,* says that a good rule is "to adopt the
> foreign pronunciation insofar as it can be rendered by customary English
> sounds in the phrasing and rhythm of an English sentence."

Rarely in a speech is it necessary to cite volume number and page. Nor is
the popular habit of saying "quote" and "unquote" necessary or graceful.

Voice and manner of speaking can usually distinguish quoted matter. If not, then plain statements are best: "I shall quote;" "That is the end of the quotation."

Form of references

When a reference list is called for, it should accompany the speech outline and is usually placed at the end. The following form of arrangement, punctuation, and capitalization represents standard practice:

I. References to One's Own Experience, to Conversation, and to Lectures
   A. Briefly describe the experience:
      "My experience as a department store salesman."
   B. Briefly describe the conversation, interview, and lecture. Be as *specific* as possible:
      "Conversation with students."
      "Interview with Professor A. F. Jones."
      "Lecture notes in American history."
II. References to Books
      Marckwardt, A.H. *Scribner Handbook of English,* New York, 1940.
      If a book has two or more authors, treat them thus:
      Jones, R.F., and J.S. Black. . . .
III. Reference to Articles
   A. Magazine articles:
      Wilson, J. "Handling the Apostrophe," *The English Journal,* 21 (June, 1923), 178-200.
   B. For articles appearing in books:
      Hazlitt, William. "On Going on a Journey," in R.S. Loomis and D.L. Clark (eds.). *Modern English Readings.* New York, 1942, pp. 117-122.
   C. For articles appearing in general reference books:
      "Rhetoric." *Encyclopaedia Britannica.* 14th ed. London, 1929.
      In citing any *Britannica* since 1932, it is preferable to use the date of printing; thus:
      "Rhetoric." *Encyclopaedia Britannica.* 1952.
   D. For citation of newspapers:
      1. For the signed article and editorial:
         Steinbeck, John. "The Attack on Salerno," The *New York Times,* September 1, 1943, p. 32. (If the paper has numbered sections, alter the citation thus: . . . November 1, 1943, sec. 3, p. 32.)
      2. For the news article and unsigned editorial or article:
         "Moscow Conference a Great Success." The *Washington Post.* November 5, 1943, p. 1.
IV. Reference to Pamphlets Where No Person Is Cited as Author or Editor
      Colonies and Dependent Areas. Boston: World Peace Foundation, 1943

CHAPTER 5

Development:
Enlarging the Subject Statement

Informative discourse attempts to answer three basic questions: What? How? and Why? What is to be understood? What is the nature of the subject—that is, how and why did it become that way? If what is to be known is the operation or function of something, we ask, How does it behave and why does it behave as it does? The speaker achieves understanding through organization and development, each executed in ways adapted to the available responses of his audience. We will discuss organization in Chapter 7, where we explain the speech outline.

Development—in our previous edition called what tradition has often called it, *amplification*—is the process of enlarging on a statement or some part of it in order to establish or clarify its meaning for a listener. Underlying development is the broad principle that *understanding is achieved by associating the new and strange with the old and familiar.* The audience understands when the speaker translates his understanding into the experience of the listener. In Chapter 2 we sketched the use of some of the fundamental materials of development and some of the principles of organization. Let us now extend discussion of such materials.

The basic materials of informative communication, we said, are facts, evidence, and opinions, which the speaker finds in his own experience and observation and in the experience of others. Whenever a speaker can do so, he ought to develop his statements with reliable facts and authoritative testimony. That material not only fosters understanding but also cultivates respect for the speaker.

FACTUAL INFORMATION AND ITS USE

Statistical data should be presented as simply as is consistent with the degree of precision suitable to audience and occasion, for the popular audience round numbers are usually sufficient unless the speaker wishes to be thought a very finicky fellow. Unless the difference between 974,321 and 974,253 is vital, it is better to say "over 974,000." The accountants in the U.S. Treasury must record the national debt to the last dollar and cent, but for most of us most of the time a statement to the nearest million, or probably the nearest billion, would be exact enough. The use of visual aids to help clarify statistics, such as some of those we describe in Chapter 6, is highly desirable; and it is often helpful to give the listener some ready way of comprehending unfamiliar measures. Most Americans, for example, are not used to thinking of temperature in terms of the Centigrade thermometer. If one uses it, therefore, one should suggest, for example, that 20 degrees Centigrade is a pleasant 68 Fahrenheit or that the normal human body temperature is 37 degrees Centigrade.

Even when precision is not necessary, accuracy in the use of factual materials is critical at all times. This is especially true when the information being used is common property. If a visiting speaker mentions the local population as being about 60,000 when it has been recently reported in the press as 46,000, he discredits himself.

Finally, whenever factual information is introduced, it is sound practice to name its source and date. Facts have a greater significance when the hearer gets a sense of their reliability. In speaking of the costs of higher education, one might say simply: "At Harvard in 1937 tuition was $400; in 1967 it has risen to $2,000, and in 1970 to $2,400." It would be more reassuring, more significant to the audience, however, to say: "The U.S. Office of Education for over thirty years has gathered information from colleges and universities about their tuition charges. As reported in *Time* in June 1967, Harvard's tuition was $2,000. In 1937 it had been $400. The Harvard cataloue for 1970 puts it at $2,400." From this latter quotation we learn the source of the fact, the date of the statistic, its scope, and the purpose for which it was collected. On most subjects for popular audiences the year, or the month and year, is sufficiently precise. The day of the month becomes important only when new information is published frequently. Such items of identification lend weight to the fact of tuition cost. The speaker should not take refuge in the lame words *Statistics show* . . . unless he is prepared to say when, by whom, and for what purpose they were collected. The informative speaker knows his facts and knows whether to trust them. The audience appreciates facts and likes to know they are reliable.

EXAMPLE

An example is always an example *of* something. The *something* is the statement to be developed. The example extends the meaning of the statement by supplying a particular case or circumstance.

> *Statement:* One function of advertising is to remind persons of the product over and over again.
>
> *Example:* In my town the Methodists still ring their church bell every Sunday morning.

The example, then, by definition, is a particular case, incident, or circumstance of the more general idea expressed in the statement which the example develops.

Examples are generally classified as short or long, real or invented.

Short or Long

The instance

The short example is the *instance,* a particular case a speaker sets forth in the briefest possible time consistent with making it clear to the listener. If the instance is chosen so the listener can grasp it immediately, it needs only the barest mention. An example of such an instance is the ringing of the church bell every Sunday.

The illustration

The long example bears the tag *illustration.* The illustration is used to build up and fill out the particular case by giving it a setting and supplying narrative and descriptive details. The example thus becomes a sort of compact story or a thumbnail sketch of the circumstances. The illustration is the example *illuminated* by details.

The illustration is especially useful in two types of situation. It is employed in place of the instance when a speaker wants to be vivid and at the same time give the hearer a sense of action and reality. This is what Bruce Barton did in handling the church bell example. (For the complete speech, see the Appendix.) Instead of presenting it as an instance, he chose the illustration:

> A member of my profession, an advertising man, . . . was in the employ of a circus. It was his function to precede the circus into various communities, distribute tickets to the editor, put up on the barns pictures of the bearded lady and the man-eating snakes, and finally to get in touch with the proprietor of some store and persuade him to purchase the space on either side of the elephant for his advertisement in the parade.
>
> Coming one day to a crossroads town our friend found that there was only one store. The proprietor did not receive him enthusiastically. "Why should I

advertise?" he demanded. "I have been here for twenty years. There isn't a man, woman, or child around these parts that doesn't know where I am and what I sell." The advertising man answered very promptly (because in our business if we hesitate we are lost), and he said to the proprietor, pointing across the street, "What is that building over there?" The proprietor answered, "That is the Methodist Episcopal Church." The advertising man said, "How long has that been there?" The proprietor said, "Oh, I don't know; seventy-five years probably." "And yet," exclaimed the advertising man, "they ring the church bell every Sunday morning."

The example offered as an instance would have taken about ten seconds; the illustration probably occupied about a minute and a half. Characteristic are the narrative setting, the dialogue which heightens the impression of a real event, the careful ordering of details to lead into the point—and the touch of humor.

When the content of the example is not instantly intelligible to the listener, or its information is novel and technical, the illustration is almost indispensable if the speaker is to give his listeners time to understand. For an audience unfamiliar with filibustering in the U.S. Senate, a classroom speaker used an illustration with telling effect. Quoting the dictionary, he defined the filibuster as "delaying tactics employed in parliamentary debate and usually involving long speeches on topics irrelevant to the subject." He amplified immediately:

You are all members of some organization—your literary society, your lodge, your farm club, your church, your young people's society. Now, as you know, such an organization holds a business meeting once in a while—called a deliberative meeting. If you were governed by the present Senate rules, it would be possible for any member of the organization to stand up and talk just as long as he wanted to on any motion that was brought before the house. In fact, he would not have to talk straight to the point all the time, either. He could start off by making it appear that he was going to talk about a certain point involved in the motion, and then he could say or read anything he pleased. He could recite poetry, or read a novel, or give a lot of dry statistics from some depart- mental report a hundred years old. He could do anything he pleased to kill time, and the rest of the members would have to let him keep right on for at least two days and perhaps much longer unless they could get two-thirds of the members together to put through a device for stopping him. Of course, you would not have to listen to him, for you could go out and eat and sleep and do anything you pleased. But, in the meeting, that member would have the floor, and nobody could take it away from him.

Experimental Evidence as Illustration. Today, because most people hold science in high regard, many popular speeches and articles draw information from scientific experiments. In presenting such information, the illustration is perhaps the surest road to understanding. The brief instance is probably too cryptic for most people, especially when they are listening rather than reading. In ordering such an illustration the speaker should (1) name the experimenter, place of experiment, and date reported; (2) indicate the purpose of the experiment; (3) detail the setup and conduct of the experiment; and (4) lay out the results, which is the point of information the listener is to comprehend.

Real or Invented

Examples are classified not only as short or long, but also as real or invented. The real example is real in the sense that its content is actual. It is an event, a case, a situation that has actually happened. All the examples we have so far included in this section of the chapter are real.

The invented example, often called the hypothetical or fictitious example, is precisely what its name implies. Drawing upon him imagination and judgment, the speaker makes up an example. He does not produce what has happened; he offers what *might* have taken place. A football coach, presenting the theory of the off-tackle play, explained that more than most plays it depends on perfect timing. Each man, he said, must do precisely the right thing at the right moment, and if he does, the play always gains yardage. The coach knew his faculty listeners would probably not remember an off-tackle play they had seen; so he did not use an instance of one. He felt he could not take the time to describe a case of such a play and so did not try a factual, detailed illustration. He had at hand no film of the play. So he amplified by saying, "Now if you were to execute the off-tackle play as it should be done, you would do so-and-so, and so-and-so...." In two minutes he made his audience see a perfect play through his invented illustration. The hypothetical example, then, amplifies an idea by presenting something that might be, or might have been.

Young speakers sometimes hesitate to use fictitious examples. Their reluctance is in part well grounded, for in preparing to speak on most subjects, one can usually find relevant examples in past events, and the historical instance or fact always has the ring of truth. Nevertheless, for purposes of amplification, there are times when the invented example is superior to all other kinds. They are the occasions on which one is trying to explain the theoretical and the ideal condition. For the ideal house or electoral system there can be no real example; the communicator must construct one.

Thorough invented material the speaker may give rein to his imaginative powers and he may create not only fictions nearer to perfection than actuality can provide, but fictions more real, more engaging, and perhaps more amusing than actuality. The poet and the dramatist in the speaker may come out to good advantage. It never occurs to us to care whether Christ was reporting an actual robbery on the Jericho road when he told the illustrative story of the Good Samaritan. That tale has engaged more interest and has illustrated a point better and longer than any newspaper story ever written. Plato used myths to clarify the more difficult of his philosophical and ethical ideas. Myths are fictions which draw the reader or the listener pleasantly and surely into a grasp of the ideas being presented. The myth of the chariot, for example, in the *Phaedrus*, illuminates Plato's idea of the struggle of spiritual love and sensual love in the soul of man. What Christ or Plato did, and good speakers have always done, the student with a spark of inventiveness can attempt with profit.

Selection of Examples

Certain considerations should govern the selection of examples.

Emphasis

In a speech the most important statements and points—those which would be fatal to clarity if the listener did not understand them—deserve examples. The illustration, with its specific, vivid details, is the longest-lived reminder of an idea. When minor ideas are to be exemplified, the short example—the instance—is usually preferable.

Relevance to statement

Although it is obvious that examples should be directly relevant to the statements they amplify, speakers are constantly tempted to squeeze and torture examples to try to make them fit. Perhaps they have found fascinating illustrations; so they feel they ought to use them somehow. Straining an example into a bad fit only puzzles an audience. Like the funny story dragged in, it may be interesting, but it always distracts from the main point.

Relevance to listeners' experience

A number of examples selected so that they will touch the different interests and experiences of the audience are effective in developing an important idea. Examples drawn from country life will strike the imaginations of some members of a general audience; those drawn from city life, others. Examples from mechanics and science will help clarify ideas for some kinds of persons; those from business and the arts will appeal to others. Very few examples will be equally effective with all persons found in general audiences. There was a time when examples drawn from the Bible would be familiar to almost all Americans. Today there seems to be no single source of examples effective with all audiences. The wise speaker, therefore, will know as much as he can about the experience of his audience and will choose his examples to fit the main areas of that experience.

The particular, recent experience of his audience, if the speaker is aware of it, is a good source of examples. For instance, is there any connection between his subject and the highway or airplane accident nearby, a strike in a local industry, Saturday's football game, the latest murder or divorce, or the current lesson in algebra, history, or zoology? To make effective use of immediate, familiar events and to avoid misfiring, a speaker must be sure that he knows his ground thoroughly and accurately. He should thus be sure that he will not arouse feelings disadvantageous to him and that he will not discredit himself by incorrect or incomplete knowledge of the situation.

Interest value

Examples tend to be interesting in themselves. In selecting the material for examples, however, the speaker may enhance their capacity to stimulate interest if he will associate them with fundamental human values. Any of the materials of development, of course, may be associated profitably with values and interests, but examples, because they are specific and concrete, are especially effective when they touch such springs of interest as sex, health, wealth, sensual pleasure, humor, sentiments, human beings, and activity.

Love, marriage, procreation, the beautiful human form are components of the most universally interesting of all stories. Anything, therefore, associated with the relations between the sexes is a potential source of interest. A picture of a beautiful woman is apparently a valuable part (sometimes the only part) of advertisements intended to interest both men and women. A few years ago in the London subway stations an advertiser pictured a beautiful blonde in a scant green bathing suit climbing out of a swimming pool smiling—not to advertise bathing suits, or suntan lotion, or a vacation resort, but a patent medicine! A resourceful speaker will not neglect the discreet, fitting, and honest use in his examples of this, the liveliest of all sources of interest.

Likewise, people's normal goals are directed toward preserving life, health, and well-being, and toward promoting wealth. The speaker, therefore, should associate his examples with these goals when he can. For example, workers in a factory never listen with so much ready interest to a lecture on safety methods as they do just after one of their fellows has been injured through careless handling of the machinery. "There's a right way and there are many wrong ways to write a check," says a speaker who is cashier in a bank. "Only last week we paid a check for *ninety-three* dollars against the account of one of our depositors because he had been careless in writing a check for *three* dollars." Here the pocketbook interest with the added interest of the concrete example is associated with instructions on how to write a check.

So also the interest of people in things affecting their pride and their sentiments may be enlisted to give strengthened force to examples. The competitive interest in grades in school can often be converted into an interest in the subject matter of study. Again, examples touching the glories of the old Alma Mater interest loyal alumni; those which call up memories of the "old gang" interest most people; and except in times of the utmost cynicism, reminders of our affection for our country interest all of us.

The appeal of activity should also influence the speaker's choice of examples. In the explanation of a process or a machine or a maneuver in football, tennis, or war, for example, the interesting speaker will not stop with the essential details of bare exposition. He will describe someone performing the process or will show an article of manufacture going through the process; in this explanation he will have the machinery running, and if possible someone running it; he will describe armies or players maneuvering or men fighting battles.

We are all interested in what people are doing and saying. Wherever practicable, therefore, a speaker should associate his subject with people. The university photographer, wishing a picture that will interest the public in the mechanical engineering laboratory's new power press, poses two or three engineering students with hands on the levers and controls of the machine. He is giving a *human* touch to what otherwise might have been a fuller, clearer picture, but a *dead, unhuman picture.*

Interest in personality, like any other valuable avenue of access to people's minds and feelings, can be overworked, cheapened, and discredited by the uses to which it is put—from advertising useless facial preparations and patent medicines to exploiting the ephemeral marital jaunts of popular entertainers. The perennial, irrepressible interest we all have in our fellow man, however, may be as readily directed to the worthy and the important.

Humor and the Example. Humor is undeniably one of the most valuable sources of interest in examples. What has been said about emphasis and relevance, and the advice on appropriateness that follows, apply with special force to the use of the humorous example.

Not everyone who can appreciate a joke has a talent for telling one, and the person who is a poor raconteur generally is not likely to shine in telling a humorous anecdote. The student speaker, nevertheless, should experiment with humor in his examples. Perhaps, guided by the principles of relevance, propriety, and freshness, he will cultivate a real talent.

Stories and anecdotes, of course, may be funny independently of the context in which they are told, but unless they are relevant to the speaker's ideas, the audience's interest in the stories will not extend to the ideas. The freshness of a humorous story depends, of course, upon who is telling it to whom, when, and how. The story which went very well in the freshman history lecture (for everyone *has* to hear a story for the first time!) may be pretty stale fare at the senior banquet. Nevertheless, on some after-dinner or sportive occasions a speaker, especially if he has the reputation of being a wit, can get a laugh with almost any threadbare wheeze or feeble pun. People laugh at such times simply because they want to laugh and are waiting only for an excuse. Most of the time, however, audiences want fresh humor or fresh application of old humor. An inexperienced speaker, at least, will avoid thumbing through jokebooks and anthologies of wit and humor, not because the contents of such books are not amusing (or at least were not amusing originally), but because they are everyone's property, the audience's as well as the speaker's. Likewise retelling stories and jokes published in such popular magazines as *Reader's Digest* and in the comic strips is not always as effective as the speaker expects it to be. The humor was very good when published, but most of the audience has already read it and has heard others repeat it again and again since its publication. An old story, in order to be effective, should be given a new twist or a new application or a disguised setting. Then the audience may be interested in recognizing the essentials of the story and be pleased at the surprise elements.

We conclude, then, that in managing his examples the speaker will do well to consider the factors of interest and to associate what he wants to make interesting with what is already interesting to audiences in general and to his audience in particular.

Appropriateness to subject and occasion

Tact and taste are not easily made subject to rules. Should one use humorous illustrations in sober circumstances? Does copious use of fictitious examples indirectly tell an audience that the speaker does not know enough to have discovered factual examples? It all depends on whether a speaker enjoys the respect and confidence of his hearers. Within very wide limits examples may properly be drawn from any areas of common knowledge or common experience. A speaker should exercise care, however, that in his choice of examples he does not depart widely from the tone and spirit which the occasion demands and his purpose requires. Extreme cases of faulty taste may easily be cited. In a speech honoring Washington's Birthday, it would seem incongruous for a speaker to couple Washington's conduct at Valley Forge with Benedict Arnold's at Quebec in illustration of the various kinds of courage evinced by a great hero. It is impossible to lay down rules for good sense and tact in choosing examples, but inexperienced speakers should err on the side of caution.

Appropriateness to speaker

Many examples that seem proper to the subject and the occasion may offend a particular audience or may seem to that audience inappropriate to the speaker. An audience composed largely of churchgoers may be antagonized by an illustration from a lay speaker pointing up the fallibility of the clergy; yet the same audience would probably take no offense at the same example were it to be used by a popular clergyman. The trouble with the example would not be that it failed to exemplify the speaker's idea, but that it raised distracting and competing ideas in the listeners. Well-informed college students, speaking before audiences of businessmen, sometimes make the mistake of choosing their examples, however pat, from those areas of business about which they themselves will seem too young and inexperienced to know anything. The natural response of those audiences is not, "I see the point; he hits the nail on the head," but, "What does that youngster know about business?"

Handling Details of Examples

Order of details

No detail should be introduced before its proper place in the structure, nor should it be delayed beyond the point where it fits the story. Examples and illustrations are *picture-forming*, and the *pictures will be formed* once the speaker has set the audience's imagination working, whether he provides the ingredients or not. Hence, if he does not provide details at the proper time, the audience will invent its own details which may not be the ones the speaker wanted. Very seldom can repair work by done afterwards, no matter how often the speaker inserts, "By the way, this house I am speaking of was built on sand." The audience already has built it on granite, and there it will stay.

Number of details

Examples, and particularly illustrations, should include a sufficient number of details to be clear, and details unessential to clarity should be edited out. The speaker has to judge how much knowledge and experience his audience can bring to bear on the example. If his listeners have much knowledge, he need suggest few details; little knowledge in the audience will demand more detail from the speaker. If he were talking to a city audience and drew an example from farm life, he would have to use a larger number of descriptive details than he would if he were speaking to a rural audience.

Speakers who draw illustrations from their personal experiences are tempted to include too many details and some that are completely unnecessary. How often have we heard the exuberant storyteller interrupt himself with "Oh, that's not important anyway," or with some other parenthetical self-correction such as "No, I believe that it wasn't Wednesday, the third; I think it was Thursday, the fourth."

COMPARISON

As a means of development, a comparison extends the statement by pointing out its likeness to another idea, object, or situation. A concise expression of likeness is often a simile or a metaphor. A likeness developed at some length is usually called an analogy. As an instance of the short comparison, Joseph

Wood Krutch asserted that protoplasm is the simplest form of life, and amplified the idea immediately with the statement, "it is a shapeless blob of rebellious jelly." Much of our conversation is filled with comparisons, and much of our slang consists of metaphors. The special virtue of comparison is its power to make an idea strong, sharp, and intense as well as larger through the addition of information.

Analogy

The short comparison mentions only a single point of likeness. The analogy, or long comparison, recognizes a number of points of likeness between objects or situations. One of the masters of analogy in the popular lecture was Thomas Henry Huxley, who often tried to make ordinary English workingmen understand what a liberal education is all about. One of his favorite statements was that education consists in learning about Nature. Then, knowing that his audience knew something about chess, he would say that learning about Nature is like learning to play chess. The world is the chessboard; the phenomena of Nature represent the pieces; and the laws of Nature are the rules of the game. Education, then, is mastering the rules of the game of life.

In pondering this example of analogy, observe the precise points of likeness. First is the controlling idea of the comparison: learning is to chess what learning is to Nature. Then this idea is amplified by three points of similarity: world and chessboard, phenomena and pieces, laws and rules. The successful use of analogy depends on seeing precisely the points of comparison and stating them clearly.

Literal analogy

Analogies, like examples, may be either real or fictitious. When the analogy is real, it is called the *literal* analogy. When fictitious, it isnamed the *figurative* analogy. The literal analogy always draws comparisons within the same class of things; it compares man with man, flower with flower, game with game, machine with machine, and the like. So Jones' behavior can readily be compared with Smith's, city government in St. Louis with that in Detroit, one farm with another, one dress with another, and so on. Within a class of things, there are always many points of correspondence. Hence a speaker has a rich mine of comparisons when he can liken his subject, say the sports program at X university, with a sports program his hearers know all about.

Figurative analogy

The figurative analogy compares objects and events which fall into unlike classes. Strictly speaking, it states an identity of relationship between two unlike contexts. The short figurative comparison is a *simile* or a *metaphor*. The new street lights are electric moons. Huxley was using a figurative comparison when he likened the game of chess to the game of life. Successful chess playing and successful living are two quite different orders of things, yet with respect to the act of learning he found a number of similarities. In speechmaking, the analogy is especially useful, because no matter what one's subject may be, it is always possible to compare it with something. Any two ideas or objects may at first thought seem entirely unlike, yet upon probing they may reveal a similarity in function, in purpose, in materials and qualities, in the causes which produced them, or in the effects which they produce. At first glance, for example, race horses and athletes may appear to have nothing in common, but if one considers their treatment and training, one can discern some interesting comparisons. The Biblical parables, such as the Prodigal Son and the Talents, are familiar analogies. So is Aesop's fable of the boy who cried "Wolf!" As an instance of a figurative analogy, consider Lincoln's comparison between Blondin, the tightrope walker, and the position of the federal government during the critical days of the Civil War.

> Gentlemen, I want you to suppose a case for a moment. Suppose that all the property you were worth was in gold, and you have put it in the hands of Blondin, the famous rope-walker, to carry across the Niagara Falls on a tight rope. Would you shake the rope while he was passing over it, or keep shouting to him, "Blondin, stoop a little more! Go a little faster!" No, I am sure you would not. You would hold your breath as well as your tongue, and keep your hand off until he was safely over. Now, the government is in the same situation. It is carrying an immense weight across a stormy ocean. Untold treasures are in its hands. It is doing the best it can. Don't badger it! Just keep still, and it will get you safely over. [2]

The figurative (invented) analogy may serve admirably (as may the fictitious example) to modify the tone of an exposition which runs the risk of becoming too serious and sober and consequently dull. Thomas Huxley wished to exemplify the notion that the laws of scientific induction and deduction come within the scope of everyday experience. To underscore his point he drew a figurative comparison, not from his own invention but from literature: "There is a well-known incident in one of Molière's plays, where the author makes the hero express unbounded delight on being told that he had been talking prose during the whole of his life. In the same way, I trust that you will take comfort and be delighted with yourselves, on the discovery that you have been acting on the principles of inductive and deductive philosophy during the same period."

[2] Carl Sandburg, *Abraham Lincoln: The War Years* (New York, 1939), II, 125.

CONTRAST

As a method of development, contrast is the opposite of comparison. It carries out the idea of a statement by showing how it is *unlike* another idea. Basically contrast involves two objects, conditions, or ideas which in some way stand opposed to each other. Any contrast therefore always entails *some* degree of difference.

The following example of contrast comes from a speech by the former Secretary of State, John Foster Dulles. Speaking to the American Federation of Labor in New York City, he used contrast simply and effectively to underline what a production worker's time was worth in New York and in Moscow:

> To buy a pound of butter in New York, it takes 27 minutes of work; in Moscow over 6 hours of work. For a pound of sugar, 3½ minutes in New York, 8 minutes in Moscow; for a quart of milk, 7 minutes in New York, 42 minutes in Moscow; for a dozen eggs, 25 minutes in New York, nearly 3 hours in Moscow; for a cotton shirt, nearly 1 hour in New York, 22 hours in Moscow; for a man's suit, 3 days in New York, 47 days in Moscow; for shoes, 1 day in New York, 13 days in Moscow; and for a woman's wool suit, 22 hours in New York, 22 days in Moscow.

A special use of contrast is called *definition by negation*, which speakers find effective in pinning down the meaning of a fuzzy word or concept and in making clear the purpose of a speech. In partial explanation of the old notion that man is a rational or reasoning animal, one student said:

> When I refer to man as a *rational* being, I do not mean that he is distinguished from other animals because of his ability to reason—at least they *learn,* and learning often calls for reasoning. Nor do I mean to set man off from animals because he can generalize and discover principles, for the dog will show much "generalizing" behavior, based on analogy, when he stops chasing skunks. He may have chased two or three with unfortunate results; so he "reasons" that all skunks will give him pain, and he keeps his distance thereafter. No, man is not rational, in contrast to other animals, if we mean only that he learns, reasons, and generalizes.

Another student, who talked on the process of flue-curing tobacco, gave emphasis to his special purpose through negation, somewhat as follows:

> Perhaps I should say that I am going to speak only about flue-curing tobacco. Interesting as the process of sun-curing tobacco is, I am not concerned with it now. Furthermore, we shall assume that the tobacco has been harvested and has been brought to the flue shed ready for handling. Also, we shall stop with the process as soon as the curing has been finished and the tobacco is ready to be taken down and carried to market.

Contrast is a means of development that builds up the meaning of an idea by increasing its precision and accuracy. It enhances precision because it helps prevent ambiguity and misunderstanding. Comparison promotes understanding in a positive way, for the listener is told that his experience applies to the idea. He is helped to grasp the new or strange information by adding to it the old and familiar. Contrast, on the other hand, enhances understanding in a negative way. The listener is asked to set aside his experience, to rule it out, as not being applicable at the moment. The difference in the psychological effect of comparison and contrast is compressed in this example: "My house is ranch type, but it is not L-shaped." Comparison helps us see a statement in the right light; contrast prevents our seeing it in the wrong light.

CAUSES OF EFFECTS

Another means of development is explaining an effect by its cause. If the statement calling for amplification asserts some condition or event to be accounted for, a curious person would want to know *why* it came about. So it is natural for a speaker to follow such a statement with a discussion of the cause or causes of the condition. For example:

> States seem reluctant today to make large increases in funds for educational uses. (Why?)
> The burden is supported chiefly by property taxes in most states.

To explain an effect by its cause or causes is an important and fundamental way of extending information. We are ever curious, always asking why. It rains—why? The temperature soars to 100 degrees—why? One substance we may eat is nourishing, another poisonous—why? Uranium 235 is more readily fissionable than other atoms—why? One person is an "A" student, another a "C" student—why? Almost any state or event or condition we think about or learn about can be regarded as an effect, and when it is so regarded we inquire into how and why it came about. Students of communication, particularly students of speechmaking, should reflect that they are right in the middle of cause-and-effect relationships. We say that a speech is effective. What is its effect, or effects? What are the causes?

The amplification of effects by their causes is useful in informative speeches and for a wide variety of subjects. Hence in preparing for speeches, it is well to keep a sharp eye out for materials that help to explain the events and conditions encountered: in particular, relevant principles and laws, especially the general principles of natural phenomena which the natural and social sciences deal with and which the audience may be familiar with or have at least heard about. For example, in explaining the operation of the slide rule, one would draw upon the mathematical laws of logarithms. The improvement of one's tennis game involves the application of the familiar laws of learning. Wages and prices depend, in part at least, on the economic law of supply and demand, and the maintenance of health and avoidance of disease on principles of exercise and nutrition. A felony or a crime, juvenile delinquency, and divorce reflect habits and principles of human behavior, of motivation and social status. It would be hard to find a subject, even for a short speech, that would not lead the speaker to consider effects and their causes.

Two words of caution ae in order. First, any effect may have not one cause but several. Hence a statement that asserts an effect may be developed by a number of statements, each pointing out a cause. How many causes should a speaker present? How complete should he be? There are no pat answers. In the short speech to a popular audience, probably he does best to point out and discuss the single cause that in his judgment seems most important. He would know that superior intellect has something to do with and "A" record, yet talking to an audience of average students he might appropriately emphasize habits of hard, persistent study. The old rule of action applies here: Do one thing well rather than three things superficially.

LOGICAL DEFINITION

As a method of development, logical definition illuminates a word or an idea in a statement by first placing it within its class and then distinguishing it from its class. The method combines comparison and contrast and through them makes clear the special meaning the speaker is attaching to the word. In discussing the nature of religious experience, a speaker said that "it always involved faith." "And faith," he added promptly, "is belief that cannot be verified scientifically." Thus he swiftly put faith into the classification of beliefs and then pointed out that it differs from some beliefs because it cannot be proved scientifically. Later he tried to distinguish faith from superstition and prejudice. Another speaker, talking about a new kind of synthetic rubber, defined rubber as an elastic substance—a kind of substance having the power of resuming its shape after being compressed. Thus he implicitly compared and contrasted rubber with other substances in order to point up its special characteristic, elasticity.

Requirements of Definition

In using definition well, there are four essential conditions:
1. It should cover all cases or instances of the word, idea, or thing being defined. If *elasticity* is said to be a property belonging to all rubber objects, it must be true that every rubber object is elastic. If the use of language is said to distinguish man from other animals, then it must be true that every man uses language.

2. The definition of the word or idea must *exclude* all else not bearing the same name. If *elasticity* properly distinguishes rubber, it must not be applicable to any other substance. If the use of language really distinguishes man from other animals, then it cannot be characteristic of any other animal. By observing these two requirements, a speaker can do much to make his meanings accurate and precise.

3. The word or idea being defined should be amplified in language that is familiar and clear to the audience. To say that a conservative politician is one who rarely thinks beyond the status quo would not be so clear to most persons as to say that he is one who prefers whatever is settled and established and who distrusts what is new and untried.

4. The definition should be as brief as is consistent with accuracy. In a short speech there is rarely time to define exhaustively. Instead, the speaker picks out the essential defining idea, which he can do if he observes rules 1 and 2 above. He omits the less significant characteristics. Jonathan Swift did this in defining style as "proper words in proper places." There are other characteristics of style, but in the context in which he was using the word, he was content to name but one of its essential features.

RESTATEMENT

We have set forth various methods of development: factual information, example and illustration, comparison, contrast, causes of effects, and logical definition. These are ways of expanding a statement by adding significant substance and information to it. In turning attention now to other means, we shall deal with three basic ways of enlarging upon a statement itself. The principle is that of *restatement:* One makes the statement again in different language, either in different words or in different form.

An example of saying the same thing in different words occurred in a student speech explaining how an architect goes about his work: "Before he can start to draw at all, he must have a design in his head. He needs a plan. He must have something to aim at." Obviously the second and third sentences are repeating essentially the same idea announced in the clause, "he must have a design in his head." For an example of restatement involving a shift in the form of expression, observe this simple case: "He must have a design in his head. A design or plan he must have clearly in his mind." Repetition of this sort occurs frequently in extemporaneous speaking and in conversation. We can scarcely avoid it, for we feel that the hearer must fix his attention on the idea and grasp it firmly before he is ready to hear it discussed and amplified in other ways.

If not abused, restatement is of real advantage in speechmaking. The use of different terms often gives a statement a fresh slant. Furthermore, restatement may strike a chord in the listener which the original words did not.

No doubt, as some propagandists and advertisers believe, incessant repetition of a statement produces acceptance or consent, provided that competing ideas are excluded. The honorable speaker, however, wants to illumine matters for his audience, not to stupefy it.

In using restatement a speaker should follow firm guides. First, as soon as the most important statements of the speech appear—that is, the statements of purpose and central idea, or theme, and the main head which leads off a unit or block of ideas, a unit corresponding roughly to a written paragraph— he should restate them. Then should follow substantial amplification. Second, the speaker can close a unit of closely related ideas with a version of the statement that started the unit. For example, if the unit began with, "An architect has in mind a design from which he works," it might close with the restatement, "Before he does anything else about a house, an architect tries to conceive a guiding design." Third, restatement finds a ready place in the conclusion of a speech if one finishes by summarizing the substance of the central idea and the main heads.

Synonym

A synonym is a word whose meaning is the same or nearly the same as that of another, and thus it can make a strange word intelligible. The use of the synonym probably springs from the desire to be precise. An informed speaker regards himself as an expert on his subject. He is related to his hearer as an expert is to the novice. As a result of his study and experience, he has acquired exact and precise ideas. He respects these ideas and takes pride in them. So he desires, quite rightly, to use the precise word in his speech even though he knows it will be strange to the hearer. What must he then do? He has two courses—logical definition, which we have already discussed; and the use of synonyms. If he were to employ the latter in explaining, say, the chief ways people respond to other people, he might say: "One of the typical ways of responding to another person is with aversion, a feeling of dislike, a sort of running away from the person and avoiding him." Thus *aversion*, the special word of the psychologist, is associated swiftly with the more familiar words, *dislike, running away*, and *avoiding*.

When does a word need clarification by synonym? There is no rule that will dictate. A speaker must develop a feel for his audience—for its knowledge and its experience—and he must realize that the more technical the language, the less likely it is that a general audience will comprehend it. For concrete suggestions for handling such language, see Chapter 9.

Quotation

Viewed as a technique of development, quotation is simply restatement through the use of a statement by somebody other than the speaker. In discussing some of the problems of intercollegiate athletics, suppose one said:

Planning a program of intercollegiate athletics and carrying it out is a complex business.

The idea could be restated by quotation, thus:

> In making a general appraisal of organized athletics in the United States, Harold Stoke observes: "Most of the larger colleges and universities, private and public, are organized into athletic conferences managed by highly paid commissioners. Through them, complicated athletic schedules are worked out with all these finesse of the international bargaining table, and considerations of finance, publicity, the prospective careers of coaches and even of presidents, are balanced in equations which would baffle electronic computers."

A speaker uses quotation principally because its language expresses an idea better than he can. The superiority of expression may represent a happy marriage of conciseness and clarity. The quotation, to use a slang expression, may say a mouthful. For example, one might restate the idea that modern architecture is functional by drawing on Francis Bacon's terse language: "Houses are built to live in, and not to look on." Or the superiority of another's words may rest in some striking quality that rivets the listener's attention. This quality may be evident in a sharp image, a simile or metaphor, an antithetical contrast, or some neatly balanced language. In other words, the quotation may have some literary excellence the speaker wants to take advantage of. If, for instance, he were to state that authorities on children's literature always remind us that some books are good, some less good, he might follow with another familiar statement from Bacon: "Some books are to be tasted, others to be swallowed, and some few to be chewed and digested."

In handling the quotation, it is well to avoid the barbarous distracting device of introducing it with the words, "Now I quote," and concluding it with "Unqote." Of course the speaker must make clear that he is using the language of another. But he can manage the acknowledgment more deftly by naming the author. He can preface the quotation with a quick phrase, "As Francis Bacon said . . . ." A short sentence giving the setting will also work well before the quotation, as, for example, "Francis Bacon expressed the idea in this manner." Note how the quotation from Harold Stoke at the beginning of this section was introduced. Furthermore, naming the author is not only a good way of signaling the quotation; it also gives the effect of authority.

DEVELOPMENT AND INTEREST

The methods of development are more than ways to clearness and understanding. They are also ways of controlling attention and maintaining interest. The informative speaker who observes them need not worry about being uninteresting if he will but keep in mind the basic principle of interest—the association of what is novel with what is familiar—and if he will respect the need for variety and identify the values inherent in the occasion.

Novelty and Familiarity

The novel and the familiar may be combined in two ways. A speaker may first present what he thinks is new to his audience and then immediately relate it to something familiar, or he may offer the old idea and then show its new application. To Americans of recent generations, assembly-line methods of manufacture are familiar, and shipbuilding is an old and well-known process. What made Henry Kaiser's procedures interesting was the application of assembly-line methods to the building of large ships; the familiar principle had been put to new use. Architects' blueprints are completely uninteresting to many persons until the one who is trying to explain them says, for example, "Here is the kitchen, here is the door to the basement, here is the window we will put the sink under." Then the listener becomes interested because he begins to find something familiar in the unfamiliar.

Variety

We know that action and movement help control attention. Nevertheless, movement is ineffective unless it is varied. Monotonous action can be as deadening as inaction. Hence, as his speech unfolds, a speaker will endeavor to give variety to his ideas. Two ways of securing variety are especially to be noted: (1) varying the *kinds* of development used, and (2) changing the *point of view* from which the audience looks at the materials presented.

Variety in kind

Examples, we advised, should be chosen from a variety of fields. The principle of variety should be extended to all kinds of development. A chain of explanatory statements, for instance, should be varied by the introduction of example, or testimony, or comparison. The presentation of information, especially of statistics and figures, should be varied by the offering of examples of the significance of these figures or of the application of these figures. Statistics offered to show that rise in position in the business world is accompanied by increase of vocabulary should be followed or preceded by specific cases of measurable vocabularies of people at various levels of salary and authority in business. A presentation of the specific benefits to accrue to the agricultural states from a Missouri Valley Authority should be varied by the citation of opinions of persons known to be familiar with the needs of the

Central states, the Plains states, and the Southern states. Furthermore, examples should be presented of the way the MVA would help a farmer in Kansas or a cattle raiser in Montana; and comparisons should be made with the benefits obtained in the Tennessee Valley.

Variety in point of view

In describing the campus of the university, the interesting speaker might take his listener on a walk along the campus paths. Before the listener is weary of walking, the speaker might put him in a car and whisk him over the campus roads and around the outskirts. The speaker might then take him up in the library tower or up to the top floor of the high-rise residence hall and let him look out over the campus, or he might give him a bird's-eye view from an airplane. In explaining the new state constitution the speaker who wished to avoid wearying his audience might turn from description of the executive department to the effects the revision would have on farmers. From farmers he might turn to urban property owners, and from them to labor and to business and to education. In short, a speaker will maintain one view long enough to fix it clearly in his audience's mind, but not so long as to stupefy his audience with monotony. Otherwise interest will give way to jumble and confusion.

Values

Interesting above all, as we have pointed out, are the things people value—the things they will go to great pains or sacrifice much for. On any particular occasion the speaker who is sensitive to those concepts and those materials that are significant to both himself and his audience will have little trouble in sustaining interest.

SUMMARY

An informative speech consists of a sequence of statements, the most impor-tant of which—the subject statement or central idea—cannot be fully under-stood without development. The development will consist of ideas and materials that add substantially to the central idea: information, examples, comparisons, contrasts, effects with their causes, and definitions. The means of emphasizing an idea—restatement, synonym, and quotation—are also useful in development. The means of development are especially effective when they can be put in ways that command interest and also appeal to the basic values of an audience.

INQUIRIES

1. As a university or college student you listen to and read much informative discourse. Much of it (especially in required courses!) you incline to call dull or unclear; some of it, clear and interesting. What in the methods and materials of development seems to make the difference? Don't pass the question off with the remark that the professor has or doesn't have a fascinating personality, that he has or lacks charisma! That may be true of course, but it is something in the lecture or the exposition that makes you think so, that makes you either listen and understand or doze and not understand. Be as a specific as you can about what.

2. Find in magazine or newspaper articles six or more passages you find unclear because they lack, or have the wrong kind of, developing materials. Show precisely what the deficiency consists of and how you might remove it. Would the passage be clear to a different sort of person from you? What sort? Why?

3. Comparison, we know, can be a very effective means of clear development, but it can also bring about fake clarity. For example, consider the following professedly factual statement: "Sprinko gets clothes four times whiter." Whiter than what? Blue clothes? That is an example of what one of the popular magazines some years ago described as the "agency comparative"—because it is a favorite device of advertising copywriters. They, however, are by no means the exclusive users of it. What effects does the usage produce in listener or reader? Observe yourself and others to see. Perhaps you'll be reminded of the response to the question, "How's your wife?" "Compared to what?"

4. One of the reasons why people and nations frequently make agreements and then fail to abide by them is that it is very difficult to agree completely on the meanings we give to words. Investigate the concept of "operational definition." Try your hand at complete definition of the following: *ghetto, mental health, cease-fire, liberal arts* or *liberal education, charisma, living wage, poverty level, soul, speech.*

5. During the Senate committee's Watergate hearings in 1973, Senator Sam Ervin demonstrated great facility at quoting aptly from the Scriptures and from Shakespeare, and in alluding to examples from those sources. Where do *you* go for quotations you are reasonably sure your audiences will respond to?

FURTHER READING

Baird, A. Craig, Franklin H. Knower, and Samuel L. Becker. *General Speech Communication.* 4th ed. 1971. Chapters 8-10.

Bryant, Donald C., and Karl R. Wallace. *Fundamentals of Public Speaking.* 5th ed. 1976, Chapter 9, "Development of Materials in the Informative Speech."

Monroe, Alan H. and Douglas Ehninger. *Principles and Types of Speech Communication.* 7th ed. 1974. Chapters 11 and 12.

Phillips, A. E. *Effective Speaking.* 1908. Chapter 3, "The Principle of Reference to Experience."

Reid, Loren. *Speaking Well.* 2nd ed. 1972. Chapters 14 and 15.

Winans, James A. *Speechmaking.* 1938. Chapters 7-10 on interest.

CHAPTER 6

Visual and Audio Materials

Although speech is the principal medium of oral communication, often there is profit in employing mechanical devices and visual aids. The use of such materials almost invariably makes for both clearness and interest. In our culture people have become accustomed to these aids and appreciate them, provided they are worked in swiftly and deftly and do not interrupt the progress of ideas.

In both elementary school and high school, audiovisual materials have become commonplace. At the college level, there are even greater resources that student speakers can draw upon readily and at little or no expense. The departments of art and music and the department of speech and communications are usually well supplied, and frequently there is also a department of audiovisual materials. They have collections of tape recorders (including both reel-to-reel and cassette), taped speeches, slide projectors and slides, and overhead projectors. Usually these can be borrowed for short periods without charge. Many students, of course, have their own recorders and projectors.

About the invention, selection, and use of audiovisual materials, experts have written many books. A few are mentioned at the end of this chapter. We shall limit ourselves, however, to the information and suggestions that most speakers can put to use without having to call in the experts.

VISUAL MATERIALS

Although visual materials are of many kinds and may be classified in different ways, we shall group them as simply as possible. Each group has its principal advantages, proper uses, and common abuses.

Charts

A chart is a drawing, a sketch, or any arrangement of lines and colors on paper or cardboard prepared prior to the delivery of a speech and exhibited during the speech as the speaker needs it. Since charts are extraordinarily useful for presenting all kinds of information in many different forms, speakers representing business and industry have long used them widely. Student speakers could well employ them more often than they do. Some of the kinds of charts, easily and inexpensively prepared, are mentioned and illustrated below. All of them show how rather difficult ideas, such as those dealing with the structure and arrangement of clubs, societies, and institutions or those dealing with data and statistical information, can be made concrete and clear.

Organization Chart. Figure 4 shows how a speaker, wishing to explain the basic organization of a university, might visualize its structure. Note that the chart is functional, for each group (enclosed in blocks) has duties and purposes which distinguish it from every other group.

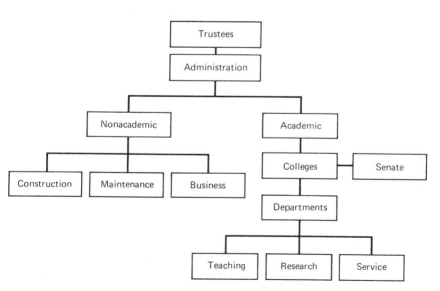

FIGURE 4. Organization Chart
The structure of a university

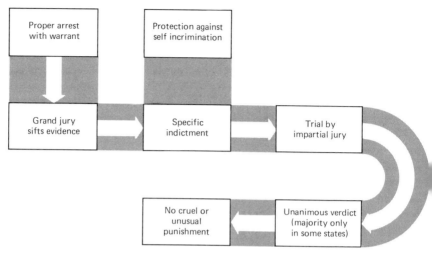

FIGURE 5.   Flow Chart

Protection of the accused

Source: A V Instruction Media and Methods (New York: McGraw-Hill, 1969), p. 168. Used with permission of McGraw-Hill Book Company.

Flow Chart.   The flow chart is particularly useful when one is explaining processes and operations, especially the making of simple products—things not too difficult for oral presentation. It may also be used with good effect in social and institutional procedures, such as that illustrated in Figure 5.

Cutaway

Figure 6 is a neat illustration of the cutaway technique, which permits one to show essential aspects of the interior of an object. Observe that the sketch is designed to make clear the *spatial* arrangement and *positions* of one part with respect to another.

Observe, too, how uncomplicated a complicated setup can be made to appear when only the essentials required to reveal basic parts and their operations are selected. The result for both speaker and audience is simplicity and clarity. Animated cutaways have come to be used often on TV, both for serious exposition and for advertising.

Maps.   A map is designed to show certain features of land and sea. The mapmaker includes only the features that serve his purpose. In producing road maps, for example, he assumes that the prime purpose of a motorist is to get from place to place without getting lost and to drive on the best available roads. A speaker, similarly, makes a map to suit only *his* purpose. He includes only the essentials, uncluttered by useless and irrelevant details.

Our example, Figure 7, is a map designed to accompany an article dealing with census taking.

Graphs. The charts we have mentioned are devices for visualizing factual materials whose functions, operation, structures, and positions must be seen to be understood. The arrangement of charts to illustrate these factors would be impossible without our notions of time and space. The graph, however, is a visual device for presenting facts generally involving number and quantity in relation chiefly to time. The graph is the eye of statistics. We will briefly consider the most ocmmon kinds of graphs, those that speakers themselves can readily construct from data they discover in their reading and investigation.

The *line graph* is best adapted to showing how related sets of facts change and develop according to some common measure of reference—usually that of time. The graph in Figure 8, for example, shows the projected growth of the nation's population over almost a quarter of a century. The *profile graph*

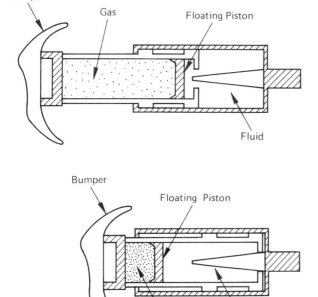

FIGURE 6.   Cutaway Diagram
General Motors energy-absorbing bumper system
Source: Reproduced by permission of the General Motors Corporation.

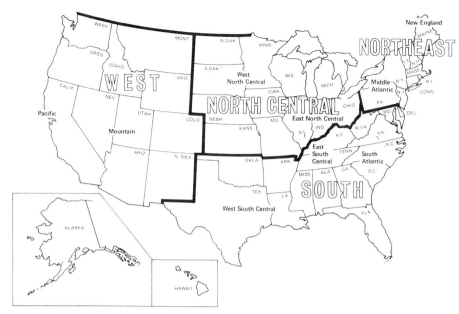

FIGURE 7.   Map
United States census regions
Source: *Statistical Abstract of the United States, 1972.*

is the twin of the line graph, and can be used to present the same data. By
shading or coloring the area under the curve, the effect is made sharp and
dramatic as in Figure 9, which shows the growth and distribution of United
States' investment abroad.

The *bar graph* is also a device for presenting two facts in comparison with
each other, but unlike the line graph it does not usually show how the facts
change over time. Instead, the bar graph simply confronts one fact with
another, one set of results with another set. It presents the final results, the
end product, without trying to show the intermediate data. Observe that the
bar graph in Figure 10 is concerned only with comparative shifts of large
urban populations of white and nonwhite families.

The *pictograph* is designed to present and compare numerical facts by
using a simplified picute or pictorial symbol, as in Figure 11. The symbolic
picture, moreover, is directly associated with the objects, events, or situations
to which the statistics refer.

Advantages of the Chart.   The chart has four distinct advantages over
the blackboard sketch or diagram. It can be used faster in the speech than
the blackboard can, and, accordingly, makes possible a swift-running
speech. Even when a speaker employs a series of charts, he can display the
right one at the right time, say what is needed about each, and move on. The

chart also makes it relatively easy for a speaker to keep his eyes on his audience; the blackboard, on the other hand, requires him to attend to it as he draws, rather than to the audience. The chart, furthermore, can be more readily used in rehearsal than the blackboard. Few speakers have available a sufficiently large blackboard when they are ready to rehearse, and student speakers cannot always find an empty classroom to rehearse in when they want it. Finally, charts provide and opportunity to use color and lines of different breadth. Contrasting colors can be employed to secure both emphasis and interest; heavy lines can be used to outline prominent features, light lines for subordinate details; shading and cross-hatching can be put in to suggest thickness. Such refinements add variety and interest, as well as promoting clearness.

In the classroom student speakers sometimes are troubled about where to place a chart—whether to thumbtack it to the blackboard frame or desk edge, to prop it up on a desk, or to pin it to some nearby handy surface, such as a curtain. Wherever a special stand for holding charts is not available, the

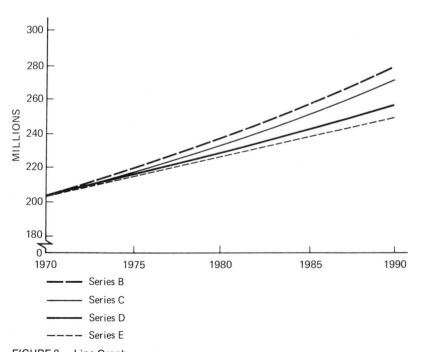

FIGURE 8.   Line Graph
U.S. population projections to 1990
Source: *Statistical Abstract of the United States, 1972.*

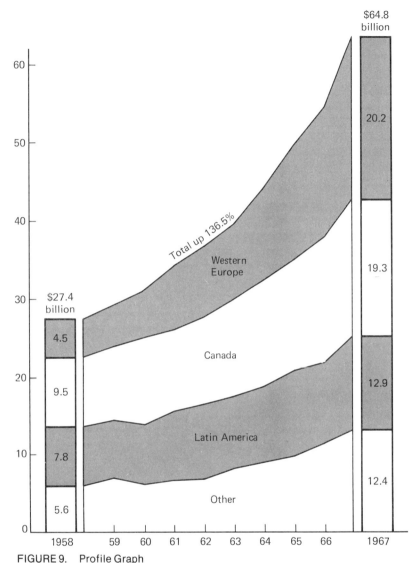

FIGURE 9.   Profile Graph
U.S. investment abroad (book value), 1967
Source: Reprinted by permission from TIME, The Weekly Newsmagazine; Copyright
Time Inc.

best solution is for the speaker to manage the size and material of the chart
so that he can hold it in front of him when he wants it. For this purpose, the
largest practicable dimension seems to be about 24 x 30 inches. The material
need be only stiff enough to support itself. A chart like this, if its features are

bold and uncluttered with unnecessary detail, can be easily seen by a group of fifty persons. A speaker can readily learn to glance down at his chart from above and point out its features with a pencil.

The blackboard sketch or diagram, the model, the object, and the chart all hold great possibilities for securing both clearness and interest in a speech. Speechmakers often use other types of visual aids, such as photographs, lantern slides, filmstrips, and motion pictures. We have restricted our suggestions here to the aids which student speakers themselves can manufacture without technical assistance and can use without special projectors and darkened rooms. Of course the photograph is often employed effectively, but in our experience the student speaker has found its merits outweighed by its drawbacks. Most photographs are too small to be seen, even by an audience of fifteen persons. They must be enlarged, and enlargement is costly—far more expensive than the materials for a chart. Unless originally taken for the special purpose of the speech, moreover, the

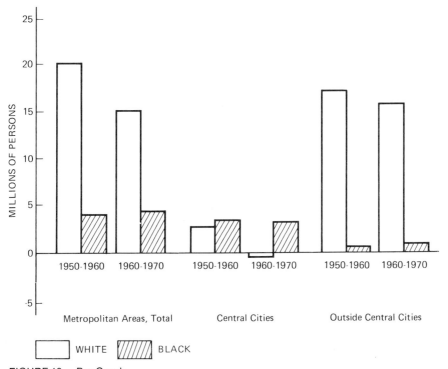

FIGURE 10.   Bar Graph
Population changes in metropolitan areas by race, 1950-60 and 1960-70
Source: Dept. of Commerce, Bureau of the Census.

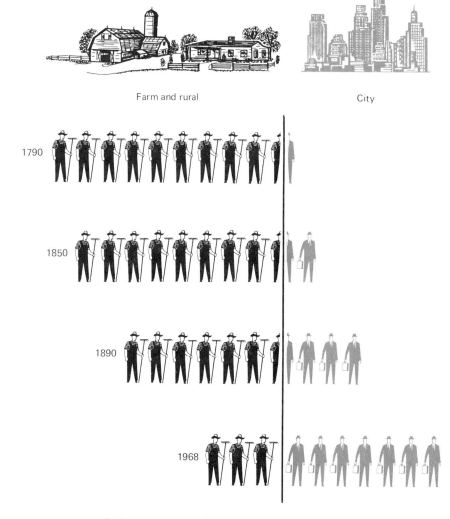

Each symbol represents 10 percent of the total population

FIGURE 11. Pictograph
America, a country of city dwellers
Source: Pictograph Corp.

photograph usually contains more features and more detail than are needed. Thus the audience, if not confused, is often distracted from the business at hand. In fact, the more unskillful the speaker the more his hearers will welcome any excuse to explore a picture for features which recall familiar pleasant associations.

Blackboard diagrams and sketches

Blackboard diagrams and sketches are best used when a speaker needs to build his sketch, step by step. He draws the first feature and explains it, draws the second, and so on, until the illustration is fully developed. The device is especially adapted to the explanation of processes and procedures (if they can be stripped down to their essentials) and to simple operations and machines.

The great advantage of the step-by-step diagram is that the listener can see only what is being talked about at the moment. He does not suffer the temptation to explore other features of the illustration before the speaker wants him to, as he does when a single, complete diagram appears before him early in the speech. The serial diagram, then, controls attention economically. It also creates anticipation and interest, for the audience is curious to see what the next features will be.

Preliminary planning and methodical rehearsal make the blackboard sketch effective. First, the prospective speaker should see the diagram as a whole. Then he should determine how many separate parts are needed and in what order to present them. Finally, he must make the diagram part of the language of the speech by incorporating it into the rehearsal period. In rehearsal, indeed, there is no substitute for a blackboard. It allows one to judge how large one can make each feature and still complete the picture without crowding. It shows one how best to work and not unduly block the view of the audience. Above all, this kind of practice gives the best chance of learning to look at the audience as much as possible.

The ineptitude of some blackboard speakers needs only the briefest mention. Who has not seen—sometimes in his teachers—a person who addressed his blackboard rather than his audience? Who has not seen a speaker cover up his drawing, thus forcing the listener to crane his neck, to peer and squirm, and, finally, to resign himself to confusion? Has anyone escaped blackboard work that was too small or too faint to be seen easily, or so badly planned that repeated erasures were necessary before some feature was just right? Have we not all endured wasted periods of flat silence with speakers who never learned to talk and draw at the same time? Persons need not be so unskilled if they remember that effective blackboard illustration needs planning and practice, and if they actually plan and practice until they can proceed with assurance.

Models and objects

A model is a materialized example. It is a three-dimensional representation of an object, small enough to be displayed in place of the real object or large enough to be seen when the object would be so small as to be invisible. The small-scale airplane and railroad, miniature furniture, the tiny house with its landscaping, and the stage set are familiar illustrations of models reduced in size. Oversized models are often used by the anatomy teacher in his discussion, for example, of the heart, the ear, and the larynx. Occasionally, also, some models may be taken apart and reassembled in order to show the innermost parts of an object, or the parts may be moved about to show how they work or how they appear in different positions. A student very effectively used a model of a living room with scale furniture to show the principles of arranging furniture in a house. Sometimes, of course, models may not look much like the real thing, for they may be designed to show the structural relationships between the parts of an object. Chemistry teachers, for example, use models of various kinds of atoms and molecules which resemble tinkertoy constructions more than they do their unseeable counterparts.

Another kind of model is the mock-up, used with great success by teachers in the sciences, in engineering, and in the armed services. It usually consists of real objects, or parts of objects or machines, mounted on a board to illustrate how the parts function. For example, light bulbs, wire, a dry cell battery, and switches are often arranged to show the fundamental principles of electric circuits.

Occasionally a speaker finds he can employ objects themselves. In demonstrating the fundamentals of the golf swing or of tennis strokes there is no substitute for the club or the racket. In recent years student speakers have displayed disassembled ribbon microphones, a baseball cut in half, the parts of a shoe, a cutaway carburetor, a book in the various stages of binding, the silent mercury light switch, magazine advertisements, musical instruments, and drawing materials. One can readily guess from the objects displayed what purposes the speakers had in mind.

The great advantage of the object and the model lies in their three dimensions. A solid object represented on a plane surface, even when drawn in perspective, is not easy to visualize. But the object itself or a model is readily perceived as solid no matter how a speaker handles it. Visually, the difference between a model and a diagram is the difference between a picture of an airplane and a model of one. Another special advantage of the model is that a speaker can move the thing and its parts about in any way he wishes at any moment to exhibit precisely what he wants to show. Whereas he might need three or four diagrams to demonstrate the parts and operation of a rotary pump, and consume valuable time to sketch on a blackboard or to draw on charts, the pump or a model can be manipulated swiftly. The model is maneuverable; it is dynamic. The speaker who finds himself with a subject that involves three-dimensional objects should face this question again and again during the early stages of preparation: Can I secure—or make—a simple model?

In learning to use models skillfully, speakers should (1) rehearse with the model until it can be handled easily and surely, with each part being introduced precisely when needed; (2) point out with a pencil or in some manner each feature and part as it is introduced. *Identify it unmistakably.* Naming the part is not enought; the connection between the name and the thing must be made visually; (3) keep their eyes on the audience as much as possible, rather than on the model; (4) make the model large enough to be seen by everyone. An object too small to be easily seen is worse than no object at all; it only irritates the audience.

Transparencies and Slides

Overhead projectors are readily available in most school and college settings. They make it possible to present an enlarged image of material that would otherwise be too small to display before an audience. They are particularly valuable because of the opportunity they offer for presenting display material on transparent sheets, 8½ x 11 inches in size, of either plastic or acetate materials. These are ordinarily obtainable, at a few cents apiece, from a store specializing in art supplies. Many college book stores carry them in stock. The only other materials needed are felt-tip markers or grease pencils in the desired colors.

From a magazine, book, or some other source one selects the illustrative material desired for the speech, places the transparency over it, and traces the features he wants. The sheet is then ready for the projector. Some student speakers, artistically inclined, draw their own illustrations on the sheets. Two or three minutes of practice with the machine just prior to the speech should insure smooth and ready use of the illustration. If a number of transparencies are desirable, a special practice time should be arranged and perhaps an operator secured from the class.

Transparencies are not only easy to use, they can be made under conditions too dark or too difficult for a camera. One can select only the features one wants and leave out all others. And finally, the user should be aware that most audiovisual centers can take the information on a book page and copy it directly on a transparency sheet.

The 35 mm. slide is a good device when one takes the pains to plan for its use. If the speaker does not have slides already at hand that fit his subject, he must take his pictures and have them processed. So he must judge his lead time. He must also decide whether he should use a manual projector or an automatic one. For the short classroom speech, six to eight minutes long, the manual type is preferable. It is simpler, faster to get into operation, and less likely to develop bugs at crucial spots.

Using Visual Materials

In discussing visual materials we have offered some suggestions for their effective use. We restate and group them here and add further advice.

Size. Whatever kind of visual material is used, it must be *large* enough for everyone to see clearly and easily. Don't guess; be sure.

Details. Include only those features and details which are *essential* to clearness. Above all, avoid useless labels and names on a chart or graph. If labels are to be seen, their lettering must be large, and a multitude of labels will therefore give a cluttered effect.

Artistry. Any chart or sketch, no matter how simple, must be *precise* and *neat.* An impression of carelessness and sloppiness reflects unfavorably on the speaker. Furthermore, a chart that is elaborate with extra decorative touches of line and color is as ineffective and inefficient an aid to verbal communication as is muddy drawing. Even if a speaker happens to be superior at picture-making and draftsmanship, his job is to communicate ideas, not show his hearers what a fine artist he is.

Eyes. The audience's eyes, not the speaker's, are to be kept on the visual materials. The speaker's eyes should not stray from his hearers longer than is absolutely necessary.

Setting. Any visual device needs a verbal setting when it is first displayed, just as a verbal illustration or story needs a setting if its point is to be understood. Perhaps the best swift setting is secured when a speaker follows this formula: (1) state first what the device is intended to show; (2) point out its *main* features, so that the listeners have some grasp of the whole. It can be helpful also to ask the audience some leading questions before explaining the visual aid. The questions will get the audience to participate at once.

Pointing. Use a pointer, pencil, or finger to *locate* the specific feature or detailed part being talked about at the moment. Even some veteran speakers assume that a properly labeled, clear chart held prominently before an audience is sufficient and that all eyes will spot each feature as the speaker refers to it. But because any sketch, chart, or graph is found to contain more than a single item, spectators' eyes roam over the illustration; they are visually curious. To control roaming and to direct focusing, pointing is necessary. But when the spot is located, the speaker should look at the audience.

To use or not to use visual materials

Many earnest persons who take their speechmaking seriously find it easier to organize ideas, to manage details, to present them orally—in other words, to apply the methods and techniques of speaking—than to judge what ideas and materials are the most appropriate and effective for a particular audience and occasion. The problem of selecting the right idea, right phrase, right word for the right time and right persons is not easy. Nor is it easy to decide in a particular speech whether to use visual materials. Two fundamental principles, however, may help a speaker make his decision. Helpful, too, may be a list of some of the kinds of subjects for which usually—but not invariably—a speaker should appeal to the eye as well as to the ear.

Visual materials should be used when speech is not likely to secure clearness and understanding without them; this is *the principle of effectiveness.* Visual devices should be called upon when speech alone takes considerably more time to achieve clearness than would be necessary with visual aids; this is *the principle of efficiency.*

The following kinds of subjects usually cannot readily be made clear through speech alone, and visualization is almost always a requirement for audiences who are hearing about them for the first time:

> The how-something-is-done subject. *Examples:* laying out a garden; planning a house; conducting a laboratory experiment.
>
> Explanations of operations, machines, physical and natural events. *Examples:* commercially separating cream from milk; the carburetor; drilling an oil well; the universe of an atom; the vacuum tube; development of the human embryo; transmission of nerve impulses.
>
> Subjects dealing with the structure or organization of something—how one part is related to another. *Examples:* The Chicago Board of Trade; county manager form of government; the Red Cross; the university players club; the X Chemical Company; the Illinois Central Railroad.
>
> Subjects requiring much information in the form of statistics and demanding summaries of factual material. *Examples:* The law of supply and demand; income tax versus sales tax; purchasing power of the dollar—1976 versus 1938; steel profits and wages; crop rotation and yields; grades as related to intelligence; pure metals versus alloys.

Through observation and experience we know that some factual materials, in both the informative and the persuasive speech, may be communicated more swiftly and efficiently by visual devices than by speech. In a few seconds the eyes may see and comprehend what the ears might require two minutes for. Suppose, for example, that a speaker were arguing that the Federal budget should be reduced. If one of his supporting points were that "the proportion of national income needed to pay the federal bill has become uncomfortably large," he might wish to amplify as follows:

> In 1930, out of each dollar of income, the government took 6 cents; in 1935, 10 cents; in 1940, 12 cents; in 1945, 30 cents; in 1950, 33 cents.

This would not be unclear, when expressed orally, but the full force of the comparison might not be instantly grasped. So, to secure greater emphasis and attention, the speaker decides he will try to put the ideas this way:

> In 1930, out of each dollar of income, the government took 6 cents; twenty years ago each one of us paid to Uncle Sam 6 percent of every dollar we received. In 1935, five years later, we paid 10 cents, or 10 percent. In 1940, we were contributing 12 cents, and by 1945, because of World War II, the 12 cents had more than doubled—it had become 30 cents. In 1950 we were supporting our government with 33 cents. In twenty years, our government bill multiplied over five times.

The second statement is less compact, easier to follow, and probably more effective communication than the first. The speaker realizes, however, that he is devoting over twice the time to the same material. He has other similar passages in the speech. Must he stop speaking on time? He doesn't want to cut the evidence or an entire section of his talk. Therefore, he decides to appeal to the eye, and with the first passage uses a bar graph (Figure 12).

He produces the graph as he starts the passage and by the end of the passage he has used only a little more time than he would have used had he spoken without the graph. He has made his hearers' eyes do what in the second passage he had to do through restatement and some diffusion of language. In brief, by using visual aid he has become more efficient.

Audio Materials

These are essential and useful when a speaker is explaining sound phenomena of one kind or another—say music, speech sounds, or animal sounds. Most audio materials are best handled on tapes. The speaker records only what he needs. He then plays it on his own recorder or a borrowed one, carefully timing and integrating it with the text of his speech.

A speech correctionist talked on stuttering, illustrating its kinds and degrees of severity and distinguishing stuttering from hesitation phenomena. Not trusting her powers of mimicry, she had all of her illustrations on tape. Students of languages often talk on some aspect of a language as spoken, say its intonational features, or the critical difference between a tone language, such as Chinese, and spoken English. In such cases tapes are almost indispensable.

When music students talk on some aspect of music, they will ordinarily use their own instruments—if portable—to illustrate what they are saying. A

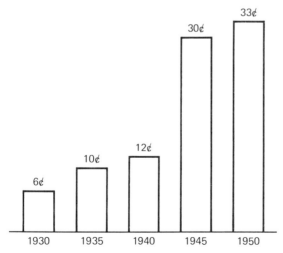

FIGURE 12.

violin or clarinet or flute will illustrate many basic features of scales, keys, melodies, and the like. But one speaker, wanting to illustrate the special sound qualities of the piano, harpsichord, piano accordion, and harp, put the material on a tape recorder and worked the examples into his speech. Students of acting who have deplored the inappropriate and extravagant oral delivery in TV advertisements have made their own examples from TV, using their own microphones and tape recorders. Theater sound effects have been recorded on tapes and have illustrated talks on their production and use.

Audio illustrations invariably claim attention and should be employed when one is talking about sound. The illustrations must be prepared carefully, and must be intergrated with language until all goes smoothly. And above all other considerations, sound should serve language, rather than language serving sound. The speaker is not preparing a script for a film story or documentary accompanied by a language line or commentary. So all kinds of examples and illustrations in whatever media—verbal, visual, or audio—*support* the message and are subordinate to it.

Audiovisual materials serve to supplement and reinforce verbal communications. They are vivid and powerful, aiding the audience's understanding and advancing the communicator's explanations and arguments. Their successful use depends on their effectiveness; and effectiveness in turn depends largely on the skill with which they can be integrated with what is said.

INQUIRIES

1. You want to explain the layout of your college campus. What existing map or maps would you use? Would you do better to prepare your own map or maps?

2. What kinds of visual aids would you use in describing the anatomy of the larynx? In explaining how changes of pitch depend in part upon the behavior of the vocal cords?

3. Plot on a graph the grades of all the courses you took in high school. What conclusions do you draw from the graph? Can you represent these conclusions on another graph?

4. You want to explain to your parents how you spend your time in a typical week at college? What graphic means would you find most effective?

FURTHER READING

Brown, James W., Richard B. Lewis, and Fred F. Harcleroad. *A V Instruction Media and Method.* 3rd ed. Chapter 12, "Audio Materials."

Carskadon, Thomas R., and Rudolf Modley. *U.S.A.: A Measure of a Nation; A Graphic Presentation of America's Needs and Resources.* 1949. A fine example of visual materials in use.

Communication among Scientists and Engineers. Ed. Carnot E. Nelson and Donald K. Pollock. 1970. Done mostly in color; highly imaginative and suggestive.

Dale, Edgar, *Audio-Visual Methods in Teaching.* Rev. ed. 1961

Deutsch, Herbert. "Transparencies, the Simplest Teaching Tool." *Library Journal,* 95 (Jan.-Mar. 1970), 1167-68.

Hamilton, Edward A. *Graphic Design for the Computer Age: Visual Communication for all Media,* 1970.

Minor, Ed, and Harvey R. Frye. *Techniques for Producing Visual Instructional Media.* 1970. Chapter 5, "Producing Transparencies for Protection and Display."

Weaver, G.G., and E.W. Bollinger, *Visual Aids: Their Construction and Use.* 1949. Chapter 4, "How to Make, Display, and Use Charts."

Wilson, William, and Kenneth R. Haas. *The Film Book for Business, Education, and Industry.* 1950. Chapter 8, "Film Script Preparation." Underlines the difference between messages carried primarily by audio-visual means and by means of speech and language.

CHAPTER 7

Structure and Movement:
Outline, Introduction, Conclusion

Fashioning potential materials into a speech fitting to subject and audience requires selecting and rejecting ideas—making choices of materials and tactics—turning the ideas into statements, forming those statements into a systematic, orderly whole, and shaping that whole into a pattern of presentation that seems appropriate and interesting. The instrument for facilitating this sequence of processes is the *speech outline*. That outline is, first of all, a building instrument and guide for preparation of the speech. After it is completed and worked out, prompting notes may be drawn from it for assistance in delivery, if the speaker feels the need. Making the outline, however, as we treat the process, is the final fashioning of the speech before putting it into language in delivery.

The initial, or skeletal, outline should help the speaker focus his attention on the *purpose* of his speech and the bare bones of his ideas. Those ideas will appear as *subject statement* and the main heads of *development*. We have sketched this minimal pattern in Chapter 2, "The First Speeches."

PURPOSE

A clearly worked-out statement of purpose, in the form of an infinitive phrase, can help a speaker greatly in determining his direction and in selecting and rejecting materials. Statements of purpose serve at least four functions:

1. It reveals the response or effect the speaker seeks. *Example:* "To get my audience to understand what term insurance is." This would both result in and guide an informative speech. *Example:* "To get my audience to prefer term insurance to endowment insurance." This would help the speaker build a favorable attitude toward term insurance and thus fashion a persuasive speech.

2. It establishes the goal, or the goal-image, which guides the speaker in preparation and delivery. He is looking ahead, as it were, in what I. A. Richards, the rhetorical theorist, called "feedforward."

3. It reveals the constraints that the speaker has had to put on his subject matter. Usually time is the chief constrainer. If a speaker had five minutes, he could probably make clear the chief features of term insurance; he would need more time to argue its advantages over endowment insurance.

4. Once it is determined and precisely formulated, it becomes the guide by which one selects and rejects ideas and materials and determines the relevance of Subject Statement and materials of Development.

Appropriateness of purpose is a matter of real concern. Student audiences do not like to be preached at by student speakers unless, perhaps, the sermon is well disguised. Speakers ought to consider potential long-term results in formulating their purposes: "I may sell my customer the product today, but will he buy again next month or next year?" The choice of one's purpose determines the dominant features of one's ethos. Purpose ultimately reveals how responsible, how accountable, a speaker is willing to be.

SUBJECT STATEMENT

The subject statement is the single declarative sentence that forms and shapes the ideas and materials used in developing the purpose. Subject statements in (1) informative speeches characterize or epitomize, or capsulize, the basic materials that develop them; in (2) persuasive speeches, they assert the position the speaker takes on a problem or his stance in controversy. A subject statement in informative discourse is as factual and neutral as the speaker can make it. In persuasive discourse it is a partisan statement presenting the belief or opinion the speaker wants his audience to accept.

Formulating Subject Statements for Informative Speeches

The subject statement for an informative speech is usually one of the following:

1. *A complete definition.* This states all the features distinguishing the subject from closely related subjects.

   Burglary is "breaking and entering the building of another in the night time, with intent to commit felony in the same."

A cooperative store is a "store or shop belonging to and supported by a cooperative society, with the purpose of supplying its members with goods at moderate prices, and of distributing the profits, if any, among the members and regular customers."

The definition of a process, a mechanism, or an operation will probably include purpose of process, materials used, and manner of handling materials. For example: "The manufacture of plain linoleum is accomplished by mixing linseed oil, ground rosin, and cork, pressing the mixture into a burlap foundation, and allowing it to oxidize, thereby making a floor covering that is resilient, durable, and waterproof." Such a definition furnishes natural main heads for the Development.

2. *A partial definition.* The subject statement can focus on one important way in which the subject—whether it be an object, a play, a novel, a process, a mechanism, a word, a person, or an institution—is distinguished from other closely related subjects.

Boys' Town is an institution for training in citizenship.

The Constitution of the United States was the result of an economic movement.

Elihu Root's career was governed, not by political expediency, but by principle.

Silas Marner is the story of a man redeemed from greed by the love of a child.

Behrman's play, *End of Summer,* is the portrait of a woman without a mind.

A distinguishing feature of the University of Virginia is its Honor System.

3. *A statement of* the principle (or principles) on which the explanation of the subject depends.

A modern reformatory operates on the assumption that vocational training, good food, and proper environment can make a bad boy into a good citizen.

The jet engine applies, in a new way, the laws governing the behavior of gases under pressure.

In determining and phrasing the subject statement, ill-considered statements should be avoided, for example: "Polo is a unique game"; "A holding company is not as complicated as it seems." Such statements do not point out the distinctive features of their subjects. Almost always, they are signs that the speaker has not taken the trouble to decide what he really is talking about.

Formulating Subject Statements for Persuasive Speeches

The subject statement for the persuasive speech is usually one of the following:

1. *The evaluative or critical statement* reflects the speaker's belief arising out of the arguments that have clustered around a problem.

Rarely does the college newspaper represent the opinion of students as a whole. The college newspaper ought to lead student opinion.

2. *The statement of policy* asserts the speaker's view of the way a problem is to be solved, whether specifically or more generally.

Any candidate for national office should be permitted to speak on campus. Leading politicians of any party should be allowed to speak on campus.

DEVELOPMENT

The selection and phraseology of the main heads of a speech involve two problems: choosing heads that are directly *relevant* to the subject statement; patterning the heads so clearly that one head suggests other, related heads.

Relevance

The problem of relevance is easily solved. A main head directly amplifies a subject statement if main head and subject statement make sense when *for, because,* or *in that* is used as a connective between them. For example:

> *Subject Statement:* The gaseous content of a city's smoke blanket impairs health.
>
> [*for*]
>
> I. It irritates sensitive membranes.

Patterning

The second problem, that of organizing main heads into a pattern, is more difficult. Yet its solution is essential to both speaker and audience if clarity of idea and ease of utterance are to be attained. A *pattern* is an arrangement of ideas or things into a system such that any one item in the system suggests and implies other items and such that all essential items have been included and all unessential and irrelevant items have been excluded. In the example that follows, the materials have been organized so that (1) any one head implies another, and (2) the parts of the whole take in all the classes of people implied in the subject statement.

> *Subject Statement:* Group hospitalization insurance is designed to spread the costs of hospital care so as to benefit everyone.
>
> I. It benefits the patient.
> II. It benefits the physician.
> III. It aids the hospital.
> IV. It benefits the community.

The better the pattern of main heads in the speech, the easier it is for the speaker to recall and react swiftly to ideas as he talks.

As a speaker sets to work at organizing the material of a speech, probably a pattern will not occur instantly to him. His mind will be engaged in shuttling—in going back and forth from possible main heads to subject statement to purpose. He may hit upon a neat pattern for the main heads only to see a moment later that one or two of the heads are not directly relevant to the subject statement. So he adjusts the phraseology of the subject statement—and perhaps also rephrases the main heads. And so the process of critical synthesis goes on, with frequent shifts and adjustments until a whole is planned and knit firmly together.

Though some subjects almost automatically fall into obvious patterns, there are times when the obvious divisions do not serve the speaker's purpose as well as other divisions would. A speech on healthful menus would divide itself almost without help into breakfast menus, luncheon menus, and dinner menus. If the speaker, however, were mainly concerned with balanced meals (whether breakfasts, luncheons, or dinners), he might wish to emphasize his purpose by taking as the basis for main divisions the different essentials of diet, such as starches, proteins, vitamins. He might then *subdivide* his main divisions according to breakfast, luncheon, and dinner menus.

Standard patterns

Through long experience, speakers and writers have found that a comparatively few plans or patterns serve satisfactorily for breaking down the majority of subjects.

The Time Pattern.   Narrative details and such speeches as involve the explanation of a process, for example, or instructions on "how to do it," are more or less naturally chronological. One item comes before another in the speech because it comes before it in the process. For such a speech, the speaker should try to find a limited number (two or three in a short speech) of time-divisions into which to group the chronological items. He should avoid having many main divisions. Grouping helps him remember and helps his audience grasp the entire speech. For example:

Subject Statement: There are four literary landmarks in the history of free speech in England.

   I. Peter Wentworth was tried by the Star Chamber for calling for freedom of speech in Parliament in 1576.
   II. John Milton wrote the speech "Areopagitica" in behalf of liberty for printing in 1644.
   III. Thomas Erskine defended Thomas Paine's right to publish *The Rights of Man* in 1791.
   IV. John Stuart Mill, in his essay *On Liberty,* 1858, argued that liberty of thought and action should be curtailed only when it directly harms others.

Subject Statement: Ballet had its origins in the Italian Renaissance and it spread rapidly to other European countries.

   I. The first ballet performance took place in Tortona, Italy, in 1489.
   II. Catherine de Medici introduced ballet to France in 1581.
   III. The English Masque evolved into a form very similar to the French during the reign of Henry VIII.

IV. Ballet was well established in Russia by the time of Catherine the Great, in the early eighteenth century.

In using the *time* pattern, it is not necessary, of course, to maintain the chronological sequence. The reverse of the chronological would equally represent a time *relation,* or a speaker might start with one period of time and move on to what came before that time and then to what came after.

The Space Pattern.   The division on the basis of *spatial* relations is natural and obvious for some kinds of subject matter. For instance, most newscasts are so divided: international news, Washington news, other national news, local news. Besides geographical subjects, others may profitably be organized to proceed from front to back or back to front, top to bottom or bottom to top, inside to outside or outside to inside, near to far or far to near. For example:

Subject Statement: The Sea of Cortez (the romantic name for the Gulf of California) is a fisherman's paradise.

I. In the northern end of the gulf totuava, grouper, and pompano are plentiful.
II. In the middle region the waters abound in yellowtail, roosterfish, skipjack, and black sea bass.
III. La Paz, in the south, is noted for its billfish: sailfish, marlin, and swordfish.

Subject Statement: The atmosphere, or the sea of air which surrounds our planet, has several distinctive layers.

I. The part of the atmosphere in which we live and in which our weather occurs is the troposphere.
II. Above the troposphere is the stratosphere, in which the temperature is constant.
III. In the mesosphere, temperatures first increase with height and then decrease with height.
IV. In the ionosphere, temperatures increase with elevation, reaching almost 200° F.

Subject Statement: The control panel of the powerhouse is arranged for the greatest convenience of the operator.

I. Close in front of him are the instruments that he uses most often.
II. Farther away to the sides are the less used dials and levers.

Because many persons are strongly visual-minded and are likely to connect things they want to remember with places, the *space* pattern of analysis has another distinct advantage. During the explanation of a process, for example, if the listener can visualize part of the process going on in one place and part in another, he often finds it easier to keep track of details and to remember them.

Topical Pattern. Any speech in which the heads spring from the natural or conventional divisions of the subject itself is topically organized. The broad divisions in medicine, for instance, are based on *structure* and *function;* in matter and in science, on *animate* and *inanimate;* in law, on *civil* and *criminal.* Narrow specific subjects break into logically appropriate divisions also. Accordingly, the forms of the topical pattern are greater in variety than those of other patterns. The following samples further illustrate the qualities of the topical pattern:

Subject Statement: The United Nations is made up of four basic parts.

I. The General Assembly is made up of all member nations, each of which has one vote.
II. The Security Council is made up of fifteen members.
   A. There are five permanent members.
   B. The other ten are elected by the General Assembly for two-year terms.
III. The Secretary-General is the chief administrative officer.
IV. The Specialized Agencies carry on a wide variety of nonpolitical functions.

Subject Statement: The North Pole is not necessarily the cold, snowy, stormy place you think it is.

I. Winter temperatures are only slightly lower than North Dakota's, while the climate of some regions could be called "tropical" in the summer.
II. We think of lots of ice and snow, but when the snowfall is converted to inches of water, an average winter yields only eight inches.
III. The Arctic is one of the least stormy large regions of the world—violent gales are extremely rare.

One kind of *topical* pattern, so often useful that special attention should be given to it, analyzes the material on the basis of the *persons, groups,* or *categories of people affected.* For example:

Subject Statement: The daily newspaper provides something for each of many kinds of readers.

I. It serves those persons who want information and opinion on public affairs.
II. It provides for those who want to be entertained.
III. It guides the shopper.
IV. It serves the businessman.

The speaker is most likely to discover various "natural" divisions of his subject through reading. Accordingly, even if he is working on an expository subject that he knows intimately through personal experience, he would do well to dig up a book or article related specifically or generally to the topic, and to read enough to become aware of the author's divisions and classifications.

Causal Pattern.   In dealing with events and their forces, one can often use a pattern like the following:

Subject Statement: A run on a bank has many causes.

    I. Its ultimate cause is lack of confidence in the ability of the bank to honor deposits.
    II. A contributory cause may be a financial depression.
    III. An immediate cause may be rumors that the bank is in danger of bankruptcy.

Subject Statement: Race rioting is one of the products of a society of unequal opportunity.

    I. A feeling of despair and hopelessness is often at the basis of riots in our big cities.
    II. Inferior schools, a lack of job opportunities, and slum housing contribute to the hostile attitude of rioters.
    III. Despair and hostility build up until a relatively minor incident precipitates a riot of enormous proportions.

Purpose-Means Pattern.   This is especially useful in arranging the essentials of a process or an art.

Subject Statement: Flower arrangement is an artistic endeavor.

    I. There is an attempt to present a pleasing picture.
    II. There is an attempt to apply the principles of visual harmony and balance.

Subject Statement: Arbitration is an arrangement settling a disputed matter without taking it to court.

    I. The purpose of an arbitration board is to find a compromise between the positions of the disputants.
    II. Both sides present their arguments to an individual or a board that they have selected and whose decision is regarded as final.

Patterns for persuasion

There are, in addition, some ways to pattern main heads that are especially well adapted to the speech that is primarily persuasive. In speeches centering on statements of policy, for example, three patterns are useful:

Problem-Solution (or Disease-Remedy).

Subject Statement: A job-training program should be instituted for unskilled workers

    I. There are few jobs available for unskilled workers.
    II. There are numerous unfilled positions requiring skilled labor.
    III. Training programs for unskilled workers would make them available for these positions.

Theory-Practice.

> *Subject Statement:* Narcotics addicts should be committed to civil institutions for rehabilitation.
>
> I. The rehabilitation of addicts of all kinds is a slow, painstaking process that can only succeed in an institution designed for that purpose.
> II. The rehabilitation of narcotics addicts would work out the same way.

Desirable-Practicable.

> *Subject Statement:* Urban renewal can meet the problems of big-city deterioration.
>
> I. Neighborhoods can be kept intact.
> II. Revitalization of old buildings is technologically feasible.

Other patterns for organizing informative and persuasive speeches serve particular kinds of subjects, purposes, and audiences; but those we have illustrated are probably the most generally useful for the beginning speaker. For others, see our *Fundamentals of Public Speaking* (5th edition), Chapter 16.

MAKING THE SPEECH OUTLINE

With the broad pattern settled on, the speaker will proceed to fashion the structure of his speech to serve his purpose as well as possible. The visual product of this patterning will be the speech outline, which will contain sketches of all the ideas he plans to use, in the order in which he plans to use them.

Logical Skeleton

The first step will be to construct a logical skeleton of Purpose, Subject Statement, and main heads of Development on the basis of the pattern he has chosen. Schematically that skeleton should appear as follows:

Purpose: _____
_____.

Subject Statement: _____
_____.

DEVELOPMENT

I. _____
    A. _____
        1. _____
        2. _____

        B. _____
    II. _____
        Etc. _____
    III. _____
        Etc. _____

The number of main heads, subheads, etc. will depend on the nature and scope of the subject.
The rules for filling out the skeleton are few but important:

1. The purpose relates to the subject statement as result does to sufficient condition; that is, the subject statement must be so presented that once the audience agrees with or accepts it, nothing else is needed to realize the speaker's goal.

2. The subject statement relates to the development (the main heads and subheads introduced by "for," "because," "or," "in that") as effect relates to cause; that is, the reasons and explanations given in the development must be closely tied to the subject statement, so that the audience is caused to accept or agree with it once they accept or agree with the development.

3. The main heads when viewed together should show a logical pattern, division, or classification of ideas used to develop the subject statement.

4. All elements in the skeleton—and also in the full speech outline—except the purpose, will appear as complete declarative sentences (usually simple rather than compound or complex), not as phrases, labels, or captions.

I

Purpose: To explain the meaning of *solution* as the chemist sees it.

Subject Statement: A solution is a fluid of homogeneous character whose composition may be varied continually within certain limits.

DEVELOPMENT

I. Homogeneity is an essential state of all true solutions.
   A. *Homogeneity* means "identity or similarity of kind or nature."
      1. The particles are alike in kind.
   B. Any salt solution is a good example.
II. The composition of true solutions can be varied continuously within certain limits.
   A. This is illustrated by the addition of salt a little at a time to a glass of water.
   B. In certain cases the limit may be infinity.
III. True solutions are differentiated from other mixtures.
   A. Turbid water is not a solution.
   B. The mixture of milk and cream is not a true solution.
   C. Metal particles suspended in water do not make true solutions.

II

Purpose: To warn of the dangers of sunburn.

Subject Statement: Getting a suntan should be done sensibly.

DEVELOPMENT

I. Sunburn can be very harmful.
  A. It is usually an aesthetic liability.
    1. Bright sunburn goes ill with women's formal gowns.
    2. Sunburn gives the skin of both women and men that crusty, weather-beaten look.
  B. It can be very harmful physically.
    1. A sunburned skin may send poisons to the whole body.
    2. Blistering one-third of the body may cause death.
II. Sunburn is a cause of significant economic loss.
  A. Vacations are often wasted because of excessive sunburn.
  B. Post-vacation and post-weekend absenteeism is high in business and industry in the summer because of sunburn disability.
  C. In one year, New York City laborers lose as much as 200,000 working days' pay because of sunburn.
III. People can get a good tan safely.
  A. Exposure to full sun should be gradual—a little at a time.
    1. People with dark complexions may take as much as 10 to 12 minutes at a time, initially.
    2. People with light complexions should not take more than 5 to 7 minutes of continuous full exposure initially.
  B. Persons whose skin will not stand direct sun, or will not tan under exposure, can use effective "suntan" cosmetics.

The Speech Outline

The logical skeleton made, the speaker will then proceed to composing in reasonable detail the speech outline. It will represent conceptually and visibly the pattern and movement of the speech as the speaker plans to present it to his audience. The thought-structure for the outline, as for the speech, is what we have been calling the logical skeleton. It will often furnish the pattern of subject statement and development for the speech outline without any considerable changes or additions except for some introductory and concluding remarks (see the conclusion of Chapter 2).

Full speech outlines, however, are as various as speeches themselves, for no two speeches, even by the same person on the same subject, are exactly alike. The most carefully prepared outline, anticipating and providing for feedback from the hearers during delivery, does not guarantee that a speaker will not be inspired to adapt some of his material in new ways. An old argument may suddenly appear with a new meaning, a concept may need a different definition or illustration, an idea may require additional emphasis. Most such adaptations will be made by the perceptive, venturesome speaker from a base provided by the skeleton. The speaker who feels ready to depart from traditional form and to experiment with imaginative modes of development is advised to do so only if he can reasonably expect the result to be clear, as well as novel and interesting.

Most speakers most of the time—and inexperienced speakers

especially—do well to expand the skeleton and follow its order. The major adaptations to audience and circumstance will come in ideas and materials for introductions, conclusions, and transitions.

INTRODUCTIONS

The introductions to most speeches serve either or both of two functions: (1) to engage the interest and attention of the audience and (2) to prepare the audience for the speaker's purpose and point of view.

Interest and Attention

The familiar reference

Reference to the Occasion or the Place. Is there any relationship between the subject and the date of the speech? A scientist lecturing on meteorology at Charlottesville, Virginia, on Jefferson's birthday might well refer to Jefferson's interest in recording data on the weather.

Observe Woodrow Wilson's recognition of the occasion and place in his address on "The Meaning of the Declaration of Independence."

> We are assembled to celebrate the one hundred and thirty-eighth anniversary of the birth of the United States. I suppose that we can more vividly realize the circumstances of that birth standing on this historic spot than it would be possible to realize them anywhere else. The Declaration of Independence was written in Philadelphia; it was adopted in this historic building by which we stand. I have just had the privilege of sitting in the chair of the great man who presided over the deliberations of those who gave the declaration to the world. My hand rests at this moment upon the table upon which the declaration was signed. We can feel that we are almost in the visible and tangible presence of a great historic transaction.[1]

Reference to a Recent Event or to a Familiar Quotation. To start with a reference to a local or national event that has made a deep impression on the community and to link it logically with the subject makes a very easy and effective opening. The speaker, however, must guard against the temptation to stretch an event, to squeeze and torture a happening or a quotation, in order to show a connection between it and his subject.

Good use of the local incident was made by a student in an oratorical contest at Evanston, Illinois. Four days before the contest, the assistant state's attorney had been machine-gunned. The student, speaking on the breakdown of the home as a cause of crime, was thus presented with a fitting event that he turned to his benefit. This was his opening sentence:

[1] J. M. O'Neill, *Models of Speech Composition* (New York, 1921), p. 554.

The murder of your prosecuting attorney, last Wednesday, has made my subject an unusually timely one for this audience, for beginning with the first recorded human crime—the murder of Abel by Cain—and coming down to this murder in your city day before yesterday, the perplexing question of crime has baffled society.[2]

Reference to the Special Interests of the Audience. What is the connection between the subject and the hearers' vocational and professional interests? Their political affiliations? Their local and community problems?

Reference to What a Preceding Speaker Has Said. Where several speakers appear on one occasion, as at banquets, conventions, and in the classroom, an alert speaker can often take his opening remarks from something that has already been said.

At least two possible ways of managing the reference should be considered. After starting with a swift report of what an earlier speaker has said, one can:

1. Explain how his subject fits into the earlier speech, by stating that he will develop a different aspect of the subject. At a meeting of small-home architects, one man spoke of new plumbing layouts, and later in the afternoon another speaker alluded to the earlier topic and added that he was going to report on a new type of valve that regulated water pressure.
2. Show a plausible association between his subject and the previous one. In a round of class speeches lasting a week, one speaker on the first day talked on the proper design of a fireplace. Later in the week an aspiring geologist spoke on how to find water. His approach was somewhat in this vein:

   A few days ago my friend Mack Taylor told you how to build a fireplace that wouldn't smoke. Now I'm going to speak on something that's far more fundamental than designing fireplaces. It's important if you should sometime decide to build a home in the country, you'd better look to it long before you worry about fireplaces. In fact, you'd better look to it before you even decide just where you're going to put that house.

   What I want to do is tell you where you can find water. The method used is recommended by up-to-date geologists. It is . . .

Humor

Speakers have always regarded humor as a good method of ice-breaking. The humorous story or anecdote as a means of introduction is effective if three conditions are always respected. (1) The story must be in point and not dragged in. The test for relevance is simple: Could the story be used as a supporting example of a main head or of a subhead? If so, it belongs in the speech and one can lead off with it if he wishes. (2) The mood or temper of the occasion must not be inimical to humor or to this particular humor; the

[2]M. G. Robinson, "The Eleventh Commandment," *Classified Speech Models,* ed. W. N. Brigance (New York, 1928), p. 19.

anecdote is out of place when the occasion is solemn or dignified. (3) The story must not take up more time than it is worth. If the speaker has selected his subject well, if it is reasonably appropriate to his hearers, he should get to the heart of his speech as fast as his audience will let him. The extended anecdote often wastes time.

For an example of the humorous story properly used in the introduction see Bruce Barton's speech, "Which Knew Not Joseph," which is printed in the Appendix.

Significance of the subject

Reference to the special significance or importance of the subject is perhaps the most rewarding means of approach for the novice speaker to master. It can be used for most speeches on most occasions and for persuasive as well as for informative speeches. And this kind of approach not only stands a good chance of claiming the hearer's attention; it is also likely to stir the speaker himself to greater energy, alertness, and interest than most types of introduction.

Let the attention section of the introduction be developed around this *implied* theme: my subject is important to *you,* at this *time,* and on this *occasion.* Or in other words, the speaker tells his audience *why* they should listen; he *motivates* them.

In planning to use this scheme, the speaker should note, first, that he does not actually state that his subject is important; to do so would probably result in a colorless, trite statement. Second, he should pick two or three reasons why the subject is significant; he states these and amplifies each, if necessary, to the point where he sees the audience react favorably and attention is won. The speaker can then move on to his purpose and point of view.

The success of this approach depends entirely on whether the speaker really *believes* that there are excellent reasons why his audience should listen to him, on his subject, and at that time. If he has good reasons, then his subject is truly appropriate to both his audience and himself. If he enjoys success with this method, it will be due primarily to two factors: (1) The reasons he picks—if they are significant rather than trivial—will usually reflect those motives, emotions, and attitudes which direct our lives and partially govern what we will attend to and perceive. The responses touched off may well be strong and deep. (2) Since he gives the reasons that led him to settle on this subject rather than some other, he is likely to respond strongly himself; he himself becomes interested, energetic, alert, and direct; he remotivates himself. Any speaker who is slow to warm up to his speech should try this approach.

One of the classic, short approaches of this kind is that employed by Jeremiah S. Black when he argued the right of trial by jury before the Supreme

Court, in December 1866. A Federal military court martial had tried and sentenced to death one Mulligan and two associates, all of them civilians. Mulligan appealed; and before the Supreme Court, the military tribunal maintained that it had the power to try civilians during wartime even when the civil courts were open, and, furthermore, that the civil courts were powerless to prevent the military from acting. In the face of such a contention, Black's approach is not overdrawn:

> I am not afraid that you will underrate the importance of this case. It concerns the rights of the whole people. Such questions have generally been settled by arms; but since the beginning of the world no battle has ever been lost or won upon which the liberties of a nation were so distinctly staked as they are on the result of this argument. The pen that writes the judgment of the court will be mightier for good or for evil than any sword that ever was wielded by mortal arm. 3

(Observe the basic motives and attitudes to which the speaker referred: *rights, liberty,* and the *good.*)

A student interested in insurance once spoke to a class of boys somewhat as follows:

> Perhaps you don't like to be bothered by life insurance salesmen who are always trying to sell you a policy. Forget the men and consider the thing. For the young, unmarried man, insurance can be a means of saving. Upon his marrying, he finds that he has a way of protecting his wife and family from financial worries if he should die. Insurance can also be a means of building up a retirement income that will give a man comfort and security in late life.
>
> I propose this morning to explain the advantages and disadvantages of three kinds of life insurance.

In the speech outline, prior to the statement of purpose and the subject statement, will appear an Introduction in two parts: Attention Material and Orienting Material. In making a speech outline, the speaker does well to block in under Attention Material what he intends to use for that purpose. For example:

INTRODUCTION

Attention Material
1. What does a college aim to do?
   a. Our college newspaper recently carried an article by Professor Dabney, saying that colleges should aim to produce "intellectual aristocrats."
   b. Last Monday in this class Mr. Kushner defended the not-too-serious purpose of the average student.

---

3 O'Neill, *op. cit.,* p. 84.

2. Many are the attacks on college education; and some colleges have met the criticism by various reforms and new schemes. Examples are,
   a. University of Chicago plan.
   b. St. John's College plan.
   c. Antioch College plan.

Orienting the Audience

With his attention step planned, the speaker can turn to the second purpose of the introduction, the *orientation* of his hearers.

In the orientation part of the introduction, the speaker should always make a direct reference to his subject. In the informative speech, the reference to subject may consist in stating the purpose of the speech, for example, "I shall attempt to explain how dress patterns are made." For some subjects on some occasions no more orientation than this may be needed, and after announcing his purpose the speaker can proceed to his first main idea. But for many subjects on many occasions, fuller orientation is desirable. It may be accomplished by the following materials, alone or in combination:

Present the Subject Statement. Many speeches present the subject statement fully in the introduction and then restate it at least once. The object is to dwell on it until it registers with the audience. Many a subject statement, for example, is abstract and general, even a bit complicated and profound, and an audience can't get hold of it without restatement.

State How the Subject Is To Be Developed. For example: "In explaining how domestic Roquefort cheese is made, I shall mention first the ingredients, and then take you step by step, from the beginning to the finished product that is ready for boxing and shipment."

Supply Background Information. A bit of history often helps an audience to see a subject in its perspective. If one were talking on the Frasch process of mining sulphur, he might, for example, supply a brief review of the older mining methods.

The background sketch should be placed in the introduction wherever it will fit in smoothly and logically. It might follow the subject statement; it could be part of the attention material; or if it contained unusual and interesting facts, it could be the opening sentences.

The orienting material will also be blocked out in the Introduction of the speech outline. For example:

Orienting Material

1. It is the Antioch plan that I think will interest you.
2. Founded by Horace Mann, in 1853, who left upon the college this motto: "Be ashamed to die unless you have won some victory for humanity."

3. Dr. Arthur E. Morgan, known as "Roosevelt-baiter" or "ex-TVA" Morgan, was president of Antioch from 1920 to 1936.
    a. As an engineer he had seen the failure of technical education to produce educated men.
        (1) Culture and skill didn't seem to go together.
    b. Dr. Morgan decided they could be brought together.

CONCLUSIONS

The conclusion has at least one main purpose: to summarize and draw together the chief ideas of the speech. The ideas and tone should give a rounding-off and sending-off effect.

The Summary

Some kind of summary is necessary, and we urge that the beginning speaker not leave its formulation to the spur of the moment. Any hearer will welcome a summary, because the summary appeals to his sense of order and proportion; the speech as a whole, the multitude of ideas he has heard, suddenly are revealed again as orderly and systematic, rather than chaotic.

It is of course true that the short speech which is extremely well organized and methodically presented may not require the concluding summary; the speaker may simply stop after he has completed discussion of his last point. But one should not be in a hurry to abandon the summary; in an overwhelming majority of speeches, it is an effective way of rounding off ideas, of securing clearness, and of stimulating action.

Summaries may be formal and concise, or informal and somewhat discursive. In either case, the summary should be managed by *restatement* (recurrence of old idea in different words) rather than by *repetition* (recurrence of old idea in the same phraseology). Accordingly, the shortest possible recipe for a summary is this: Deftly restate the ideas expressed in the subject statement and in the main heads.

To illustrate the summary, suppose the subject statement and main heads were as follows:

The control panel of a powerhouse is arranged for the greatest convenience of the operator.
    I. Close in front of him are the instruments which he uses most often.
    II. Farther away to the sides are the less used dials and levers.

The formal summary might be this:

In short, the instruments that control the machinery of a powerhouse are arranged on a large panel to suit the convenience of the operator, the instruments most used being in front of the attendant and ready to his hand, the instruments least used being at the extreme sides of the panel.

The less formal summary might run something like this:

> To conclude, then: If you were to visit the control room in Urbana's powerhouse, you would see Mike Williams, on the night shift, seated before the large control panel—a panel that is arranged like most control panels in powerhouses. Immediately in front of him, and easy to reach, are the instruments he may need five or six times during the night. At the far sides of the panel are the dials and levers that may be used once a week, or even less often.

Subject Statement as the Conclusion

When a speaker discovers that his subject statement is too complicated and unwieldy to handle easily early in the speech and perhaps too difficult for his hearers to understand without much restatement and preliminary explanation, he may save the statement until the end of the speech and use it as his conclusion. If he does so, he must be sure to retain in the orientation step the statement of his purpose.

The Detailed Illustration as a Summary

Perhaps the most interesting type of conclusion by summary is a detailed example which illustrates the meaning of the entire speech. The informal summary cited above is really such an illustration. It would become detailed had the speaker given Williams three or four typical operations to perform, if Williams were to use two or three of the dials and levers near at hand and to use each for a definite purpose, and were he to make use of one of the remote instruments.

In preparing the speech outline, it is good practice to lay out carefully the ideas appearing in the conclusion. For example:

CONCLUSION

We see, then, that Antioch College, which Dr. Eliot of Harvard once referred to as one of the most significant experiments in American education, succeeds by correlating technical and cultural studies on the one hand, and study and life on the other.

TRANSITIONS

Inexperienced persons often find the "joints" of a speech hard to manipulate. Like most elements of a speech, transitional phrases and sentences must be planned; they don't spring, ready-made, into the mind. It is good practice to include them in the speech outline and to give special attention to them late in the rehearsal stage of preparation when one is ready to work on details of phraseology.

Introducing Main Heads

Use signpost devices. Number the main heads: *First, Second, Third,* and so on. Variations of this are: *In the first place, The first step, The first matter to be discussed is . . . , Let us first discuss. . . .* Although such labels may seem obvious and somewhat wooden here alone on the page, usually they are not distractingly obvious in a speech.

Use parallel structure in main heads and emphasize by the pause. Here are four heads whose structure is alike:

I.   On the north side of the quadrangle are the dormitories.
II. On the east side of the quadrangle are the science halls.
III. On the south side of the quadrangle are the administration and classroom buildings.
IV. On the west side of the quadrangle is the great auditorium.

Through experience and conditioning we have come to regard things similar in structure and size as equal in value, as having equal claims on attention. Hence, if the speaker phrases head II exactly as he worded head I, a listener senses that both heads are coordinate in value. He reacts similarly when he hears heads III and IV. Parallelism of structure, accordingly, holds main heads together.

Parallelism is most effective when combined with the pause. Just before stating a head, pause for five seconds or so. The pause will give emphasis to the idea of the preceding division and will at the same time advertise the beginning of the next division.

Use the flashback and preview device. This consists of alluding at the major points of the speech to what has just been said and to what will follow. Although there are many ways of managing such a transition, perhaps the "not only—but also" formula is the swiftest and easiest to handle. In the example below, the material supporting each main head has been omitted.

I. Antioch combines cultural and practical studies . . . .
. . . .
[Antioch not only combines cultural and practical studies; it also joins study with practical experience.]
II. Antioch combines academic study with work in the business world
. . . .
. . . .
[Antioch has done more than combine culture and practical studies and join study with experience; it has found that its systems works.]
III. Antioch's plan has been successful.

Keeping Subheads Distinct

Adopt a consistent set of conjunctive adverbs, and get into the habit of using them to start off the discussion of a subhead. A workable group of such words is this: *moreover, also, furthermore,* and *finally.*

In using these coordinating words with the subheads, avoid using the same words also to designate main heads; and don't use *first, second,* and so on with the subheads if you are applying them also to main heads. There's no surer way of confusing listeners than to cross them up by inconsistent labeling.

The rule of thumb, then, is this: Use one set of labels for main heads, another set for subheads. In all cases avoid, if possible, the useless, undiscriminating connectives, "and another thing," and "then too."

SUMMARY OF RULES FOR MAKING THE SPEECH OUTLINE

1. There are four distinct parts: Title, Introduction (including Purpose and Subject Statement), Development, and Conclusion.
2. Complete declarative sentences should be composed for subject statement, main heads, and subheads.
3. The logical relationships among purpose, subject statement, and main heads should be the same as those for the logical skeleton.
4. The introduction should have two parts: (a) ideas and materials designed to claim attention and stir interest; and (b) ideas that orient the audience to the purpose and give it emphasis.
5. The conclusion should summarize by restating the substance of the subject statement and main heads, and where appropriate should offer a suggestion or make an appeal to relevant values.
6. Transitions, whether as full sentences or as phrases, should appear where they are to be used and should be enclosed in brackets [ ].
7. The Development should provide the amplification of ideas and materials appropriate to the kind of speech—for the informative speech nonargumentative materials, for the persuasive speech good reasons and arguments.

Illustrative Speech Outlines

I.

What Is a Solution?

INTRODUCTION

A. Attention Material
  1. Many of you are now taking qualitative analysis.
    a. Last week you heard Professor Baker explain the nature of a solution.
    b. If you don't understand what a solution is any better than I did, perhaps I can help you.

2. I talked with Professor Baker for half an hour and then read an article on solutions in the *Journal of Chemical Engineering.* I believe I now know what a solution is.
B. Orienting Material
   Purpose: to explain the meaning of *solution* as the chemist sees it.
   Subject Statement: A solution is a fluid of homogeneous character, whose composition may be varied continuously within certain limits.

DEVELOPMENT

[The most important feature of a solution is its homogeneity.]

   I. Homogeneity is an essential of all true solutions.
      A. *Homogeneity* means "identity or similarity of kind or nature."
      B. Salt in a glass of water is a good example. [Demonstrate by mixing salt and water in a beaker.]
         1. Neither by eye nor microscope can different physical states be detected.

[The next feature of a solution is its variability.]

  II. The composition of true solutions may be varied continuously within certain limits.
      A. This is illustrated by the addition of salt a little at a time to a glass of water.
         1. The salt dissolves for a long time.
         2. Then finally it settles to the bottom and the limit of the process has been reached.
      B. In certain cases the limit may be infinity.
         1. Water and alcohol will dissolve each other in any given quantities.

[It is instructive to understand what solutions are not.]

 III. True solutions are differentiated from other mixtures.
      A. Turbid water is not a solution. (Stir soil and water in a beaker and hold to light.)
         1. It is merely a suspension of pieces of matter.
         2. It is not homogeneous.
         3. The solid will settle to the bottom eventually.
      B. The mixture of milk and cream is not a solution.
         1. Cream is merely a mass of fat globules suspended in the water of the milk.
         2. Suspensions of one liquid in another are called emulsions.
      C. Metal particles suspended in water, although they show little tendency to settle out, cannot be classified as true solution.
         1. This type of mixture is intermediate between the dispersion of the solution and that of the suspension.

CONCLUSION

[It's all very simple, you see.]

A solution is a homogeneous fluid whose composition may be varied within certain limits.

II.

(This outline, designed for an essentially descriptive, characterizing speech, was made in preparation for one of the early assignments in the autumn of 1972 in an introductory undergraduate course in public speaking. The subject was timely because of the recent murder of the Israeli athletes at the Olympic Games in Munich. The outline, though not completely consistent logically, illustrates very well the principles and forms of structure essential to the logical skeleton and the speech outline.)

Black September
by
E. D. Walker

INTRODUCTION

A. Attention Material
1. Imagine the following:
    a. You have no regard for human life.
      (1) You would readily take any person's life.
      (2) You are prepared to give your own.
    b. You have learned and lived hatred all your life.
    c. You have lost your home and have resolved to reclaim it.
2. If you were one in such a condition, you might easily have been one of the eight men responsible for the deaths of the Israeli athletes at the Olympics in Munich on September 5; you could have been a Black September terrorist.
B. Orienting Material
Purpose: To make the audience realize the character of the Black September group of terrorists.
Subject Statement: Black September is an especially violent, desperate subgroup of the militant Palestinian refugees.

DEVELOPMENT

I. The members of Black September are Fedayeen.
    A. Fedayeen can be distinguished by their nationality.
      1. They are neither Syrian, Jordanian, Lebanese, or Egyptian.
      2. They are Palestinian Arabs.
        a. They are Arabic-speaking Moslems.
        b. They have made their homes in Palestine since the seventh century.
    B. Fedayeen are distinguished by being refugees.
      1. They are part of some 1.5 million people who have been expatriated.
      2. They have fled or have been forced from their homes to refugee camps by the Israeli-Arab wars of 1948 and 1967.
      3. They live lives of hate.
        a. They hate themselves because they are helpless.
        b. They hate the Israelis for taking their homes.
        c. Their children drill and make mock battle.
        d. They have a single dream—of returning to their homes.
    C. The Fedayeen have taken up arms.
      1. They constitute the underground resistance to Israel.
        a. They are an irregular force, much like the Viet Cong.
        b. They are guerrillas.

2. They are dedicated to bringing an end to the Israeli state through the use of ambush, sabotage, and subversion.
3. The Fedayeen make up some dozen or more guerrilla organizations.
   a. Many of the groups are obscure.
   b. Some, however, have attracted international attention.
      (1) The most prominent is Al Fatah.
          (a) It is the largest.
          (b) It is relatively moderate.
      (2) A second well-known group is the Popular Front for the Liberation of Palestine.
          (a) It has a Marxist orientation.
          (b) It is among the most militant.
II. The people of Black September are different from other Fedayeen in several important respects.
    A. They are more desperate.
       1. They are frustrated.
          a. They have seen a sharp curtailment in Fedayeen activity.
             (1) The curtailment began in Jordan.
                 (a) During 1970 King Hussein ordered the suppression of all guerrilla activity.
                 (b) Guerrillas in Jordan were forced to flee or surrender.
             (2) The governments of Syria and Lebanon have begun to restrict commando activity.
          b. They have seen Fedayeen forces dwindle.
             (1) These forces peaked in 1970 at 20,000-30,000.
             (2) Their current size [Fall 1972] is perhaps one-fifth that figure.
          c. They have seen other Fedayeen forces and leaders accept these setbacks while they themselves desire urgently more aggressive action.
          d. Even their name speaks of frustration.
             (1) Black September is an expression of wrath.
             (2) It protests King Hussein's betrayal of the guerrilla movement in September 1970.
       2. They are disillusioned by failure of guerrilla tactics and activities so far.
          a. They are no closer to regaining their homeland.
          b. The Israeli position now seems stronger than ever.
    B. They are an extremist fringe.
       1. Their approach is extreme.
          a. They believe that it is futile to aim future efforts directly at Israel.
          b. Instead they intend to accomplish their goals through extortion on a global scale.
             (1) They wish to focus world attention on the Palestinian problem.
             (2) It is their plan to create an international crisis of fear and tension.
             (3) They believe that the community of nations can be forced to implement the desired change.
       2. Their methods are extreme.
          a. The crisis they plan to create is one of terror.
          b. Through irrational, bloody terror they attempt to dramatize the plight of their people.
          c. They are committed to giving the world no peace.
       3. Even their comrades in other guerrilla bands are alarmed by some of their tactics.
    C. They are deeply secretive.

1. They hide their identities with remarkable effectiveness.
   a. Unlike other groups, they have no public headquarters.
   b. Their operatives become known only when captured or killed.
   c. The world knows of their activities only when they take credit for some atrocity.
2. There is little reliable information about the size of the group.
   a. Estimates by the C.I.A., Israeli intelligence, and other sources vary widely.
   b. There is agreement that they are relatively small.
3. The nature of the group's organization is a virtual mystery.

CONCLUSION

A. Black September is a group of extremist Palestinian guerrillas who intend to outrage the world.
B. If you are outraged by events in Munich last September, they have in part, at least, accomplished their purpose.

BIBLIOGRAPHY

Sharabi, H. *Palestine and Israel, the Lethal Dilemma.* 1969.

"Black September's Ruthless Few." *Time,* 100, No. 12 (September 18, 1972), 33.

"These Are Very Desperate Men," *U.S. News and World Report,* 73, No. 12 (September 18, 1972), 21.

III.

Education for the Gifted

INTRODUCTION

A. Attention Material
   1. Michael Grost is receiving a special education.
      a. He is an eleven-year-old student at Michigan State University.
      b. He is learning more than if he were in a regular program.
   2. Michael Grost is exceptional.
      a. He has an exceptionally high IQ.
      b. He is very well adjusted emotionally.
   3. Other gifted children could be helped through special programs.
B. Orienting Material
Purpose: To show that the present programs for the gifted are not enough, and to present my plan for improved education for this group.
Subject Statement: More provision for developing individual abilities than exists at present should be made for our gifted children.

DEVELOPMENT

I. Acceleration and complete isolation of the gifted is not the best solution.
   A. Acceleration is not the answer.
      1. Professor Leta Hollingworth warns that often there are physical and social maladjustments.

    2. The student may miss fundamental knowledge and skills.
    3. The new curriculum is still aimed at the average student.
  B. Complete isolation is not the answer.
    1. The child is not always superior in all subjects.
    2. The student may not be socially or physically mature enough.
    3. Dr. Leonard H. Clark says, "The evidence does not show that ability grouping has been successful."
  [Since these practices have not been successful to develop the full potential of the gifted, I suggest the following ideas.]
II. Giftedness should be identified as soon as possible to allow for full development of the child's abilities.
  A. Gertrude Hildreth's book, *Educating Gifted Children*, says that parents could be trained to identify giftedness in their children.
  B. Children could be placed in an environment that would encourage early development.
  C. Special training could then be given to gifted pupils to improve study and work habits.
III. Students should be classified in special classes on the basis of their abilities in particular subjects.
  A. A child might be placed in a special math or science class.
  B. He might be placed in a regular English class.
IV. Better students should tutor poorer students.
  A. This helps the superior student's understanding of the subject.
  B. This brings out the leadership quality.
  C. This allows a feeling of communication between two groups.
V. Grade groupings should be abolished.
  A. A gradeless system is working at Melbourne High School in Melbourne, Florida.
    1. A student may take sophomore English, junior math, and senior French.
    2. The student may move up or down as his case warrants.
    3. Principal B. Frank Brown says, "Flowers have been blooming all over the place."
  B. A gradeless system is also working at Woodrow Wilson Junior High in Elizabeth, New Jersey.

CONCLUSION

In short, I think you can see that the present practice of complete separation of the gifted child is not doing the job. I hope that you will agree that early identification of giftedness, classification by special ability, opportunities for superior students to tutor poorer students, and the abolition of grade groupings would greatly improve our educational program for gifted children.

BIBLIOGRAPHY

Hildreth, Gertrude H. *Educating Gifted Children.* New York, 1952.

Pritchard, Miriam C. "The Contributions of Leta S. Hollingworth to the Study of Gifted Children." *The Gifted Child,* edited by Paul Witty, Boston, 1951.

Pollack, Jack Harrison. "Should We Separate Smart and Average Kids?" *Parade Magazine, Chicago Sun Times* (January 3, 1965), 4-5.

INQUIRIES

1. Observe the talk of at least twenty persons during the next day or two. Why do they talk? Try to state what you think are their purposes or intentions. How many of these purposes can be regarded as motives? How many as values?

2. None of the outlines in this chapter is perfect, and much can be gained by working them over.

   a. In the logical skeleton for the sunburn speech, for example, is the purpose quite consistent with the content of the development? If the purpose is adjusted, does the subject statement also need adjustment?

   b. Are transitions needed in the speech outlines presently without them?

   c. For what ideas in any of the outlines would you add examples? evidence? testimony? definitions?

   d. Can you make clearer the classification or pattern of the main heads in any?

3. Consider the materials, books, and lecturers in courses you are taking, or have taken recently. Of what lecture, what chapter, what discussion, could you most readily prepare a logical skeleton?

FURTHER READING

Baird, A. Craig. *Rhetoric: A Philosophical Inquiry.* 1965. Chapter 9, "Structure."

Baird, A. Craig, Franklin H. Knower, and Samuel L. Becker. *General Speech Communication.* 4th ed. 1972. Chapter 11, "Organization and Outlining."

Bryant, Donald C., and Karl R. Wallace. *Fundamentals of Public Speaking.* 5th ed. 1976. Chapters 15 and 16.

Christensen, Francis. "The Generative Rhetoric of the Paragraph." *College Composition and Communication,* 16 (October 1965), 144-56.

Monroe, Alan H., and Douglas Ehninger. *Principles and Types of Speech Communication.* 7th ed. 1974. Chapters 13 and 14.

Reid, Loren. *Speaking Well.* 2nd ed. 1972. Chapter 9.

CHAPTER 8

Materials and Methods
of Persuasion

GOALS OF THE PERSUASIVE SPEECH

The goal of all persuasion is to influence opinions and beliefs, behavior and conduct. In preparing to address a particular audience at a particular time and place, however, one does not simply say to oneself, "I want to change the belief of this audience"; but rather, for example, "I want my hearers to believe that the railroads ought to improve passenger service" or, "I want this audience to vote the straight Republican ticket." The goal of a particular persuasive speech, whether expressed or implied, always reveals (1) the speaker's belief about a state of affairs and (2) his intention that his hearers should think likewise.

PRINCIPLES OF PERSUASION

The persuasive speaker reaches his goal through the application of a single controlling principle. Writers on persuasion have expressed the principle in different ways. The three following are representative. A. E. Phillips called the principle "Reference to Experience":

> Reference to Experience . . . means reference to the known. The known is that which the listener has seen, heard, read, felt, believed or done, and which still exists in his consciousness—his stock of knowledge. It embraces all those thoughts, feelings, and happenings which to him are real. Reference to Experience, then, means *coming into the listener's life.*

J. A. Winans spoke of "common ground." A speaker is on the road to persuasion when he and his audience stand on a common ground of belief, of goals and values, and of emotion and feeling. The speaker recommends his own belief to others in terms of relevant beliefs which he and they share, of relevant values and ideals which they both approve of, and of relevant emotions and feelings which they experience alike. Kenneth Burke has asserted: "You can persuade a man only insofar as you can talk his language by speech, gesture, tonality, order, image, attitude, idea, identifying your ways with his."

In brief, the persuasive speech is likely to achieve its goal when speaker and audience can be shown to share beliefs and attitudes, motives and interests, emotions and feelings that are relevant to the business at hand. The persuasive speaker is always saying, in effect, "Accept what I say because it harmonizes with what you already accept and regard with favor." Borrowing from Burke, we shall refer to the principle as that of *identification* and shall think of persuasion as a process of identification.

MATERIALS OF PERSUASION

Knowledge of Subject

The most substantial way of identification is through ideas and information relevant to a particular problem, audience, and occasion. A persuasive speech, however, is not occasioned primarily, like the informative speech, by a speaker's superior knowledge of a subject that he wants his hearers to appreciate and understand. Rather, he has, or thinks he has, a solution to a problem that matters, or ought to matter, to them. Hearers are in doubt and are called on to make decisions and choices; they have not made up their minds or acted decisively. So the materials that unite speaker and audience, if speaker and audience are to find common bonds at all, must come from the ideas, facts, opinions, and arguments that are relevant to the problem and appropriate to the audience at a particular time and place.

Any problem, its "solutions," and the decisions made and actions taken go through well-defined stages of discussion. The speaker can get on common ground with his audience by focusing his speech on the questions and issues that concern them at the time.

Two methods of analyzing a problem are widely used. They tell the speaker what he must know and where he can concentrate his fire. The first was formulated by the distinguished American philosopher John Dewey. The second is an inheritance of the ages.

Dewey's steps in analysis

1. Becoming aware of the problem.
2. Defining the precise nature of the problem.
3. Discovering possible solutions to the problem.
4. Deciding on the best solution.
5. Testing the decision by putting it into practice.

Thinking on any problem always goes through these five stages, although the testing process, except in the laboratory under experimental conditions, cannot be carried out until the solution has been put into practice to see whether it will work. Our legislators discuss and debate and pass a law, but the law is not tested until it has gone into effect.

How does a problem arise in everyday affairs? First, some observer gets the notion that he doesn't like what is going on at present; he may not, for example, like the subsidizing of intercollegiate athletics at X college. So he complains about it; or in more formal terms, he becomes a critic of the present. He may run across others who have been vaguely disturbed over the matter, and discussion goes on. Second, discussion arrives at the point where criticism makes the problem definite. It becomes clear that the trouble with the subsidizing of athletics lies not in the awarding of athletic scholarships, but in the awarding of scholarships for athletic ability only. Accordingly the problem is made clear: "Can athletic scholarships be granted at X College on grounds other than athletic prowess only?" Third, with the problem clearly recognized, remedies are suggested; and fourth, out of suggested remedies one proposal is adopted by the college. Finally, discussion on the matter subsides and the proposal goes into effect.

Now suppose a speaker were at X College when the discussion of athletic scholarships was going on. Suppose his knowledge and grasp of the situation had led him to see the problem in its five aspects. What would he elect to speak on to a college class? *He would do well to select that aspect of the subject that reflected the current stage of discussion.* If the audience vaguely felt that the problem existed, then the speaker might decide to define the problem and bring criticism to a head, perhaps judging correctly that the hearers were not yet ready for a solution. Or if current discussion were beyond the stage of definition and students were discussing alternative proposals, a speaker might wisely advocate a specific solution. In short, analysis not only helps to understand the problem as a whole, but analysis is of practical value in determining what special view of it is best suited to the particular audience. This is true not only of campus problems but of all controversial problems—regional, national, and international. Indeed, the campus or local problem differs from the international problem only in being closer to home, more concrete, and less broad in extent.

The traditional scheme of analysis

This method of seeing the essentials of a controversy is not unlike the foregoing steps of analysis. It is, however, somewhat more detailed, and some speakers in their preparation find it more practical because it directs attention to the cause-and-effect mode of thinking and suggests statements (or their equivalents) that may often be used as the subject statement or as the main heads of a speech.

I. What criticisms are made of the present situation? Are there evils—effects or conditions we do not like?

I.' What are the causes (both immediate and remote) that have brought about the criticisms and bad effects?

II. What policy, program, or action would if accepted and put into action remove the criticisms and abolish the evils?
   A. Does the proposal for remedying the evils make a definite and clearly recognized change from the present state of affairs?
   A.' Does the proposed solution specifically recognize new causes and conditions that will remove the old causes that brought about the bad effects?

III. Is the proposal for change the best possible remedy?
   A. Is it definitely distinct and separate from other solutions offered?
   A.' Is it superior to any other remedy?

IV. If adopted, would the proposal set causes to work whose effects would be as bad as those it would remedy?
   A. What drawbacks has the proposal?
   A'. Would they really be serious and significant evils?
   B. Would the proposal be workable? Could it be put into operation?

Again this method of analysis is useful to the persuasive speaker in the same way as are the Dewey steps. The questions help him survey the possibilities of his subject and help him to decide on that aspect of it which would be appropriate to the special audience and occasion. On one occasion he would find it appropriate to concentrate on one phase of the subject, on another on some other phase.

Selecting the specific goal

Once the speaker has found an area of interest in which both he and his hearers can meet appropriately, he begins to consider his specific goal or aim. He decides what effect, what response, he wants from his audience. He states the effect as his *opinion*, his *judgment*, his *evaluation*, and builds his speech in support of it. He wants his audience to accept it, to have the same attitude toward it that he has. Technically, his opinion functions as the *subject statement* of his speech.

Knowledge of Audience

Some of the basic materials of persuasion are derived from what the speaker can learn about his hearers. He is especially interested in them as *social* creatures, in the kinds of persons they are because they have been brought up among people, not alone on a desert island.

The study of social character is complex. It is best carried on formally in the fields of psychology, social psychology, and sociology. Those who have had an introduction to these fields are in a better position to understand the character of audiences than those who have not. For the young person who has not had the chance to analyze human nature rigorously we offer a few fundamental suggestions that will put him on the road to discovery.

Norms and standards of group behavior

A person in an audience is not a member of that group only, but more importantly he is a member of other groups from which he has derived most, if not all, of his ideals and beliefs. Some significant groupings:

Family
Political groups:
   Democratic and Republican parties
   Liberal, conservative, middle-of-the-road
Religious groups
Racial groups
National and regional groups—U.S.A., the Middle West
Societies and clubs:
   Service clubs—Rotary, P.T.A.
Professional groups: teachers, lawyers, physicians
Economic groups:
   Owners and managers—Chamber of Commerce, trade associations
Farm—Farm Bureau
Big Business, Little Business
Consumers—high income, average income, low income
Labor—A.F. of L.-C.I.O., electricians, teamsters

In preparing to meet his audience, a speaker asks two kinds of questions: (1) What groups are represented in the audience? (2) What ideals of belief and conduct are the groups committed to? What do they say about their goals and values? What values may be inferred from their actions? Most speakers will find that they know a good deal about groups they themselves belong to; for example, family and religious groups. On reflection, they can list the ideals, customs, and codes of behavior by which these groups judge

the behavior of their members. For knowledge of other groups, they may
have to consult books and articles that deal with their aims and principles.
Societies of any size and scope issue literature about themselves.

Group norms are the uniformities of ideals, rules, customs, and behavior
by which the thought and conduct of group members are regularized. Norms
are *standardized generalizations*. Group pressure is behind them and individuals are expected to conform. As examples of norms expressed as ideals,
take our American values as asserted in the Constitution and in our Declaration of Independence. We respect "justice," and we stand for "liberty to
ourselves and our posterity," and for the protection of property and freedom
of religion, speech, and press. No man may be "deprived of life, liberty or
property, without due process of law," and "all men are created equal,"
having certain "inalienable rights," such as "life, liberty, and the pursuit of
happiness." These are some of the ideals and concepts that bind Americans
into a national group.

The force and appeal of group standards are manifold. Norms not only
bring social pressure to bear on an individual, but they are bundles of many-
sided experience. They announce or imply deep-seated goals and desires.
They are associated with motives and emotions. They are responsible for our
strongest attitudes—those mechanisms we recognize when we say we are for
or against something or regard an object, person, or idea with favor or
disfavor, liking or disliking, desire or aversion. And because they channel so
much experience into broad streams, they are the chief means by which
members of a group can successfully communicate with each other in ways
that ensure the preservation, solidity, and unity of the group. One of the
widely respected social psychologists, Theodore Newcomb, some years ago
pointed up the impact of group standards in this way:

> Group norms . . . determine individual behavior in two ways. They provide
> both meanings and goals. They provide meanings because . . . the individual is
> dependent on group norms for his meanings; without them he cannot
> communicate. They provide goals because the individual cannot be indifferent
> to the approvals and disapprovals which are associated with the norms.
> Inevitably, he becomes motivated toward or away from objects, people,
> institutions, and ideologies whose meaning is provided by the norms.[1]

How are group norms employed in persuasion? They supply the fundamental ways to identification. The speaker draws on norms that are relevant
to the ideas he presents. The identification works in two ways. Knowing that
individuals identify themselves with the ideals of a group, he connects his
proposals and arguments with their ideals wherever he can logically do so.
Thus he establishes identity through common ideas. He also suggests a

[1]Theodore Newcomb, *Social Psychology* (New York, 1950), p. 275.

personal identification, on the grounds that persons who approve of the same ideas are to that extent alike.

A striking example of identification is in George William Curtis's speech, "The Puritan Principle," delivered when feeling ran high over the Hayes-Tilden election controversy in 1876. Responsible, thoughtful people were so aroused that they spoke openly of resorting to arms to determine who should be President. Before about 400 influential citizens gathered in New York, Curtis advocated that Congress set up machinery whereby "a President, be he Democrat or be he Republican, shall pass unchallenged to his chair." He singled out the chief national groupings in the audience—the Irish, French, English, and German—and reminded them of their old-world allegiances by mention of their national flowers. He shifted to their new-world values, to their traditions as New Englanders and as Americans, and to their respect for liberty and for liberty under law. Then he asserted that the traditions of law were directly applicable to his proposal, and Congress should find a legal remedy. The address is supposed to have stopped all talk of a civil war. Serious students of persuasion ponder it as a classic appeal to ideals, values, and emotions that held speaker and hearers in common bond. Somewhat less emotional and less direct is President John F. Kennedy's use of identification in his Inaugural Address, January 20, 1961 (below, pp. 233-35).

Lines of Thought, Motives, and Emotions

When the persuasive speaker has analyzed his subject and has some appreciation of the group norms represented in his immediate audience, he becomes interested in finding the possible lines of thought by which he hopes to achieve his purpose. At this point in his preparation he looks again to the *precise circumstances* that gave rise to the problem under discussion. If he will regard them closely, he will find what people think are the conditions (sometimes referred to as "causes") blocking the achievement of their goals. In other words, people and groups are experiencing frustrations. When goals are not attained and frustrations appear, emotion is almost always the result. The speaker who can thus size up the problem-situation has discovered the logical basis of emotional appeal—blocked motivations and thwarted goals. Helpful in locating such lines of thought are the following guide-questions:

Are there conditions that threaten their *economic welfare?* What is hurting wages, salaries, savings, production costs, and prices?

What conditions are harmful to the security and stability of *family life?* What is injurious to the opportunity, education, and comfort of children?

Who or what is working against the *basic freedoms?* Is the situation placing unwarranted checks on freedom of speech, action, or worship? Who is being tyrannical and arbitrary?

What opportunities are being denied to the audience or to groups and persons it is interested in? Who is discriminating against whom? Are conditions in some way unjust? Illegal?

What is damaging to the status and prestige of the audience, the community, the nation? What is insulting to whom?

Is any aspect of the situation damaging to some cherished tradition or custom?

Has any person, business group, labor group, or political group been shirking its social responsibilities, or been reneging on its public promises and commitments?

Have persons or groups involved in the situation been deceitful or untruthful? Has some group or party forsaken accepted ideals of truth, virtue, democracy, religion, or codes of conduct?

The genuine concern of any audience in a problem and its solution is grounded in such motives and in conditions that interfere with the normal realizing of goals.

The speaker who thus probes a problem will be more than realistic and interesting. He will also be on the way to acquiring the language of power and emotion. If the circumstances actually *threaten* our values and modes of conduct, there is danger, and we cannot avoid feeling anxious and fearful. In the face of injustice and unfairness, we become indignant. We take pride in our accomplishments, and pride also is the feeling that permeates prestige and status. We feel pride in actions that are honorable and dutiful, and we experience shame in dishonor and unfaithfulness. When we think we can successfully cope with a situation, when we believe that we are ready to solve a problem and when it seems probable that we will, we experience confidence and feelings of security. (What emotions do students experience when they take an examination?) When persons unite, determined to face a problem and sincerely desiring to solve it for the benefit of all involved, they experience feelings of mutual understanding and good will. So the speaker who honestly faces a real problem, who understands it, and who believes that he can help an audience solve it, finds his thought and argument impregnated with emotion, and his language will bear the signs of it.

The young speaker often seems to think that he must avoid emotion and feeling and the mention of attitudes that stir men emotionally. He may even feel that it is wrong to reason other than "logically." But there is no valid basis for deprecating emotion generally, and there will be no ethical problem if the speaker's view represents his *considered* opinion. The sincere speaker cannot avoid emotion unless he schools himself against it. He will reveal it in his face, his voice, and his movement. And as he responds to his hearers and they to him, he will often unconsciously refer to "our duty and responsibility," to "our sense of fair play," to what is "right" or "good" to do. If he quotes a well-known passage from the Bible, most listeners will experience a slight feeling of reverence—and so may the speaker, as he quotes it. The sincere speaker cannot be a machine.

Furthermore, the divorce between "logic" and "emotion" is more supposed than real. When one sets out to reason most logically, one may discover that *what* he says speaks as loudly as its logical form and framework. Suppose one were speaking in support of the annual Red Cross drive and decided that the effective line of attack was to emphasize the little-known service that the local chapter rendered in putting a serviceman in touch with his family when the normal means of communication had broken down. So the speaker took this as subject statement: "The local Red Cross chapter kept servicemen in touch with their families when other means failed." He knew of a number of instances and arranged his material thus:

I. The chapter did this in the city.
    A. A well-to-do family was put in touch with their son.
    B. A poor family was put in touch with their son.

II. The chapter also performed such service in the rural area.
    A. A well-to-do family, etc.
    B. A poor family, etc.

He concluded after four minutes, most of which was devoted to factual description of the four instances. In such a speech the subject statement is a limited generalization that is supported beyond reasonable doubt by four instances, and the instances are meant to be typical because the selected cases included both the rich and the poor. Now is it possible to tell whether the perceptions of the audience were controlled *primarily* because of reasoning? Or was the main effect secured through what was said—the ideas used and the associations they stirred up directly or indirectly? Did there come into play the listeners' sense of duty and obligation to servicemen, their desire for the soldiers' happiness and well-being, their affection for home and family relationships, and their sense of justice (no discrimination because of differences in money and position)? Even when we aim at the logical connections among ideas, the ideas themselves control attention by calling up our accumulated experience of motives, emotions, and attitudes.

The Speaker's Character and Personality

When Emerson said of a speaker, "What you are thunders so loudly I cannot hear what you say," he was only expressing anew what speakers and audiences have always known—that personality and character exert as strong an influence (perhaps an even stronger influence) on the reception of ideas as do other means of persuasion. Quintilian so keenly appreciated the force of the speaker's character in persuasion that he believed no bad man could secure any honor whatsoever with an audience. Bad character and persuasion excluded each other; consequently, he defined the orator as a good man skilled in speaking.

The impact of character is derived partly from the speaker's prestige and partly from his manner of presentation, his bodily activity, facial expression, and vocal qualities that mean sincerity, earnestness, modesty, courtesy, and geniality. These desirable qualities of personality, not revealed on the surface of language and behavior, shine through presentation and help paint the speaker's portrait.

How can the speaker paint a desirable self-portrait? There are no formulas, no rules-of-thumb. Socially acceptable qualities of personality and character are built up through long training in the home, the school, the church, and association with others. All we can do is to offer some advice which may make these qualities more evident to a person who has them and may show the person who lacks them what is needed.

Prestige and esteem for the speaker

One of the significant characteristics of any group is its social structure or system. The structure is evident as soon as well-defined positions have developed, positions whose status can be located on a social scale from low to high. Persons who hold high-prestige positions enjoy the esteem of other members of the group. Hence esteem becomes a factor in persuasion.

The speaker-audience situation is a real, though relatively simple, group structure. The social position of the speaker is a dominant one and carries prestige largely because he is expected to possess some, if not all, of the qualities of a leader. One of the chief qualities is that of knowledge, because the speaker, relative to the audience, is supposed to have had the opportunity to know and think. Enough has been said in this chapter and elsewhere in this book about information and knowledge as essential ingredients of speechmaking.

Knowledge is of course made evident by what the speaker says, through the information he reveals on the subject of the moment, and through the general background of knowledge an educated person is supposed to have. To the extent that a speaker possesses the *special* knowledge of the expert, his esteem is heightened and he wields the influence of *authority*.

Other factors that significantly influence the prestige and esteem of the speaker fall into two general categories: (1) traits of good taste, and (2) moral traits that are expected of speakers in a free society. In the former category we shall emphasize courtesy and modesty.

Courtesy

There are two principal *cautions*. Avoid offending the sensibilities of a group by being risqué, by being irreverent toward people they respect or toward religion and God, by using humor when the occasion is solemn, or by attacking cherished ideals and deep-seated opinions by recourse to ridicule and to sustained satire and sarcasm.

The following approaches to the revered authority, the cherished belief or tradition, recognize the hearer's attitude without condoning it:

> We all respect Thomas Jefferson's views on education and find them especially sound for his day and time. But we should not extend less respect to John Dewey whose mature judgment on modern education leads him to say . . .

> We may all believe that the American army is the greatest in the world. The opinion is a credit to our pride and loyalty. Nevertheless, if we examine the opinion carefully, we may see it in a new light.

The second caution is this: Avoid convicting an audience of ignorance. Present the information hearers don't have, of course, but don't make such mistakes as saying, "You didn't know that, did you?" Don't dismiss an objection with a shrug, or with a smart-alecky "So what!" Rather, some formula like this is to be preferred, "I am sure your opinion is well-founded, but my information leads me to another conclusion."

Modesty

A speaker with a know-it-all attitude is a trial to everybody, anywhere. He is even more obnoxious on the platform. Signs of his immodesty are especially evident in his flat, dogmatic assertions, in his sweeping generalizations, and in his voice and manner which plainly imply, "I can't be wrong." The cause of such immodesty lies principally in his failure to recognize that he may possibly—just possibly—be wrong once in a while. He fails to appreciate what most educated persons learn: that in pro-and-con matters, neither pro nor con has a monopoly on truth. Our opinions can be called "possibly true," "probably true," "in all probability, true," but never "certainly" or "universally" true. Scientific conclusions and laws probably carry the greatest certainty. The physicist may have proved that all bodies will fall in a vacuum at a uniform speed. But even for this observation he will not claim too much, for he will preface most of his laws with the phrase that admits the possibility of doubt: "*So far as we know*, all bodies will fall in a vacuum at a uniform rate." Why should the persuasive speaker, without the laboratory experiment to test his conclusions, be more certain than the scientist? Remember that the speaker is often recommending a policy—a belief or action to be applied in the future. How can he, without being immodest, say dogmatically that he will prove, or has proved, what will hold true in the future "beyond all shadow of doubt"? Even in the law, where most questions are decided by reference to past happenings and can be testified to by witnesses, documents, and so forth, juries are specifically charged to reach a verdict that is "beyond *reasonable* doubt." Doubt, accordingly, can seldom be banished. A sensible speaker knows this—and so does his audience.

The young speaker should avoid phrases like "I shall prove conclusively," "No one can take exception to this conclusion," "This is proved beyond question." Let him be more accurate and more modest, with such phrases as "It seems to me," "Probably," "Perhaps we can accept this," "My opinion is . . . ."

The modest speaker who does not claim too much for his conclusions will avoid another sign of immodesty: exaggeration. He will not say carelessly that "all men are honest" when he really means that "most men are honest"; in other words, he will avoid the sweeping generalization. He will, furthermore, appreciate the value of *understatement* as opposed to *overstatement*. A sailor who described his rescue from a torpedoed merchantman concluded by saying that the experience was "pretty rough." He let his hearers supply the high-flown adjectives, "harrowing," "terrible," "miraculous," "amazing." Indeed, it should be observed that one value of understatement is that the hearer is often ready to concede more than he would permit the speaker to claim.

Moral Values

The persuasive speaker should reveal in himself those moral qualities and social values we normally expect of ourselves and our friends. Persuasion always involves ethical problems, because an audience must necessarily *trust* a speaker to seek only worthy ends and to use only honest, socially desirable means of persuasion.[2] The audience must be convinced that the speaker is a man of integrity, good will, sincerity, and good sense. The audience will be likely to see these qualities in him if, in addition to being modest and courteous, he also strives for the general welfare and not simply for his own, respects the opinions of others but respects his own judgment as well, and plays fair with his audience, his opponents, and the issues at stake.

---

[2]For a fuller discussion of the speaker's ethical problem see above, pp. 8-11, and Chapter 5 of our *Fundamentals of Public Speaking,* 5th ed., 1976.

HANDLING THE MATERIALS OF PERSUASION

The speaker who can assure himself that he has found and considered the essential materials for a persuasive speech is ready to think about ways of treating and presenting his ideas.

First, the *methods and techniques of development* are as useful in the persuasive speech as they are in the informative speech. As a general rule, it is not easy to persuade an audience to belief or action without making clear what belief is to be accepted or what is to be done. Indeed, if a group is convinced that the time for action has come, sometimes all that is needed is a description of the desired action, presented pointedly, unambiguously, and vividly. Furthermore, the best argument is ineffective if it cannot be understood, and all the skills of identification go to naught if hearers do not see what is being identified with what.

Second, all the *resources of language and style* help in producing persuasion. Particularly important are those ways which impart *impressiveness* to style—the sharp, intense, vivid phrase, image, and illustration.

Third, the attitude of the audience toward the speaker's goal and the position he recommends will greatly influence strategy and tactics. Before he decides finally on what ideas to use and how to handle them, a speaker should ask: How does my audience regard me and my basic position? Are they neutral, partisan, opposed? Are some groups for me, others against me? So at some stage of his preparation, the persuasive speaker should consider his goal, his basic position (to be expressed as a subject statement), and his chief lines of thought with relation to the partisanship of his audience. "Now," he tells himself, "I know what I want my hearers to accept and here are the arguments I have about decided to use. How many of my listeners will probably find them congenial? How many will reject them? How many are neutral, ready to be informed, and willing to judge on the basis of what I can say?"

To answer such questions accurately would require the speaker to make some kind of attitude poll of his audience, or to discover the results of such a poll. Except under the most favorable and unusual conditions—in the public speaking class, for example—it is impracticable to conduct one's own poll. Consequently, the alert speaker is alive to any polls reported in the newspapers which in any way relate to the subject and materials of a speech he may be planning to make. These will tell him something about the population of which his audience, or some of it, may be a part. Better yet he will discover that by reading widely and by talking with as many people as possible, he will learn what people *say* they believe. With such information he can turn his attention to his prospective hearers and group them into at least three main classes: *partisans, neutrals,* and *opponents.*

Rarely will hearers be all partisan, all neutral, or all in opposition. They will usually exhibit shades, tints, and colors of all three opinions. Although no one has discovered sure-fire, scientific formulas for selecting and handling materials for *any* audience, we shall try to present some guiding considerations that have met the test of experience.

Influencing Neutrals

The neutrals, whether well-informed and judicious or ill-informed, haven't made up their minds, and a speaker has a real chance to guide them. In general, these people are the so-called independent voters whose decision to vote one way or another—or not at all—decides elections. If they have had too little information to enable them to commit themselves, they will welcome information. It is therefore easier to cope with neutrals than with opponents, a fact that political campaigns invariably recognize. The election campaign aims at two things: to hold the interest and support of partisans and to swing into camp those who are vacillating.

Select the primary objection [or objections] that has prevented decision, and answer it with the best evidence and argument available. Often we vacillate because there is one aspect of a situation or problem that bothers us. We say, "Yes, so-and-so and so-and-so are true, but there's one matter I'm still doubtful of." Some doubters want to be sure on all important aspects of a problem, and if one aspect bothers them, they will reserve decision and refrain from action.

One of the commonest objections raised by conservatively minded people is this: "In theory," they say, "your idea is all right and we're for it, but you simply can't put it into practice—it won't work." Consequently, if the speaker can show how his proposal has actually worked elsewhere, or if he can draw a vivid sketch of how it might work, with enough detail to make the plan seem alive, he can often win favorable response. The greatest virtue of the public speaker has often been considered his power not only to make people *understand* but to make them *see.*

Give special emphasis to one aspect of the problem or to one solution, and subordinate or omit other sides of the question and other solutions. Judicious neutrals frequently find no great objections one way or another, but all sides and alternatives look equally attractive; at one moment they lean one way, at the next moment, another. Consequently, the speaker makes his solution look as attractive as possible by (a) great concentration on it, and (b) largely excluding rival ideas. Of special importance here will be motives and attitudes that will give force and strength to argument and evidence. Keep at-

tention undivided, and exclude competing, unfavorable ideas. This is not
deception unless the speaker is dishonest; it is merely sensible economy.
*In addressing the judicious element, use as many facts and as much
evidence as is consistent with* a *and* b *above.* Thus a speaker will tend to
satisfy those neutrals who are undecided because of insufficient information.
[*Note:* In discussion with potential members of an audience, watch for such
responses as "I don't know" (a sign of inadequate information?), "I just
can't make up my mind" (a sign of vacillation?), and "I agree, *but* there's
one thing that . . ." (a sign that a special objection is hindering decision?).]

Neutrals and Partisans

In addressing the neutrals, one cannot afford to ignore partisans.
Make the entire speech as interesting as possible. Some of the ideas used
to address the neutrals—perhaps all of the ideas—will be old and familiar to
the judicial and informed partisan. Accordingly, avoid alienating supporters
by boring them.

In being interesting one is employing good tactics on the partisan whose
indifference and lethargy keep him from active partisanship. Furthermore,
by including information for the ill-informed neutral in the group, one also
appeals to the tepid partisan, for his lukewarm attitude may be the result in
part of his not having had any real knowledge of or argument dealing with
the problem.

Avoid ideas that will alienate partisans. Suppose a speaker were arguing
that longer vacations with pay would be a boon to labor and to the country,
and some of the hearers were generally sympathetic to labor but didn't like
George Meany. To mention his name or to cite him as an authority would
hurt both the speaker and his argument. Let sleeping inhibitions lie unless
there is a real reason for awakening them. This is especially true in addressing prejudiced partisans.

The speaker need not appeal to or condone the prejudice of the irrational
partisan. The attitudes that feed his prejudice—such as loyalty to his class
and social group—are likely to be so broad that he will apply them automatically to almost anything said or implied.

Influencing Partisans

Often a group is already persuaded of the soundness of an idea or of the desirability of an action. The audience is overwhelmingly partisan. A speaker
accordingly will concern himself with one of two goals: (1) to impress upon
his hearers the old truth and thus encourage them to act upon it whenever the
opportunity comes; (2) to urge them to a definite and specific action to be

undertaken immediately or in the very near future. In either case the speaker seeks *to intensify* attitude. Most preachers seek to accomplish the first purpose; they try to keep the virtues of right conduct and of religion bright and appealing to a congregation whose presence indicates sympathy and respect for religion. The advertiser and the salesman ordinarily have in mind the second purpose.

For sharpening the impression

The general method is to give the old theme new interest. Accordingly those ideas and methods that elicit imagery and enliven the old idea with new information and interpretations are especially valuable.

Associate the old with the new. (1) Seek a new angle or point of view; (2) use novel illustrations; (3) build up vivid and sharp images.

A good illustration of a speech calculated to impress is Bruce Barton's "Which Knew Not Joseph," printed in the Appendix. Mr. Barton spoke of the value to business of persistent advertising, of the wisdom of always being sincere, and of the need for being warm and friendly—all "old stuff" to his audience. What made it effective were his illustrations—the humorous story which has real point, the familiar story of Joseph given a new interpretation, and examples drawn from personal experience.

Apply the old truth to the present situation. For example, what does the old Christian maxim, "Do unto others as you would that they do unto you," mean to modern business (if one were addressing a businessmen's club)? To student relationships (if one thought it appropriate to talk on this to his class)?

For securing action

Again the speaker's primary job is to keep his listeners' undivided attention on the conduct desired, and avoid ideas that suggest alternative action. An idea of an action, keenly perceived and understood, tends to result in the action.

Of particular value in moving listeners to action are the following methods:

Making the hearer imagine himself doing what is desired. If one would get a friend to shove aside books or beer and go to the movies, one might say, "Just think of that cool, comfortable theatre. Remember the last Bergman we saw? There's another one on. Then there's one on with Marlon Brando—not to mention a special with the Roaring Rocks. Just think—comfort, Brando, and music out of this world!" Of course, pleasure and sex are effective motives here, but imagery so chosen as to put the hearer imaginatively into the action desired does the real work.

Awakening the confidence of hearers by showing them that the action is practicable. Perhaps nothing so promotes confidence as to show that other groups, similar to your audience, have acted as you propose and have enjoyed *success.* On an occasion when an all-fraternity council was considering whether or not to recommend requiring a "C" average for initiation into a fraternity, the strongest appeal was made by a student who took five minutes to explain that the adoption of the measure at X University had been a signal success. Concern and worry were replaced by confidence and considerable enthusiasm.

Enlisting the pride of hearers. Pride is an emotion centering on the self and is stimulated chiefly by the high regard in which others hold the self. Consequently, we cherish our reputation, are cordial to admiration, and expand under anything that enhances our prestige and self-importance. One can enlist pride by showing that the desired action will enhance or protect the reputation and prestige of hearers.

Here the speaker reminds his audience that others—individuals or groups—have regarded them as progressive, as people of good will or of honor, and suggests that in the face of such regard they will not want to re-frain from acting as suggested. A speaker who engineers an appeal to his hearers' reputation must always take two steps: (1) logically associate the action desired with one or more basic motives and values, and (2) definitely indicate that other persons respect the audience for holding the attitudes.

Prior to a local election, a housewife illustrated both steps well. A citizen of Brown Township, stumping for the bond issue that would finance a new school building, she reminded her hearers that they had always supported measures that preserved and enhanced the educational opportunities of their children. "In fact," she said in substance, "you have a reputation for guard-ing the opportunities of our youth. The *Record* [the newspaper of the neigh-boring county seat] last month said this about us: 'Some persons are asking whether Brown Township will pass the school bond proposal. We think its people will. They not only can afford it, but more than the people in most districts we know of, the citizenry of Brown Township are mindful of the edu-cational welfare of their children.' "

Making the audience face squarely the arguments—and especially con-ditions and facts—that call for the desired action. Here the speaker briefly reviews the reasons that have led his hearers to accept the idea of the action that they have not yet taken. In particular he gives great emphasis to the facts—unpleasant though they may be—and to the excuses and evasions that have led his audience to sidestep action. One of the weaknesses of human nature is to forget, to put out of mind, unpleasant evils that cry for remedy. We don't like to think of the deplorable conditions in the slums or the poverty and malnutrition in underprivileged countries. We sometimes excuse our failure to hold an opinion on the grounds of "having an open mind," our shady financial deals as being "good business," our laziness and procrastination as a result of being too tired or too ill, our own destructiveness as being students' fun, or dissipation as evidence of being good fellows, and our cheating on examinations as a sign of cleverness rather than of immorality and ignorance! There are times when a speaker can and should speak bluntly and plainly; such a time comes when people fail to act as they should because they shut their eyes to facts that demand action and indulge in conscience-saving evasions. Some of the extreme rhetoric of recent years was prompted by the failure of the Establishment to listen.

One of the most direct and telling examples of making an audience face the facts of a situation occurred in the course of Clarence Darrow's argument to the judge who was to determine the sentence of two college students, both confessed murderers. Darrow sought life imprisonment for the defendants, rather than execution. He said:

> Your Honor, it may be hardly fair to the court, I am aware, that I have helped to place a serious burden upon your shoulders. And at that I have always meant to be your friend. But this was not an act of friendship.
> I know perfectly well that where responsibility is divided by twelve, it is easy to say:
> "Away with him."
> But, your Honor, if these boys hang, you must do it. There can be no division of responsibility here. You can never explain that the rest overpowered you. It must be by your deliberate, cool, premeditated act, without a chance to shift responsibility. [3]

The direct suggestion or command is especially effective when an audience is ready to act. A speaker can quite frankly say, "Go and do so-and-so." A student once interested a class in reading *The Grapes of Wrath* and at the end of his speech offered an explicit direction:

> All you need to do now, if you are interested in Mr. Steinbeck's book, is to go to the library during the next vacant hour you have and fill out the call card. The call number of the book is PN6167 S112. There are six copies available, and in three minutes you have the book. If you have no class next hour, go at once and be sure of a good book you can start reading this afternoon or tonight.

The oblique form of the same suggestion would have been: "I think you will want to read the book at the first chance you get." Or, "Isn't this book sufficiently interesting to be read at the first opportunity?"

The beginning speaker should always remember this: When an audience is ready to act and wants to act, supply explicit directions. If he can rouse

[3] Defense of Richard Loeb and Nathan Leopold, Jr. In W. N. Brigance, ed., *Classified Speech Models of Eighteen Forms of Public Address* (New York, 1928), p. 141.

real interest and enthusiasm for the proposal—as he very often can with the partisan audience—he can give the hearers something definite to do. If he wants them to sign a petition or endorse a resolution, he should give them a chance to sign as soon as possible. If he wants them to write their Senator or Congressman, he should give them definite directions and information so that they can. Supply his name and address, and perhaps suggest what they should say. When a speaker fails to capitalize on the readiness of his hearers to act, he blocks and frustrates them. There are few disappointments so great as to want to do *something* and not know just what to do or not to be able to do it.

Influencing Opponents

Conditions

Ordinarily it is futile to try to make converts out of opponents in a single speech. People usually change their beliefs on a subject, if at all, only over a considerable period of time. The process of radical change-of-front is almost always slow and requires substantial education, exposition and persuasion, many speeches and books and articles, and much discussion.

Nevertheless, the zealous speaker need not feel discouraged about his chances with the opponents in his audience. First, even in the single speech it is always possible to get persons to believe less surely. Merely to *soften opposition* in a single effort is a positive accomplishment, and the veteran speaker, as well as the beginner, should regard it as such. Second, converts can sometimes be made on a subject to which opponents do not respond emotionally and which does not deal with fundamental economic, social, or political questions having wide implications. One would be foolish to try to convert conservative businessmen and industrialists to state socialism, or even to persuade them to take a *limited* step toward socialism, such as to accept government ownership of railroads. But on less touchy and fundamental questions, there is a fair chance of success. The auditing of the finances of extracurricular societies, changing the grading system, shortening the Christmas holidays, altering rushing rules and the regulations governing parties—to mention only a few campus perennials—do not involve social upheavals. These are limited in their social implications, and opponents who are not strongly prejudiced can sometimes be brought around to the advocate's view in a single speech.

There is another time when a shift of attitude is quite possible: it is at that stage in a controversy in which discussion concerns *means and methods* of change, rather than the desirability of change. When almost everyone agrees that there are deplorable evils, that the disease has reached a point at which something must be done, discussion turns to the means of cure. Since most people have recognized the need for change, there is a big area of agreement. Hence, there is a favorable attitude toward solution of some kind, and this promotes rational consideration and choice of the best cure. Such an atmosphere even permits acceptance of a cure that is not perfect. For example, the United States Senate accepted the United Nations Charter, an imperfect instrument of world peace.

In framing the subject statement of the proposal do not ask hearers among whom are influential opponents to make a radical change from their habitual conduct and attitude; choose a statement that requires but little reorientation of habits of action and belief. Be moderate rather than extreme.

Methods

The judicious opponent

Meet the chief objections of the judicious opponent, so far as you can discover them through discussion and reading. The judicious opponent has weighed and considered the question under discussion and, in all probability, has looked at it from all sides—at least he believes so. Since he has reasoned to a conclusion and respects reason, the speaker can meet him directly on rational grounds, can recognize his objections and reason with him directly about them.

New facts and new conditions may lead an opponent to reconsider his opinions. The judicious opponent is usually willing to consider any and all material that is relevant to the problem. He has tried to overlook nothing important in making up his mind. Yet often on problems that keep recurring in different form, such as the best kind of taxation, he has been unable to keep up to date and hasn't fully realized that fact.

Mention ideas and opinions that both speaker and opponent have in common. Those experienced in conciliation and arbitration techniques say that conflict is intensified when contending parties emphasize their disagreements and that opposition is minimized when agreements are clearly discerned. Consequently, it would be wise to determine what speaker and opponents have in common, and briefly but clearly review the common ground early in the speech, probably in the introduction.

Meeting the casual opponent and the prejudiced opponent

If a study of an audience reveals that such opponents are in the minority, the speaker does not have an insuperable problem. First, the casual opponent—he who has happened to hear more against the speaker's opinion than for it—probably lacks information. Consequently, the reasoning and information designed for the neutrals will be fairly effective for him. Second, since one is not likely to make a convert out of a prejudiced opponent, one's job is simply to avoid rousing his prejudices and increasing his opposition. A speaker cannot disregard and neglect the prejudiced listener; he simply takes care not to offend him by a careless remark or phrase.

In the lone persuasive speech, a speaker should remember that his major task is to keep his partisans interested and if possible swing the neutrals into line. As for opponents, a speaker does not ignore them; he deals frankly and tactfully with his judicious critics and avoids hardening the hostility of his prejudiced opponents.

Much of what we have been advising may seem like no more than common sense. It is buttressed, nevertheless, by the findings of some experimental studies that were designed to determine the effectiveness of recognizing and arguing "both sides" in a controversial situation. It is better to present both sides rather than one side only when listeners possess intellectual and critical ability and when they will continue to be exposed to many-sided arguments.[4]

Logical Modes of Persuasion

We have identified thus far three methods of handling persuasive materials: the means of development, the style of language, the adjustment of ideas to the attitudes of the audience. We consider now one other way of handling materials and ideas. It is the logical mode.

The mode takes advantage of man's tendency to believe when statements (and the ideas they carry) are so arranged as to call attention to their consistency, relevancy to each other, and reliability. The form and support of the combination of statements appeal to *reasonable* men. The force of the appeal is evident in the remark, "That sounds reasonable," or "That makes sense."

The basis of logical support is fact and opinion. If the basis is shaky, doubtful, and untrustworthy, and reasoning built on it will seem weak and unconvincing. Hence when the speaker considers facts and opinions as support for his statements, he has a special concern for their accuracy and reliability. Indeed, in a close argument he may be forced to indicate why they can be depended on. He should therefore be aware of the rules of evidence, which we have presented in Chapter 3 (pp. 41-42).

Forms of Argument

When reasoning is conducted logically, the speaker works his ideas and evidence into the patterns described in the following.

[4] For example, see Carl Hovland, Irving Janis, and Harold H. Kelley, *Communication and Persuasion* (New Haven, 1953), p. 294.

Deduction

The deductive pattern applies the meaning of a general idea to a more specific, relevant idea, and thus permits a conclusion to be drawn. The process is one by which the particular is brought within the significance of the general so as to suggest a consequence. For example:

> Contracts should be honored. (*General Premise*)
> Room leases are contracts. (*Specific Premise*)
> Room leases should be honored. (*Conclusion*)

(In deduction, the general idea may be conveniently named the *general premise*, the more particular idea the *specific premise*.) In the example above, room leases as an idea is brought within the meaning of contracts. This done, whatever may be asserted of contracts may also be said of room leases—not all things, of course, but those things thought to be relevant and fitting as measured by the experience of the speaker and listener. The notion of "should be honored" can be applied to contracts, at least as a general rule. Ergo, room leases should be honored.

In use, the deductive pattern is seldom presented as it is above, with the general premise starting the pattern and the conclusion ending it. Usually the order is this:

> Room leases should be honored. (*Conclusion*)
> They are contracts. (*Specific Premise*)
> Contracts should be honored. (*General Premise*)

This is the order and indentation of the logical skeleton and often of the speech outline as well. It is also the order observed in conversation more often than not. Because the sequence seems "natural," we shall observe it in the illustrations below.

To every instance of deductive reasoning, the speaker applies three test questions:

1. *Are the meanings of the premises unequivocally clear?*

2. *Is the predicate-idea of the specific premise properly included within the subject-idea of the general premise?* In the example above, "contracts" in the general premise is taken to mean *all* contracts; so the same word in the specific premise is necessarily included within the meaning.

The necessary connection is ideal and a speaker rejoices when he can show one. If there be any condition which he can claim is "conclusive," "beyond all shadow of doubt," this is it. But in much argument about human problems and behavior, as distinct from matters of science, the perfect general premises—the generalizations without exception—are few and far between. General premises are likely to be true almost always, or in most cases. In other words, they are *probably* true, not invariably true. Hence, the wise, perceptive speaker must often be cautious about claiming too much for his general premises. He does well to keep in mind an ever possible qualification, as for example, "All contracts should be honored except in unusual circumstances." Then he can show, if necessary and if conditions suggest it for the case at hand, that the conditions are *not* unusual or peculiar. We all subscribe to the belief that *no person should lie*; yet there are instances when some high humanitarian motive justifies an exception.

3. *Which premise needs supporting?* In many contexts the general premise is so obviously acceptable to the audience that it barely needs mention, if at all. It is the specific premise which, as a rule, demands support and needs to be established as true.

Example

A general idea may be supported by examples. The process is often called generalization from example, or argument from example. In the process, an idea that is wider in scope than the example carries the notion of the *many*. The example bears the notion of the *one*. In addition, the connection between the one and the many derives its force from this implication: what is true of the one is also true of the many. For instance:

> Wars are triggered by provocative incidents. (*Generalization*)
> Firing on Fort Sumter started the American Civil War. (*Example*)

> Students gain confidence in public speaking through experience in public speaking classes. (*Generalization*)
> Jones did. (*Example*)

> Tests of vocational aptitude are useful in choosing one's life work. (*Generalization*)
> They were for Jones. (*Example*)

If the argument from the example is to be convincing, at least three key questions must be answered affirmatively:

1. *Is a single example sufficient?* Because of their cumulative force, a number of examples usually carries more weight than a single one. As in a statistical inference, the larger the population under observation, the more probable is the truth of the generalization about the population. In numbers there is strength. In a speech, of course, there is not time for anything like an exhaustive enumeration of cases. Yet the lone instance is seldom convincing. The listener is too likely to respond, "But that's only one case; what about the others?" The persuader should keep in mind the distinction between the role of the example in exposition and in persuasion. In explaining a general

idea, the example *illustrates*, and a single one may be enough to secure clearness. In argument, the example is intended to prove.

The argument from example is most effective when the instances can be followed by statistical evidence. To illustrate:

> Most students buy their textbooks at X Bookstore. (*Generalization*)
> Peterson does. (*Example*)
> Rhodes does. (*Example*)
> In our largest dormitory, 11 out of 12 students do. (*Statistics*)
> A survey of buyers at X Bookstore last semester showed that 9 out of 10 of them were students. (*Statistics*)

2. *Are the examples truly comparable and relevant?* A generalization arises out of a number of similar instances and asserts what the instances have in common. Sometimes it is relatively easy to see in what respects examples are similar to each other and to the general idea. One can readily recognize, for example, a single point of comparison. In the illustration above, there is but a single point of likeness, the buying of textbooks. On the other hand it is more difficult to perceive clearly and to state exactly *several* points of similarity, particularly when they are buried in an abstract word. For example:

> Students in Y fraternity are responsible persons. (*Generalization*)
> Barnes of Y fraternity is a responsible individual. (*Example*)

What is entailed in responsibility? Various traits of behavior are associated with it, and one would have to make sure which traits before he could know they were common to both the general idea and the example. Upon the presence of the same traits would depend the soundness of any comparison between Barnes and his brothers in the fraternity.

3. *Do the exceptional cases, if any, weaken the generalization?* We recall the old proverb, "The exception proves the rule." It does, in the sense that it *tests* the rule. So any exception must be regarded critically. Is it unusual—so far out of line with other instances that it weakens the force of the generalization? If it cannot be accounted for satisfactorily, a general statement less wide in scope had better be used, or the generalization abandoned entirely.

Argument from analogy

A comparison brings together two ideas, objects, or events and makes the most of their similarities rather than their differences. The argument from analogy is built on a number of similarities between two sets of conditions or circumstances. It specifies that one set of conditions has characteristics A, B, C, D, and E, and that the second set of conditions also reveals A, B, C, and

D. Then it concludes that *E* either is true or will be true in the second set. For example:

> Jones will do good work at X University. (*Conclusion*)
> He did good work at Y University. (*Specific Premise*)
> X and Y Universities are comparable in ways that affect grades. (*Comparative Premise*)
> Both have similar scholastic standards. (*Condition 1*)
> Both have similar faculties. (*Condition 2*)
> Both place studies ahead of social affairs and campus activities. (*Condition 3*)

Note that the argument from analogy is well named, for it derives its strength and cogency *from* a comparison which is expressed as a premise. Note, also, that the comparative premise is a conclusion with respect to the items of similarity that support it.

Analogical argument is a powerful tool of persuasion if two requirements are met:

1. *The greater the number of similarities between two particulars, the more convincing is the conclusion.* In reasoning intended to demonstrate that true-false tests will prove successful in elementary economics because they have been successful in elementary physics, the more points of likeness between the two courses, the sounder the conclusion. Both courses are designed for freshmen and sophomores; both courses assume that students are of about the same age and have the same academic preparation; both deal with principles and laws that are matters of fact; both aim to impart knowledge rather than skill.

2. *The dissimilarities between the particulars must not be more significant than the likenesses.* Do the laws of economics—the law of supply and demand, for example—admit of so many qualifications and special conditions that they cannot be tested by a simple true or false answer? And are there fewer exceptions and special qualifications in the laws of physics? If the answers are yes, then the single dissimilarity is far more significant than all the similarities noted above.

Effect to cause

A causal relationship is held to exist whenever one event or condition controls and accounts for the occurrence or behavior of another. In the effect-to-cause pattern, some present or past condition is accounted for by an event or condition that preceded it. The statement to be supported is treated as an effect. The supporting statement, or statements, is regarded as the cause or condition. For example:

Brezhnev's speeches to the West have not been extreme. (*Effect*)
He wants to gain favor. (*Cause*)
Persons who desire favor almost always avoid extreme language. (*General
Rule*)

Often, as in this example, the credibility of a cause depends on the credibility of the generalization relevant to it. The general rule expresses the audience's knowledge of similar causal conditions and makes the application to the case at hand. In such situations, the cause to be established is an educated guess. It cannot be taken as a fact. Hence, the speaker must be confident that the generalization is acceptable.

In other situations, the speaker is better off. When he can draw on more exact knowledge than that of opinion and belief, when he can pull in the findings of science and experiment, he can establish the fact of the cause. This, combined with the law or general principle, is highly convincing. For example:

Williams is a dependable student. (*Effect*)
He always completes his assignments on time. (*Cause*)
Prompt discharge of commitments always attends dependability. (*Principle*)

Here the statement of cause could be substantiated by enumerating instances and by statistical evidence.

Probably the most convincing situation of all arises when it can be shown that in the absence of the cause there was a contrary effect. For example:

Farmer X produced more wheat per acre than his neighbor. (*Effect*)
He used chemical fertilizer. (*Cause*)
His neighbor did not. (*Absence of Cause*)
Chemical fertilizer always increases the yield of a crop unless some circumstance interferes. (*Principle*)

In selecting a causal argument and in presenting it, a speaker will be guided by a number of questions:

1. *Does the argument deal with events or conditions?* Whenever a speaker can deal with real causes, the argument is more convincing than when he has to depend on favoring conditions only.

2. *Is the effect accounted for by a single cause or condition?* In locating *the* cause—if there be an only cause—the speaker weighs the possibility of other causes. Human problems are seldom simple. Obviously forest fires, high grades, world peace, radiation effects, and high prices cannot be explained in terms of single causes.

3. *How direct is the connection between cause and effect?* To consider this question is to see the difference between an immediate or trigger cause and a more remote but compelling condition. The immediate cause of a for-

est fire may be a lighted cigarette thrown from a car, or an unextinguished campfire. The more remote condition is a habit—carelessness.

4. *In the absence of the cause, would the effect be as probable?* Too often we confuse coincidence and chance with cause and effect. Few people today believe that carrying a rabbit's foot, crossing the fingers, or knocking on wood will keep away bad luck. But some athletes still wear lucky socks and lucky numbers. And some persons say that atom bomb tests have been responsible for the outbreak of unusually violent storms and floods in many parts of the country for the past few years. As yet we do not know of a connection between storms and A-bomb explosions, but there were similar periods of abnormally bad weather long before the A-bomb was invented. Our friend the basketball coach actually does win some games without wearing his lucky socks.

Cause to Effect

This logical pattern involves a prediction about the future. The effect-to-cause pattern, on the other hand, is based on the present and past. By the nature of his task, the persuader must employ both patterns. To see why this is so helps in understanding and in using the patterns.

The logic of the problem-solution state of affairs can be put simply: a speaker must address himself to either the problem or a particular solution or both. If he talks on the problem, he has these alternatives: He says, "I think present conditions are bad and I want you to think so too." Or he says, "I see what the problem is, and it is of this nature because of certain causes and conditions." If he talks to the solution, he says "I have a solution, and it will remove the causes and conditions which created the problem." Or—if the audience has reached this stage of discussion—he says, "My solution is better than a rival solution, for the rival solution won't take care of the causes that produced the conditions you complain about." One can see at a glance that causal relationships are inherent in recognizing, establishing, and solving a problem. One can see, also, that the problem-solution circumstances entail two dimensions of time. If the speaker deals with the problem only, he is concerned with present conditions and what has caused them. He looks to the present in the light of the past. If the speaker deals with a solution, he says in effect, "If you accept my proposition and act in keeping with it, the consequences *will be* desirable." He looks to the future. Like a physician, the persuasive speaker is a diagnostician; he recognizes the symptoms of the disease—the accompanying conditions and their signs—and determines their cause. He prescribes a remedy. Consequently, when a speaker talks about a problem and its sources, he is reasoning about effects or conditions and their causes. When he is reasoning about solutions, he thinks of his proposition as a cause or condition that will bring desirable consequences. He is then within the framework of the cause-to-effect pattern.

In the cause-to-effect pattern, statements direct attention to a cause or condition and the predicted effect. In the advocacy of a solution, there are two typical kinds of structure:
1. A single statement may join both cause and effect.

> Independent audits of labor union funds would eliminate dishonest union officials.

Note that the subject-idea designates the cause; the predicate-idea names the effect.
2. One statement asserts a condition that entails more than one effect; succeeding statements specify the effects.

> It would be desirable to have union officials elected by secret ballot.
> The requirement would prevent intimidation of members at election time.
> It would restore democratic procedures to labor unions that have lost them.

In using a cause-to-effect argument, the speaker encounters two questions: Has the causal relationship held true in the past? If it has been true in the past, is there any reason why it should *not* operate as expected in the future? The relevancy of these questions can be perceived from the following example:

> Independent audits of labor union funds would eliminate dishonest union officials. (*Conclusion*)
> Independent audits of the funds of any organization discourage dishonesty among officials. (*General Premise*)
> Unions do not differ from other organizations in ways that would make an audit ineffective. (*Comparative Premise*)

The general premise is combining two ideas: (1) it implies that a union is an example of an organization in which (2) the cause has produced the effect. Then the comparative premise says that a union, taken as an example of an organization, reveals no condition that would make the cause ineffective. Thus it is apparent that the cause-to-effect pattern involves a prediction whose force depends on comparable conditions in the present and the past.

The speaker who is familiar with the five logical patterns and who gains experience in applying them in his speeches will gradually realize the source of their effectiveness. He will see that they cannot make sense to a reasonable person unless the meanings they carry are clear, stable, and unequivocal.

INQUIRIES

1.   Consider a problem now being discussed on campus or elsewhere. When and how was it recognized as a problem? At what stage of discussion is it

now? or what is the *status* of the audience? If you were to enter the discussion, what aspect of the problem would be *appropriate* for you?

2. Consider the customary language in which issues are referred to in political campaigns: "The issue is taxes"; "The real issue is peace in the Middle East"; "At issue is control over inflation." What is meant by *issue* in such usage? What might you do to point up issues with greater accuracy? Would you find the idea of *position* useful?

3. Look closely at the analogy between the health of the human body and the health of society. Extend the analogy as far as you can. That is, invent as many similarities and dissimilarities as you can. Can you discover a better analogy for pointing up the ailments of society?

4. We hear it said of someone that he is a reasonable person; and we are enjoined not to be unreasonable. What is it to be reasonable? Does being reasonable depend, in part at least, on being informed? Cite cases you think relevant out of your experience or the experience of others.

5. Consider carefully the notion of good reason. Then consider the last "argument" you encountered that you would call good. Is a good argument the same as a good reason?

6. What do we mean when we say we are reasoning logically? illogically? When we offer good reasons, are we reasoning logically? Does logical reasoning involve the factor of consistency?

7. Consider the idea that it may be more important how a person is persuaded than what he or she is persuaded of. On what grounds could you support that idea? Think of examples or situations.

8. Consider what values are relevant to you in your daily living and in your aspirations. Rank them on a scale from high to low. Are they mainly those of American college students, or are they peculiar to you?

FURTHER READING

Bettinghaus, Erwin P. *Message Preparation: The Nature of Proof.* 1966. Chapter 6.

Cohen, Morris, and Ernest Nagel. *An Introduction to Logic and Scientific Method.* 1936.

Dewey, John. "Authority and Social Change," in *Authority and the Individual.* 1937.

Ehninger, Douglas. *Influence, Belief, and Argument: An Introduction to Responsible Persuasion.* 1974.

Eisenson, Jon. *The Psychology of Speech.* 1938. Chapter 17, "Motivation."

Frye, A.M., and A.W. Levi. *Rational Belief.* 1941.

Gray, G.W., and C.M. Wise. *The Bases of Speech.* 3rd ed. 1959. Ch. 9, "The Semantic Basis."

Gray, G.W., and Waldo Braden. *Public Speaking: Principles and Practices.* 1951. Chapters 3-4, "Motivation and Interest"; Ch. 5, "Occasion and Audience."

Hovland, Carl J., Irving L. Janis, and Harold H. Kelley. *Communication and Persuasion*. 1953.

Minnick, Wayne. *The Art of Persuasion*. 2nd ed. 1968.

Monroe, Alan H., and Douglas Ehninger. *Principles and Types of Speech Communication*. 7th ed. 1974. Chapter 20.

Oliver, Robert. *The Psychology of Persuasive Speech*. 1957. Chapter 2, "Ethics"; Chapter 8, "Identification"; Chapters 9-12, on modes of appeal.

Packard, Vance. *The Hidden Persuaders*. 1958.

Ruby, Lionel. *Logic, An Introduction*. 1950.

Wallace, Karl R. "The Substance of Rhetoric: Good Reasons." *Quarterly Journal of Speech*, 49 (1963), 239-49.

Whyte, William H. *Is Anybody Listening?* 1952.

Winans, J. A. *Public Speaking*. 1917. Chapter 8, "Influencing Conduct."

CHAPTER 9

Style

Speeches are, first and foremost, tissues of words—words supported by bodily expression and vocal cues, of course, but principally words. Style, therefore—language and the management of it—makes a speech the thing it is and gives it its final refinement of meaning. There can be little doubt, therefore, of the importance of the speaker's skillfull use of language, and hence of what is called *good style*. It would seem to be equally obvious that the quality of style depends on the qualities of the words chosen, and how they are worked together and made to function in connected speech.

Whether as words or as connected passages, the speaker's language, should serve efficiently the purposes of speaking. That is, it should assist the speaker in getting the audience (1) to understand his meaning, (2) to believe him, (3) to remember his message, and (4) to want to accept his ideas and his recommendations. To promote these ends, good style will be (1) clear, (2) appropriate, (3) attractive and interesting, (4) impressive. These four qualities, of course, do not correspond precisely to the four functions of speaking we have just listed; but, speaking broadly, to be understood a speaker must be clear; if his language fits the subject, audience, occasion, and himself, his audience is most likely to respect and believe him; interesting and attractive language tends to make listening easy; and impressiveness tends to secure memory and motivate action.

SELECTION OF LANGUAGE—INDIVIDUAL WORDS

"Proper words in proper places make the true definition of a style," wrote Jonathan Swift; and it should be obvious that the quality of linguistic choices may make or break a speech.

Clearness

Clear language is language that is meaningful to an audience as it is spoken. Through experience and knowledge of the capacities of audiences, a speaker develops a feel for clear and easy expression; but he may deliberately accelerate the process.

Familiar words

Words in current general use carry more lively meanings to most people than stranger or more "elegant" words. People may well have some sense of what is meant by *fallacious reasoning,* though normally they do not use the expression. Nevertheless the speaker before a general audience who wants to be sure that he is clearly understood will probably say *faulty thinking* instead. *Pernicious precedent* may be the more exact expression, and in some ways preferable, but a speaker had better say *bad example* unless he is absolutely sure that his audience knows the meaning of both pernicious and precedent. The skillful speaker might say, "This legislation will constitute a pernicious precedent; such laws will leave a bad example for future congresses to follow."

Strange words

Strange words, of course, may pique the curiosity of hearers, and in moderation they seem to enhance an audience's respect; nevertheless, they almost always hinder understanding. Even such relatively innocent usages as *film* for *movie,* and such slightly foreign expressions as *holiday* for *vacation* and *van* for *pickup* may delay comprehension.

One may find statistical accounts of the relative familiarity and the frequency of occurrence of various classes of English words. The speaker may find such accounts suggestive, but he cannot be governed by them. He must speak in the language he can command, and should beware of seeming to talk down to his audience. Whatever language a speaker uses, he should use as if it were the natural and obvious thing to do.

Technical words

Specialized and technical terminology, or vocational jargon, likewise presents problems of familiarity. In handling definitions, for example, a speaker must not expect an audience to understand technical language just because he does. The fact is that most people receive only vague and remote impressions from the special language of an occupation or profession or social climate other than their own. On many college campuses, for example, the term *grade-point average* has a definite meaning and is immediately clear. To unacademic persons, however, it has only a nebulous meaning, if any. We cannot even safely expect a general audience to have an exact idea of what is meant by such common commercial expressions as *inventory, trial balance, requisitions, flow sheet, form letter,* or such frequently used political expressions as *autonomy, social justice, logrolling, unicameral.* Terminology of this sort should be used wherever necessary, although many times when it is used a more common expression would serve the purpose just as well. When it is used, however, it should be accompanied unobtrusively by explanation, or it should be used in such a context that its meaning cannot be mistaken.

Words from the social and psychological sciences, such as *fixation, psychosis, complex, freudian slip, culture, statistical significance, feedback,* have a spurious currency which the speaker must beware of. Such terms are likely to mean no more to the general audience than that the speaker wishes to be thought well-informed, not necessarily that he *is.*

A good way to make sure one's vocabulary is understandable is to develop a healthy respect for the capacity of people to *misunderstand* and to be puzzled by words and expressions that are out of the ordinary. Some conscious attention to this problem will soon result in the habit of distinguishing between language that is clear to oneself and language that is clear to one's listeners.

Concrete and specific words

The concrete, specific word carries a clear, definite meaning because it points to real objects and real events and is associated with them in common experience. Consequently, for most purposes concrete terms are better than abstract, and specific terms are better than general terms. When abstract language is necessary, it should be defined or otherwise explained swiftly. If the abstract or technical term is the most accurate for the purpose and is, therefore, necessary, it cannot be left undefined without producing fuzziness. *Democracy* is abstract; *the government of the United States* is concrete. *Creature* is abstract; *horse* or *man* or *pussycat* is concrete. *"Depart from evil and do good"* is abstract; *"Thou shalt not covet thy neighbor's wife"* is concrete. Abstract language, like abstract thought, has great values. Some of the best philosophical and scientific writing in the world would be impossible without it. In handling the subjects, however, on which most of us talk most of the time, the more abstract the language we use the less memorable will be our speech. Undoubtedly there are important meanings in such common abstractions as *virtue, goodness, sin, liberty, social equality, profit, justice, honesty,* but in themselves they hardly produce *clearness* of idea or intention. *A certain Middle Western city* is vague; *St. Louis* or *Chicago* or *Cleveland* is specific and should be used instead unless there is some special reason for not mentioning the name. *Municipal services* is general; *refuse collection, water and sewer, parks and recreation* are specific. At times, of course, a speaker will choose to be general or vague, leaving his audience free to supply, as suits them, the concrete, specific ideas the speaker avoids.

Then there is the deliberate resort to ambiguous language so often seen in public controversy and political campaigning. Consider, for example, the contrary meanings conveyed by the expression "law and order," so often the refrain in public discourse in the 1960s. They could range from "protect freedom of speech for both dissent and assent" to "keep the blacks in their ghettos," from "police brutality" to "safety in the streets." There are circumstances in public controversy in which the only way to gain initial assent is to be vague or general; and at times it seems justifiable political strategy for a speaker to use ambiguity in order to seem to be in harmony with discordant elements in his audience. Under most circumstances of public speaking, however, we may express our ideas *at first* in abstract and general terms in order possibly to get preliminary and vague general acceptance of them. But not until we become concrete and specific do we really come to grips with the minds of our audience and succeed in convincing or informing them. The clearness of meaning that comes with concrete, specific language stands out notably in the following sentence from Booker T. Washington's *Atlanta Address* (see Appendix). He wished to say that the progress the Southern Negroes had made in the thirty years since freedom had not come without struggle and difficulty. Observe the familiar, concrete, specific words he chose.

> Starting thirty years ago with ownership here and there in a few quilts and pumpkins and chickens (gathered from miscellaneous sources), remember the path that has led from these to the inventions and production of agricultural implements, buggies, steam-engines, newspapers, books, statuary, carving, paintings, the management of drugstores and banks, has not been trodden without contact with thorns and thistles.

Action words

In conformity with a familiar psychological law of attention, whenever a concrete word or phrase also suggests movement and activity, it enhances clearness.

A speaker can take at least a few practical steps to make his language act. First, he can use action words in place of words that do not suggest movement. To say that a machine *runs* is better than to say that a machine *func-*

tions; to say that something *stands up* suggests more activity than to say something *resists rough use* or *assumes a vertical position;* to say that the town council *debated and passed* an ordinance is probably superior to saying that the council *considered and approved* an ordinance. The general rule, then, is to use words, particularly verbs, that tend to conjure up momentary action pictures.

Second, speakers should prefer verbs in the active voice. It is better, for example, to say, "The gunner drops the shell into the mortar," than to say, "The shell is held over the muzzle of the mortar," or, "The shell is dropped into the mortar by the gunner." "We know we should act" is better than "It is thought that action should be taken." "Congress created a committee to investigate the problem" is superior to "The problem is to be investigated by a committee set up by Congress." "Action by the committee is desired by the chairman" represents a kind of reverse English compared with "The chairman wants the committee to act." "We ate our lunch by the pasture gate" does not leave the meaning in doubt as does the passive form, "Our lunch was eaten by the pasture gate." The active voice, in brief, almost always creates a sense of movement; the passive voice, even when clear, stops movement. Still water is less dynamic than running, rushing, turbulent water.

Appropriateness

A speaker's words may be very clear and yet be inappropriate to him, to his audience, to his subject, or to the occasion.

To the speaker

When language is unsuitable to the speaker, the reason is usually that he is either straining for elegance or impressiveness and achieving only inflation, or that he is mistakenly trying to speak his audience's language, to be one of them, and managing only to be degraded and substandard. When the agent of the light and power company, whose customer has asked to have the electricity turned off, inquires, "Were you contemplating changing your residence?" he is trying for elegance and achieving foolish pomposity. Had he asked, "Are you thinking of moving?" he would have done his business in not only the most unobtrusive but the most efficient language. When the college graduate, who is assumed to be a person of some education, affects the defective grammar and semiliterate vocabulary of the uneducated, he is not (as he may claim) getting a common ground with his audience. He is insulting his audience, as did Patrick Henry when he talked to backwoodsmen in their dialectal and ungrammatical language. Most listeners recognize the inappropriateness of such an approach. They understand simple, correct language, even if they do not habitually use it themselves, and they expect a person to speak to them in language that is normal to him.

A speaker should also be cautious in using the special terminology or jargon of a particular class of people or occupation not his own. When a college debater, discussing socialized medicine before a group that included physicians, endeavored to meet the physicians on their own verbal ground, he confused *diagnosis* with *prognosis.* He did not find out until later why some of the medical men smiled. If a speaker is to use a specialized idiom, it must be with complete assurance and accuracy unless he intends to be funny at his own expense.

Language of the speaker as a person and as a speaker

The speaker's language, therefore, first of all must be seem to belong to him, to fit him both as a person and as a speaker. What language belongs to him as a special individual, what his private habit of speech is, bears upon the fitness of his language; but most of the time listeners are not personally and intimately acquainted with the speaker. They know him as a kind of person—an educated businessman, a labor leader, a clergyman, a college student—and what seems becoming to him in that role and in his role as speaker, taken together, will be fitting and appropriate.

The sense of what qualities of language become a man as speaker over and above what fit him as an individual is a delicate matter. That there is a difference has been recognized from Aristotle's time to our own. The subtlety of the difference has led to many mistakes. On the one hand, it has trapped people into adopting a special "speaking style" (and tone of voice), which can readily degenerate into the ridiculous. On the other, and by revulsion to what is called "oratorical" language, it has led to an exaggerated ordinariness, a deliberate debasing of language below what a self-respecting person would use in careful conversation.

Language superior to casual talk

The most desirable language for public speaking will maintain a nice balance a little on the careful side of good conversation. The language that is normal in offhand, informal conversation does not seem natural in public speaking. Therefore the advice of Professor Winans is excellent, "Public speech does not require a low tone, or a careless manner, or undignified English. . . . Give your thoughts fitting garb; to plain thoughts plain expression, to heightened thoughts heightened expression." In a word, the language of a good public speaker is the language of a "gentleman conversing," whatever the prevailing standards of gentlemen or gentlewoman may be.

Language that is barely acceptable in the offhand style of ordinary conversation, because of its informality and casualness, will appear debased when elevated to the speaker's platform. Language that seems a little too formal in conversation will seem on the platform just elevated enough. The learning speaker who keeps a gentle pressure (but only *gentle*, without forcing) on himself to tone up his language will usually improve satisfactorily.

Language of the educated person

Most of the users of this book are educated people, or are on the way to becoming so. Therefore, they will be expected to use language that is not defective in grammar, usage, or pronunciation. Their language should not raise the eyebrows or divert the attention of the "judicious," as Hamlet told the players. Bad grammar and faulty pronunciation, of course, are not moral offenses. Nevertheless, because on most occasions they conflict with what listeners expect of educated speakers, they invite attention away from the intended meaning by implying that the speaker is somehow deficient in his education. Such grammatical errors as "like I said," "if I would of known," "everybody has their own opinion," widespread as they may be, do a speaker no good. Nor does he gain by such false elegancies as the "usage" of a new gadget rather than the "use" of it, "in lieu of" for "in view of," and "media," "criteria," and "curricula" as singulars.

The educated speaker, however, is no linguistic prude. As Nicholas Murray Butler told a graduating class at Columbia University half a century ago, the educated man "knows the wide distinction between correct English on the one hand, and pedantic, or as it is sometimes called 'elegant' English on the other. He is more likely to 'go to bed' than to 'retire,' to 'get up' than to 'arise,' . . . to 'dress' rather than to 'clothe himself,' and to 'make a speech' rather than to 'deliver an oration.'" Nowadays, perhaps, he would "give a talk" rather than "make a speech"!

In general, then, an audience expects in a public speech language superior to what it would encounter in casual, off-the-cuff conversation. The speaker who aims "to speak better than he thinks he can" will probably satisfy this expectation in his hearers.

To audience, subject, and occasion

Obviously audiences differ, subjects differ, and occasions differ in their demands on language; but the three are so closely related that when one changes the others change. One cannot lay down rules for making language appropriate. Probably the best one can do is to encourage taste and sensitivity in language and to call attention to the hazards to appropriateness latent, for example, in slang, jargon, and the language of extravagance.

Slang and jargon

The temptation to speak in slang is strong, for slang is often vivid, sharp, and telling. Moreover, it sounds, and often is, contemporary, and therefore seems to offer a common bond between speaker and audience. Because it is familiar and readily recognized, it seems a natural, easy means for promoting clearness. Nevertheless, speakers should be aware of the pitfalls as well as virtues of slang. First, slang is a slippery and ever changing language. Its vocabulary goes out of date even faster than popular songs and newspaper headlines. Consequently, the slang expressions that seem familiar and clear to the speaker may be Greek to an audience. The speaker, therefore, must be sure that his colloquialisms are also his hearers'. Second, the flavor of informality and casualness in slang is distasteful on many occasions and from many speakers. Rarely is slang suitable on formal occasions or in a speaker who is not well known and well liked by his audience. Third, even when accurate, slang suggests to some audiences that the speaker is just trying to be a good fellow or is talking down to them. In brief, slang, like humor, can either sweeten a speech, or sour it.

The same observations apply to the special terminology and jargon of, let us say, sportswriters and sports commentators, of the entertainment world as represented in the publication *Variety,* and of such cults as the hippies and the rock 'n' roll enthusiasts. Only very special audiences find such language desirable.

Extravagance

The language of exaggeration, of "super," so dear to advertisers, involves basically the problem of propriety. Perhaps we should not be concerned with this fantastic vocabulary, which we as listeners may tend to discount automatically. We hear so much of it, however, that, unless we are careful, it creeps into our speaking—even the speaking we do on serious occasions. We cannot dress up commonplace matters, such as breakfast cereals and laundry soap, with shouting enthusiasm and inflated diction, without seeming absurd and ridiculous, and without losing the respect and confidence of our listeners. After all, in a vocabulary where "Super Colossal" describes the normal, what does one say for emphasis?

Interest, Attractiveness, Impressiveness

Individual words, quite independently of their use in connected passages, may be interesting, attractive, or impressive. The concrete, specific word is not only clearer but more interesting than the abstract, general word. No doubt the concrete word is clearer because it is sharper. The active voice of verbs is more interesting than the passive because it means motion. Some words have special or peculiar attractiveness, are particularly pleasing, either from association, sound, or some more mysterious cause. One is reminded of the elderly lady who told a speaker that she had enjoyed his speech because he had used that blessed word which she loved, *Mesopotamia.* Most of us would agree, furthermore, that there is more dignity and impressiveness inherent in the words *constitutional convention* than in the headline writer's shorthand, *code parley.* The one word *peace* has served to focus the whole message of Christian preachers on many notable occasions, and more recently it has become one of the favorite catchwords of proponents of the new society. Furthermore, perhaps some words are beautiful and others ugly simply because of the sounds of them. It is hard, however, to isolate the inherent beauty or ugliness of words from the beauty or ugliness they have acquired through association and meaning.

MANAGEMENT OF LANGUAGE—WORDS IN COMBINATION

In the following section we again will treat language with respect to clearness, appropriateness, interest, attractiveness, and impressiveness.

Clearness

Usually, clearness is the result of casting familiar, concrete, specific, active words into familiar, direct, uncomplicated sentences. This will also hold true of larger thought-units if the structural and logical relations are easily perceptible and marked with connecting and relating words. Declarative sentences in the active voice that are not too long to be spoken easily in one breath will usually be clearer than the longer, more oblique sentences.

Observe the relative clarity of the following two versions of the same passage:

> If waves are watched rolling in and striking the iron columns of an ordinary pier, it is seen that although the larger waves are not much obstructed by the column, but are merely divided briefly and joined again, as a regiment of soldiers is divided by a tree, the short waves are blocked and scattered by the columns.

> Imagine that we stand on any ordinary seaside pier and watch the waves rolling in and striking the iron columns of the pier. Large waves pay little attention to the columns. They divide right and left and reunite after passing each column, much as a regiment of soldiers would if a tree stood in their road. It is almost as though the columns had not been there. But the short waves and ripples find the columns of the pier a much more formidable obstacle. When the short waves impinge on the columns, they are reflected back and spread as new ripples in all directions.

The use of familiar rather than strange sentence structure promotes clearness, as does the sharply constructed paragraph or basic unit in which the *statement* is easy to recognize and the *development* is marked by guidepost words and phrases: "let us take an example," "for instance," "another bit of information," "consequently," "on the other hand."

Appropriateness

As we shall observe again when we discuss cultivating and improving the handling of language, style in speaking and style in writing are closely akin. Excellence in written style, which registers chiefly through the eye, also exhibits clearness, appropriateness, interest, and impressiveness.

Thus the basis of good style in writing is the same as the basis of good style in speaking. Yet the difference between the circumstances of listening and of reading accounts for certain important differences between oral and written style. Certain elements and qualities are appropriate to the direct, face-to-face, personal encounter between speaker and a particular audience which do not fit so well the more remote relationship between writer and general reader, or even particular reader. Furthermore, the great versatility of voice and facial and bodily gesture in grouping, emphasizing, contrasting, and structuring language as it is spoken perhaps makes appropriate to speaking a less stringent discipline in the selection and visible arrangement of language than is needed in writing. In brief, we may say that though the essay and the speech are blood relatives, the essay is not simply a written speech or the speech an essay standing on its hind legs. Let the speaker never forget, therefore, that he is directing his language to a *specific audience* and not at the general reader.

Oral Style

Directness

The language of direct, oral discourse is more plentifully sprinkled with *I*, with *we* and *our* and *us*, than is most written discourse except the personal letter. It is marked also by a more copious use of the question than most readers would tolerate. Interrogation and the first and second-person pronouns suggest strongly that audience and speaker are face to face in immediate communication.

The interrogation is easy to use, once a speaker really thinks of himself as a speaker and once he finds that talking to an audience is little different from elevated conversation. The question is one of the best means of making hearers respond. The open question simply invites hearers to consider what is coming next. It usually introduces a point or a main idea. The closed, or rhetorical, question implies or dictates the proper answer and is often used to tie up an argument. Open: "We've described the urban dweller; now what of the family on the farm?" Closed: "So, isn't it high time to take significant action before we are too late?"

Profuseness

Oral language is also more profuse and repetitious than written language. It is more inclined to pile up words than to trust to finding the single exact word. A student speaker, roused by a local crime wave, was not satisfied to express a chief point only once. Early in his speech he said,

> The gangsters warred against each other.

Then, following a few statistics and an example, he restated the idea enlarged:

> The racketeers killed racketeers. The mobsters of the Capone days rarely molested ordinary people. Murder was just an "occupational hazard."

The same student speech affords an illustration of the piling up of words, words that are near-synonyms, overlapping in meaning:

> The hoodlums today are the mugger, the knifer, the rapist, the strangler, the brute attacker.

In the pressure of extemporanous utterance, eager to insure clearness, emphasis, and force, the speaker did not revise his list of hoodlums, as might the writer, to secure a neat, logical classification of gangsters.

Informal constructions

The language of extemporaneous speech, furthermore, often lends itself to sentences whose construction is less traditional and formal than would be proper for the eye alone. The eye must depend on the signs of punctuation and capitalization and on the careful placing of sentence elements, such as qualifying phrases and clauses. The ear, however, can depend on the tremendous resources of voice and gesture to set sentences straight. Inflection, pause, pace, and emphasis are the oral signs of punctuation; they tell the listener how sentence elements are related to each other. A dangling participle may dangle to the eye but not to the ear! Besides, there is greater variety in the length of sentences. A succession of short, terse sentences that would bother the eye might not offend the ear; nor do long, complicated sentences that tend to baffle the eye necessarily confuse the ear when they are spoken with a firm sense of meaning.

The following brief passage from a speech of the president to the students of the University of Bridgeport exhibits many of the qualities characteristic of the oral style of direct address. It is dignified but sufficiently intimate and is readable as well as listenable.

> We in college, both faculty and students, must keep this goal of freedom clearly in view, because it is principally from the students in college that our leaders come. You who represent the student body of the University of Bridgeport, and your fellow students in other colleges throughout the land, are a highly selected group—you are one in five of all people your age. Therefore, upon you rests a greater responsibility in this matter of freedom because you are being given greater opportunities. As the potential leaders of people in a free country, you must help us to help you toward an education for freedom.
>
> And so I would say to you today as we open this twenty-first year of our college, that each and every one of us must keep this goal forever before him. And to the members of the faculty I say specifically that regardless of what we teach, how we teach, or whom we teach, education for freedom must be the ultimate objective.

Oral style, in sum, is a matter of fitting the language of discourse to the speaking situation: to speaker, to subject, to audience, to the special dimensions which voice, facial expression, pronunciation, and gesture can add to language and to occasion.

Interest and Attractiveness

Activity

The language of action promotes interest, not only by action words and active verbs, but by short and lively sentences:

> We can't wait for the last straggler. We must not listen to the faint heart. Looking back takes our eyes from our path, and complaining of the cost confuses our purpose. We shall make no major mistake. Let us act now and correct any minor errors as we go.

Long sentences of several clauses each may suggest slow, meditative, easy movement.

Another way to heighten the sense of action is to change indirect discourse to direct: Not "God said that there should be light," but, "God said, 'Let there be light.'"

Curiosity

Both curiosity and suspense, through the management of language, can help control attention and hold interest. The building up of descriptive concrete detail stirs curiosity:

A wedding is about to take place in a remote part of the emerging world. The natives are gathering in their best attire, their dark faces contrasting sharply with their white, sheetlike garments and the light walls and sands. As the ceremonies are approaching their climax . . . .

Is the listener still curious and attentive?

Curiosity is also likely to be aroused and attention held by a well-told anecdote. To an audience of children, Booker T. Washington, the early black leader, told the following instructive story:

> There is a way for us to work out of every difficulty we may be in. There is a story told of two unfortunate frogs who in the night had the misfortune to fall into a jar of milk. Soon afterward one of the frogs said, "There is no use to make any effort; we might just as well sink to bottom and have life over with." The second frog said, "That is not the way to look at it. Where there is a will there is a way. I am going to get out of this milk." So the second frog began to kick and he kept kicking until three o'clock in the morning, when his kicking had turned the milk to butter, and he walked out on dry land. Now I am on the side of the kicking frog every time, and I believe there is a way for us to kick out of every difficulty in which we find ourselves placed as a race.

Questions may also serve to stimulate curiosity. The open question often serves well to introduce a main point or even to start off the speech itself. It opens the way for an answer the speaker immediately supplies: "Do you know what is the biggest business in the whole world? The United States Government!" A good formula for finding an effective question is: Frame the question a hearer would ask if he were to interrupt, and introduce it at that point in the speech where he might logically ask it.

Humor

Though stories and anecdotes are excellent sources of humor and within the reach of most speakers, some of the best humor arises from playing with language: a turn of phrase, an epithet, an amusing simile or metaphor, surprise in the presentation of detail, application of a familiar quotation in a new context. But each must be an integral part of argument, idea, or explanation. Thus did the famous Dr. Johnson score a point against the pompous, pretentious scientist, that "stately son of demonstration, who proves with mathematical formality what no man has yet pretended to doubt" (*Idler,* No. 36). And Robert M. Hutchins, reviewing ten years of his presidency in a speech to faculty and trustees just after the University of Chicago had been attacked by a notably unrestrained newspaper columnist, made an amusing combination of items: "Apart from fire and pestilence we have had about everything happen to us that could happen in the past ten years. Yesterday we had a robbery, today we have Westbrook Pegler." Someone who wished to break the news humorously to a famous actress commented, "Madame, your show is slipping." A speaker once defined a dilettante as a man who goes about announcing the discovery of lands that have long since been explored and mapped.

Humor in language is invaluable but perilous. It can generate an atmosphere of pleasing and telling wit, but easily it may turn into buffoonery. The perpetual "wise guy" seldom conveys a serious message or reinforces a discoverable idea, except perhaps that he is determined to be conspicuous. The student speaker, nevertheless, should cautiously try his talents; perhaps he will find that he has capacities worth cultivating for the subtle humor of language. If not, he can abandon the attempt before making a fool or a nuisance of himself.

Impressiveness

Language is impressive when expression is memorable. Words and idea compounded together stick in the hearer's memory. Speakers and listeners alike know that the commanding sentence, the lively word, the apt phrase, the vivid metaphor, the amusing or catchy epithet, of all the elements of a speech, often make the most immediate and most enduring impression on listeners. Franklin D. Roosevelt's label "horse-and-buggy," for the economic ideas he wished to reform, served efficiently for many people to summarize the gist of a series of his speeches. A generation earlier Woodrow Wilson had coined a memorable slogan for our participation in World War I and for the peace: "Make the World Safe for Democracy." The Republican slogan of 1972, "Four more years," served to unite many miscellaneous groups of supporters who might otherwise have looked in vain for common ground; and for some older hearers it may have stirred a happy nostalgia for the Democratic slogan of a generation earlier, "Four long years." Of late, "One man, one vote" has focused attention on fairness in representation.

Further examples of impressiveness come to mind in abundance: Winston Churchill's tribute to the Royal Air Force, "Never in the field of human conflict was so much owed by so many to so few," and his splendid affirmation of the stamina and will of the English people, "We shall fight on the beaches, we shall fight on the landing grounds, we shall fight in the fields and in the streets, we shall fight in the hills, we shall never surrender"; Franklin D. Roosevelt's coinage, born of the panic days of the Great Depression, "We have nothing to fear but fear itself"; Homer's "wine-dark sea"; Christ's "Render unto Caesar the things that are Caesar's"; William Jennings Bryan's condemnation of the gold standard as "crucifying mankind upon a cross of gold"; the many proverbial sayings, such as "The race is not always to the swift"; and sharp word inventions like "The inhibited don't mind being prohibited."

Imagery and metaphor

Impressiveness is greatly enhanced by the vividness of imagery, which gives the listener a substitute for actuality, or actuality of a new and more lively kind. One of the characters in a novel by J. B. Priestley attends a concert in which, for the first time, he hears a "modern" symphonic piece. The author describes the effect of certain passages upon the conventional, conservative sensibilities of the listener: "Tall, thin people were sitting around sneering at each other and drinking quinine, while an imbecile child sat on the floor and ran its finger nails up and down a slate." Thus the speaker who wishes to give force and intensity to his ideas tries to turn his abstract and general ideas into concrete and specific imagery.

A metaphor is what Henry Ward Beecher called "the window in an argument," because it lights up reason. The metaphor rouses an image, a flash picture or sensation; its concentration brings attention into a fast sharp focus and its image gives strength and intensity. Metaphor, as Aristotle observed centuries ago, though the most distinguished ornament of the speaker's style is the least teachable, because it depends on a talent for seeing significant resemblances. Nevertheless, a speaker may foster his talent for metaphor. As the literary critic J. Middleton Murry wrote, "A metaphor is the result of the search for a precise epithet. Try to be precise and you are bound to be metaphorical."

Antithesis and contrast

Antithesis is a compressed contrast that brings close together words whose meanings are at opposite extremes. "The educated man has no monopoly on knowledge; the uneducated man has no monopoly on ignorance." Usually, as in this example, the structure of the expression is exactly parallel and is strictly balanced. Thus pattern and thought reinforce each other with the force of a well-aimed blow.

The following sentence, with contrasting balance, effectively communicates the main point of the student speech on pages 27-28 and it also distills an image that provides a title for the speech. "Thus we can see that although the conscience is often called 'a little voice inside,' it acts more like 'the old crank next door.' "

Inventing impressive expressions

In order to invent impressive language, state the governing idea of the speech in the most concise and accurate way possible. Do the same for the chief supporting ideas and for the conclusion. Summarize the entire thought of the speech in twenty words. More often than not the effort to be both compact and precise results, as in poetry, in vivid, figurative language. And if the main ideas of a speech can be expressed in striking language, the listener will grasp and remember essentials rather than details, as he does with Churchill's statements on page 170. They are brief compressions of entire speeches. We will remember them. Similarly, Lincoln epitomized a speech with "A house divided against itself cannot stand." Expressions like these do for a speech what slogans do for advertisements and campaigns.

False impressiveness—the trite and shopworn

The commonest source of pallor and dullness in style, and probably the easiest for a speaker to fall into, is triteness, definable as saying the same old thing in the same old way at the wrong time. When the touring political candidate begins "My Friends [or Fellow Americans], it gives me a very real sense of pleasure to pay another visit to this fine city in this great state," he wants to appear especially direct and genuine. In fact, he is being pompous in as trite a way as is possible. Every expression is a cliché so shopworn from thousands of repetitions by hundreds of candidates as to sound utterly perfunctory. If he were to begin, "Ladies and gentlemen, I'm pleased to be here," he would probably startle and delight his audience.

For the young speaker to develop a reliable sense of what is trite and what is not, is no simple matter. Such a sense can come only from much experience with language and sensitive observation of it. After all, everyone has to encounter an expression for the first time, and then it is new and fresh to him. If the speaker is aware of the subtle danger of the cliché, however, he is on the way to controlling it. He will look out for such automatic expressions as *last but not least, blast-off, not the heat but the humidity, not the money but the principle of the thing, that's just politics, tell it like it is.*

Further Considerations

Any writer on public speaking is tempted to enlarge his discussion of language to great proportions, not only because the subject is complex but because it is very important. Under the present limits of space, however, we have thought it best to treat in the preceding pages chiefly those considerations which should govern the speaker's choice of words and some of the elementary methods of bringing clarity and force to connected speech. The student who is seriously interested in the best possible achievement will wish all the helpful suggestions he can get from the many excellent treatments of style in such works as those listed at the end of this chapter. Perhaps he will wish to begin with Chapter 17 of our *Fundamentals of Public Speaking* (5th edition, 1976), of which this chapter is an abridgment.

IMPROVING STYLE

Speaking Often

Frequent speaking is one of the obvious ways of learning to use language well. However, it may intensify bad habits as well as create good ones. The speaker, therefore, especially while he is a learner, should practice each speech aloud several times before he presents it to his final audience. He should also covet opportunities to give a speech on the same subject before different audiences in order to try changing his language to make it more effective each time. For the greatest profit, obviously, the speaker must be keen to the listeners' response to his language, noticing what is puzzling, what is amusing, what is clear, what is dead, and altering his technique accordingly. Otherwise his practice will be useless—if not harmful.

Listening and Reading

One does not come instinctively by a sense of clearness and fitness in language. Through extensive and frequent exposure one has to absorb a sense of what good language is. There are only two sources of this experience: one is hearing good oral discourse, the other is reading.

There is much good oral discourse to be heard, on the air, from the pulpit, from the public lecture platform, and even in the college and university classroom. Furthermore, good speech recordings are increasingly available. Not always, alas, are these specimens easy to find, and they are even more difficult to find when one wants them. Therefore reading good prose and poetry is the speaker's best resource for exposing his mind to excellent language.

As a means of improving the use of language, no one can overestimate reading *aloud*. We learned to speak in the first instance because we *heard* and talked long before we learned to read and write. Accordingly, hearing and speaking remain the most effective avenues to improvement in our command of the spoken word. To hear and to read orally a vocabulary wider and more precise than our own is to enhance our own oral vocabulary; to hear and mouth language that is constructed better than ours, that is more rhythmical and impressive, is to improve our own oral patterns. We urge, therefore, that the earnest public speaker read aloud—and read aloud as much as he can. He will find courses in oral reading (or oral interpretation of literature) helpful, not only because there the models of language will be exemplary, but because a teacher can help him to listen accurately and critically to himself. But if courses are not available, he can do much if he selects good materials and strives to read as if he were *communicating* with a listener.

Writing

Writing and speaking need the corrective influence of each other if either is to attain its potential excellence. A careful writer often tests his sentences by reading them aloud. He seeks to modify any unnecessarily complicated structure and to shorten sentences that would otherwise require a reader to carry too much detail in mind before he gets to the action words. A careful speaker examines critically his extemporaneous utterance. From a recording or a stenographic copy of what he has said, he can criticize his own language—discovering and repairing the fragmentation, needless repetition, and inept expression. He can write in, for future reference, those coinages he wishes he had used.

Writing is best only when it permits that lively flow of thought characteristic of good speaking, only when it conveys the vitality—the lifelikeness—of spoken language, only when it bears in mind the best lanes of approach to its audience. Conversely, speaking is excellent when it is governed by some of that discipline which controls the best writing: (1) when the speaker has so developed his usable vocabulary that the most accurate and appropriate language the audience will understand springs readily to his tongue; (2) when something of shapeliness and grace appears in his normal mode of talk; (3) when sentences take on without rigidity or complexity some semblance of structure, of subordination and coordination, clear evidence that some things come before or after others by design rather than by chance.

Rehearsal and Revision

It follows that after a speaker has begun to become really naturalized to the speaking situation, he should take to writing as a regular, substantial part of his preparation. After planning and outlining and some oral rehearsal, he should write out his speech, or considerable portions of it, just as he would propose to speak it to his audience. He should set the written text aside for a few hours or a few days, then retrieve it, read it aloud critically, and revise the language and the sentences as better or more fitting words come to him and as he discovers sentences that are either clumsy or not so clear as they could be. Once more, he should read the new version aloud to a tender and critical ear (his own).

Maintain an Oral Attitude

The main object of our attention in this book is the planned but extemporaneous speech—not the speech that is written out and read aloud or memorized. For this reason there is little in the earlier chapters that gives special consideration to language. Thinking for communication and in communication is the first consideration. If there were to be only one consideration, that would be it. We all come equipped with a usable enough stock of language to get well started. Thinking and using language, however, are so much parts of the same process—thought is so completely dependent on symbols—that improvement in the one is impossible without improvement in the other. Furthermore, the language of words, rather than thought itself, is amenable to direct study. Consequently, in improving his use of language, a speaker is improving the materials of what we have called "applied thought."

Force, vividness, memorableness, the qualities in language that give speechmaking clearness, aptness, interest, and impressiveness, are the ones most seriously missed when language falls below what the audience expects, what the subject demands, and what the occasion and the speaker's personality justify. These qualities taken together effect that fitness of language to the speech as spoken discourse which must be the good speaker's object. The philosopher, the moralist, and perhaps the scientist need only make us understand the truth; the popular speaker must make us feel the truth. The language of clarity vitalized by the language of force, vividness, and memorableness is an indispensable ally of the public speaker.

INQUIRIES

1. Compile a list of words, usages, and habitual locutions that you think your speech and that of people you frequently hear would be better without. Would you include any of the following?: *y'know, I mean* (as a filler), *in terms of, this point in time* (for *now*), *viable, by the same token.* What are others of your special un-favorites? Would most of your peer group agree?
2. Make a parallel list of words and expressions that you think would be good additions to your working vocabulary, or that of your acquaintances.
3. What in the language of speeches are you likely to notice especially, favorably or unfavorably? Incorrectnesses and what you consider blunders of language? Especially good expression? Are you more likely to be sensitive to the language and delivery near the beginning of a speech, and less so later? Why? What makes the difference, if there is one?
4. Observe the current use of slogans in the press and on television and radio and try to assess their effectiveness in this or that campaign or this or that cause. What seems to make the difference?
5. Read Lincoln's *Gettysburg Address* aloud until you have in effect learned it by heart. What in the language intensifies and deepens as you make it your own? What seems to become trite or stale? Can you account for what you seem to observe?

6. Follow the procedure of question 5, using the *Twenty-Third Psalm*.

7. Discussion or debate question: "Is the language of advertising the language of good persuasive speaking?"

FURTHER READINGS

Aly, Bower, and Lucile Folse Aly. *A Rhetoric of Public Speaking*. 1973. Chapter 4.

Aristotle. *Rhetoric*. Translated by J.H. Freese. 1939. Book III, Chapters 1-12.

Baird, A. Craig, Franklin H. Knower, and Samuel L. Becker. *General Speech Communication*. 4th ed. 1971. Chapter 12, "Verbal Systems of Communication." An excellent, interesting contemporary exposition of what language is and how it works.

Bryant, Donald C. and Karl R. Wallace, *Fundamentals of Public Speaking*. 5th ed. 1976. Chapter 17, "Style: the Language of the Speech." The fuller treatment, of which this chapter is an abridgement.

Black, Max (ed.). *The Importance of Language*. 1962. A collection of authoritative essays.

Blankenship, Jane. *Public Speaking: a Rhetorical Perspective*. 1966. Chapters 6-7 on style.

Hayakawa, S.I. *Language in Thought and Action*. 2nd ed. 1964.

Langer, Suzanne K. *Philosophy in a New Key*. 1948. Chapter 5, "Language."

Lee, Irving J. *The Language of Wisdom and Folly*. 1949.

Monroe, Alan H. and Douglas Ehninger. *Principles and Types of Speech Communication*. 7th ed. 1974. Chapter 16.

Murry, J. Middleton. *The Problem of Style*. 1925. Chapters 1, 4, and 6.

Read, Sir Herbert. *English Prose Style*. New ed. 1961.

Richards, I.A. *The Philosophy of Rhetoric*. 1936. Lecture 5, "Metaphor."

Sapir, Edward. *Language*. New York: Harvest Books, 1949.

Sutherland, James R. *On English Prose*. 1957.

CHAPTER 10

Principles of Delivery

Style and delivery are the aspects of oral communication that ultimately make a speaker's conceptions actual to him and real to his audience. After treating style—the selection and management of language—in the previous chapter, we now turn to delivery—the audible, visible aspects of the speaker's performance. The psychology of delivery is grounded in the principle that *ideas* (conceptions, meanings) *dominate utterance and bodily behavior.* In good delivery, listener and speaker fully grasp the idea at the moment of utterance. In delivery that is less than good, some competing stimulus—an irrelevant idea, for example—prevents the speaker or the audience from concentrating on the relevant idea. One cannot fully concentrate on any statement on this page if he is at the same time thinking of watching a ball game on TV.

The principle is derived from observations of the mind at work in lively, direct conversation. Of course we cannot see the mind at work; we can only make our best guesses. By minimizing distractions, a speaker can come close to achieving that characteristic of conversation, realization of idea at the moment of utterance.

From experience in conversation, almost anyone can point to things that divert listeners from the message being spoken. Those distractions may include some unusual feature of dress that monentarily commands attention. Or some mannerism of posture, movement, or gesture. Or some bothersome trait of speech, such as long pauses, frequent pauses, rapidity of utterance, indistinctness of speech, novel pronunciation. "uh"'s and "er"'s, "y'know" 's, and "like" 's. Or some sign of indirect communication, such a dullness of tone, immobility of face or body, or averted eyes. Or some quality of voice or gesture which we interpret as insincerity, affectedness, or lack of interest in us. Or perhaps an unrecognizable word or phrase. These are a few of the distractions. In conversation when we are attending *only* to what is said, we are being dominated by ideas and nothing else.

In the formal, public speaking situation, the listener may be subject to the same distractions he encounters in conversation. But because he is playing a more prominent role than in conversation, they may strike him more forcefully. Yet listeners do not *expect* a good speaker to be distracted. They expect him to claim their attention utterly and to hold it; they expect to think along with him.

Like the listener, the speaker is dominated by ideas during utterance when other factors do not compete for his attention and divert him from concentrating on his meaning. Sometimes the distraction is primarily emotional, as with nervousness, or anxiety, or (in extremely rare instances) stage fright. More often the distraction is a feeling of inadequacy, which may result from inexperience in public speaking, from a sense of having nothing worth saying, or from insufficient preparation (such as poor organization of ideas and inadequate rehearsal). Hence the struggle to concentrate gets in the way of thinking itself. When the speaker is talking in the absence of distracting experiences, he is living his ideas and his meaning.

DESIRABLE FEATURES OF DELIVERY

In keeping with the basic principle, the psychology of delivery should meet three requirements: (1) Responsiveness to meaning during moments of utterance; (2) Sense of communication with the audience; (3) Bodily action that reflects meaning and serves the needs of communication. J. A. Winans was the first to call these three standards taken together the "conversation quality" in delivery.

Realization of Meaning During Utterance

The speaker during delivery should be as fully responsive to ideas and their meaning as he is in good, everyday conversation. Now what happens when a person speaks in everyday situations? He gets an idea, he says, and just utters it. Precisely. He doesn't get the idea, frame a careful sentence that is grammatically correct and beautifully balanced, and then utter it. He doesn't decide that a particular sentence requires a downward inflection of the voice, that he must say it one way rather than another, or that he must pause at one place for one-tenth of a second, at another place for two seconds. Not at all.

He gets an idea, or the germ of an idea, and starts speaking. He thinks as he speaks; and the vocal inflections and gymnastics, often incredibly intricate as sound patterns, are at one with his thought. Utterance, accordingly, is genuine and spontaneous, and if one's acquired *habits* are good, so is one's utterance. The listener is not even aware of it as utterance unless it is in some way peculiar and therefore distracting. We call that mental activity which results in genuineness and spontaneity of delivery, *vivid-realization-of-idea-at-the-moment-of-utterance*. It is perhaps the most desirable aspect of delivery.

As we speak before a group for the first time, do our minds behave as they would in private conversation? Perhaps they do; if so, we are fortunate. Most of us, however, realize that we are no longer engaged in private, informal colloquy; the "platform" is a new situation and our minds have not been at work there. Consequently, in the face of some self-consciousness and perhaps a touch of fright, we go ahead, and by gaining experience in the speaking situation, we become accustomed to it. That is, we *learn* to think and talk on the platform as the occasion and circumstances demand. Actually our minds do not behave in a new and strange manner; they are only learning to adapt, to function freely in a new and different situation.

The beginning speaker—or any speaker, for that matter—must avoid preoccupation with delivery on the platform. His attention must be centered on ideas from start to finish. He must avoid setting up mental hurdles. The time to attend to the *process* of utterance is in rehearsal periods devoted to improving *habits*.

Sense of Communication

The speaker on the platform should have a keen sense of communication with his hearers. By a *sense of communication* we mean a *feeling* or *awareness* that two or more minds are engaged in mutual action and reaction. The feeling is evident in almost every conversation. Both parties to a live conversation are well aware that two people are engaged; neither is talking at a stone wall. Furthermore, in addition to some mental interaction, the feeling of communication, of being with another, is helped by the conversationalists' confronting and looking at each other. This identical relationship between speakers in normal conversation must also be evident in the 'public' situation between speaker and audience. Recognition of this relationship led Emerson to say that public speaking is only enlarged conversation and that the speaker is a gentleman conversing.

Like learning to think vividly during moments of utterance, learning to feel with the audience means learning to do in the audience situation what may already be normal in the private situation. Although a student may have to make a number of speeches before he feels in close touch with the audience from beginning to end, he may have moments of direct contact even in his first speech. Looking at his auditors and actually seeing them as live persons gives a speaker a sense of what they are doing, how they are responding; and it gives the listeners something useful to do with their own eyes if they can look into his. The speaker talks to others; or, to express the communicative quality of delivery in its strictest sense, the speaker talks to and with others, not at them. Speaker and hearer are in touch and know it.

Gesture and Meaning

Body and mind are so closely linked that an idea vividly experienced not only prompts speech but gesture also. But gesture does not break through into meaning, it cannot aid communication, unless the body is *free* to respond to idea. Hence, poise is necessary if the speaker is to gesture spontaneously.

Basically, poise simply describes bodily behavior that is efficient; it is movement that fits a particular situation with economy and without obtrusiveness; it is, in brief, activity that is *fully adaptive*. Like good speech, poise in behavior is never noticed. Like poor speech, behavior without poise is conspicuous because of its inadequacies; it may be random, needlessly repetitious, gratuitous, or awkward. Good platform behavior, accordingly, is bodily activity that fits the communicative situation.

Freedom to gesture

Learning to become bodily expressive on the platform does not mean that the speaker is becoming a pantomimist or an actor. Action must not usurp the role of speech. Nor does it mean that the speaker deliberately invents gestures and plants them wherever he may think them appropriate. The hallmark of good gesture, like good speech, is its apparent genuineness and spontaneity.

Learning to become physically responsive involves, in the first place, getting the body *free to respond* to the meanings of the mind. Accordingly, the beginning speaker seeks to maintain his normal freedom of action on the platform. In learning to gesture, then, the process is one of adaptation to the new situation through guided experience and practice. The beginner learns, accordingly, to handle himself so as not to *inhibit* bodily responses that ordinarily accompany vivid and vigorous thought.

Discipline of gesture

Learning to become bodily expressive on the platform, in the second place, implies discipline of gesture. After the speaker has become bodily alert and responsive, he is not utterly free to behave as his old, everyday impulses dictate. He must recognize that because he is standing before others, or otherwise assuming a more prominent place than is customary in conversation, his position has become emphatic. Consequently, some behavior that is inconspicuous and proper in daily intercourse may become glaringly evident on the platform. Such, for example, are *mannerisms.* They are repetitious behavior that is peculiar to the individual. In fact, they are so distinctive of the individual that his friends and associates have come to accept them as being part of his personality. Hence, a person's mannerisms escape notice by friends or are charitably tolerated. On the platform and in the presence of strangers, they yell for attention. What is natural and acceptable in one environment is no longer natural and acceptable in another. Accordingly. under the guidance of instructor and classroom listeners, the student may need to eliminate certain mannerisms. They may be such habitual quirks of behavior as stroking the hair, pulling the collar or the nose, adjusting the tie, wagging a hand, rubbing the knuckles, smoothing the dress, or fussing with the necklace or earring. Whatever they are, they compete with ideas for the hearer's attention.

Beyond the discipline required to eliminate mannerisms, most beginning speakers must undertake some training to smooth out gesture, to iron out such roughness and awkwardness as may distract attention. The training is begun *after* the speaker finds that his body is responding with considerable ease and freedom. Only after action on the platform begins to be spontaneous and habitual can the novice afford to be self-conscious about his gesture. In the early speeches the important first steps are (1) handling one's body so as not to inhibit action, (2) responding freely to all impulses to activity, and (3) breaking up distracting mannerisms. The refinement of gesture comes later in the speaker's development.

DELIVERY AND MEMORY

The chief problem of the novice speaker is memory. During the moments of delivery the speaker is recalling what he has prepared for presentation. But *what* is he recalling? The language he has prepared, along with accompanying bodily states and movements? Or is it the ideas and the materials that give rise to the words?

It is useful to recognize four modes of delivery: that which requires memorizing prepared language in full, which seemed to be favored by the ancients; that which arises without forethought in unanticipated circumstances, called *impromptu*; that which involves reading a prepared text from the page (or the teleprompter); and that in which the speaker is responding to a set or chain of *ideas* which he has prepared but has not tried to memorize in exact language. In this last, the *extemporaneous*, the speaker wants to recall his ideas in the order he has determined, and as in impromptu delivery, to leave their phrasing to the moment of utterance. The extemporaneous is the most widely used of all modes of delivery and is, therefore, the one with which in this book we are most concerned.

Every speaker solves the problem of memory in delivery in ways that prove most effective for him. There is, however, a common method of attack; it depends on a working knowledge of the principles of memory.

Memory may be usefully regarded as the record and storehouse of experience. The image of a storehouse implies the notion of space, in which objects and experiences have places and are arranged. In normal persons experiences are not chaotic, they are ordered and arranged. Hence the first and most important principle of memory: *Organized materials—materials ordered and shaped—are better remembered than disorganized materials.* Patterned experience governs attention and perception, and it furnishes the basic principle of successful learning and proper outlining.

The second principle is: *What strikes the individual hard has a better chance of being remembered than what does not.* This is the principle of intensity of impression. Closely connected with it is the principle of *sharpness of impression.* The image that is clear in outline and shape enhances impression and registers memorably on the human organism.

The importance of motivation to learning is too well known to need amplification. From it comes the principle of memory that *what is learned under the influence of motive or desire lasts longer in memory than what is not.* The same sense of purpose, desire, or goal that monitors the preparation of a speech functions also to recall the mainstream of materials and, later, to give direction and energy to ideas and language in delivery.

A final principle is no doubt obvious, that of repetition. Hence *whatever occurs again and again is better remembered than what does not.* "Practice makes perfect," it is said. Yes, if one practices what is perfectible. More precisely: Practice makes *permanent.*

Applying to Delivery the Principles of Memory

In all modes of delivery a speaker has one goal: to recall what he wants to say in the order determined during preparation. Except in the impromptu situation, he usually works from written materials—a speech outline, or notes, or a full text. Of course he engages in repetition. But what is to be repeated? The immediate temptation is to repeat words, either silently or orally, or both. This procedure is effective only if one practices long enough for meaning to dominate language rather than letting language dominate meaning. When one allows words to control, he is merely articulating the sounds of speech; he utters signals with little live meaning, and so burdens his listeners with translating his mere sounds into symbols before they grasp his meaning. Even if one reads silently from his outline or manuscript, he is probably repeating words subvocally. In short, the response during initial practice is likely to be a series of vocal motor events. In preparing for extemporaneous delivery, then, the repetition of words as signals is wasteful.

It is preferable to give first attention to meaning rather than to sounds. One tries to recall ideas and meanings with all the freshness and spontaneity that accompanied their birth. The speaker created the ideas he works with; so he tries to *re-create* them, knowing that in good time the signals and code of speech will fall into place during utterance, just as they do in impromptu speech.

A number of practices used in combination, emphasize meaning. One is to read over the speech outline aloud or silently or both, trying to discount words and concentrate on meanings. In order to stamp in the basic ideas, one pays special attention to statements that embody purpose—the subject statement and the main heads. One looks for patterns of thought that link the mainheads and subheads. As soon as the structure of the whole can be recollected, the speech outline may be abandoned in favor of talking the speech through from beginning to end, addressing the ideas to one's mental image of the intended audience. If the speaker keeps his body relaxed during this stage of practice and concentrates on meaning, gestures will begin to appear as natural parts of the message. So it is important to practice remembering, and to work primarily with the idea-structures that tie together one's meaning.

Continued Rehearsal

Speakers who respect the requirements of memory will discover that, during the late stages of practice, recollection of specific language gives way to the recall of ideas. A sign of this change is the appearance of new ideas, as additional details and illustrations, or as a sharper, more effective way of stating an idea. The sudden, apparently accidental occurrence of new thoughts and materials is further evidence that an organized whole not only controls its parts, but helps its master invent and create new and unantici-pated items. Other tactics that speakers find valuable are the use of headnotes on a small card, and of transition passages of the flashback-preview type. The headnotes stand for blocks of ideas, not words. The transition passages are fully worked out, connecting the blocks of ideas and keeping the whole structure clear.

Good delivery, then, is marked by full responsiveness to meanings, by the sense that one is in communication with his hearers, and by effective gestures. To realize these qualities of delivery in the prepared speech, the speaker applies the principles of memory. He tries to acquire the habit of responding to his preparation—spontaneously, fully, accurately. Doubtless his initial efforts will be attended by uncomfortable self-consciousness. But he will find this disappears once his mind is completely absorbed in the meaning of his speech; then his only concern will be the desire to share his information and ideas with others.

SPEAKING IMPROMPTU

So far we have focused on the principles of all forms of delivery, with special attention, quite properly, to the extemporaneous mode—that speaking which is carefully prepared, is preferably rehearsed, but is not committed to final language until the speech is presented to the audience. Perhaps nothing so satisfies our egos, however, as success in speaking impromptu—unexpectedly, without a chance to prepare for the occasion.

Unfortunately, most impromptu speaking is bad, because the speaker, surprised in deep water, loses his head and thrashes and flounders about. His delivery is halting and hard, and his remarks are often inane and irrelevant, repetitious and disconnected. In alarm and desperation, he clutches at any idea that pops into mind and without examining it hopes that somehow it will save him. When impromptu utterance is good, it is very, very good. Delivery, in particular, may be excellent; it may exhibit the verve, sparkle, and spontaneity that one struggles to attain in the extemporaneous speech. Most public speakers have observed that their impromptu delivery is at times superior to their prepared efforts. A speaker may recognize that he talks well when the circumstances of communication are just right. When the preceding speaker stirs him strongly or when discussion starts him thinking, when he springs to correct another speaker's information, to criticize an argument, to express a different point of view, he has simultaneously an idea to communicate and the impulse to say it—and the job is done with vigor and dispatch. He should recognize, however, that the fortuitous combination of circumstances, just the right situation, brings about his success. Indeed, when the circumstances are made to order, who can fail?

We are concerned here with the situation in which the circumstances are not perfect, in which a speaker, called on unexpectedly, must, like an aggressive athlete, make his own breaks and take advantage of the opportunity to speak instead of letting it slip by.

In coping with the impromptu situation, a speaker should recognize above all, paradoxical as it may seem, that he is not wholly without preparation. He has a background of experience and information upon which he may be able to draw. *The problem is how to make his past work for him.* In such a situation he may be able to enjoy considerable success by attacking the problem in the following ways.

Listening Carefully

This should not be difficult if the preceding discussion has claimed his interest. But if the speechmaking and the discussion do not readily interest him, and if there is the possibility that he may be called on to speak, he had better force himself to follow the talk as closely as he can. The ideas of others may touch off information and experience, and thus prompt some kind of reaction. For example: "The speaker has overlooked an important point"; "he is being inconsistent"; "that argument is weak"; "he believes so-and-so, but I disagree"; "he's right, but only partly so." When such ideas strike, one should make notes of them—brief notes, only a phrase or two, so as not to lose track of the speech or the discussion.

Controlling Alarm and Panic

Usually if the novice can control the first moments of thinking, or rather feeling, that he is in an impossible bind, he can make some headway toward bringing his resources to bear. Fright feeds on itself, but such expedients as the following should tend to moderate it.

Begin by relaxing and thus reducing muscular tension. Breathe regularly. With a little practice, you can learn to ease off thus in four or five seconds. Then turn your attention to the situation and meet it squarely. Has a specific question been asked that demands a definite answer? Start walking to the platform and decide what the answer will be. (If necessary to gain time, ask that the question be repeated. This gives the mind something to do!) Your decision will probably suggest a reason or two or at least an illustration to back it up. At this moment you have, whether you recoginze it or not, what amounts to a central idea with which to lead off, and one or two ideas to follow and support it. You can conclude by restating your opening idea. If you cannot reply to the direct question, two roads are open. Either decline to speak, excusing yourself as gracefully as you can, or say in substance, "I don't have anything to say to that question, but if I may, I should like to comment on such-and-such a point." Here is where your notes come in handy, for your decision to comment on another point may be prompted by a glance at them. You use them to recall swiftly your earlier reactions.

If, on the other hand, a general question is asked you—such as "Would you care to comment on so-and-so's remarks?"—you turn at once to your notes for suggestions. To one inexperienced in impromptu discussion, notes are invaluable here because a general question or invitation suggests no possibilities. It isn't specific enough to give one a mental start, and the review of notes may prompt an idea.

Becoming Thoroughly Habituated to Useful
Patterns of Thought

So far we have been concerned principally with suggestions that aid the impromptu speaker in selecting something to say. Now to the rapid organization of his ideas. The impromptu speech, like the extemporaneous speech, requires not only that a speaker have something to say but that he say it as clearly as he can. The least to be expected of him is that he will contrive a simple, sensible subject statement and support it with an example or two. Anything more he may be able to accomplish is clear profit.

The patterns below, intended primarily to promote clarity of expression, may also serve to suggest ideas. The student would do well to practice them so thoroughly that they become part of him; he should, in other words, assimilate them completely. They will then come to his aid, unrecognized and unheralded, in those few moments of preparation in the impromptu situation, to provide form for his thoughts.

1. Lead off with what has been said. Express your reaction. Support it. (*A variant of this:* Start with the question asked. Answer it in one sentence. Explain or give reasons for the answer.)
2. Lead off with an illustration. Conclude by stating the point it suggests.
3. Say that an important point has been omitted. State it. Support it.
4. Express disagreement with a certain argument. Give reasons for disagreeing.
5. Express disagreement in terms of the problem discussed.
   a. The evils have been exaggerated. State why.
   b. The solution is bad, for
      (1) There is a better one. State it. Give reasons.
      (2) It is impractical. Give reasons.
6. The reasoning in such-and-such an argument is in error, because of
   a. Insufficient or untrustworthy facts. Explain.
   b. Inadequate or untrustworthy testimony. Explain.
   c. Faulty analogy. Explain.
   d. Faulty cause-and-effect reasoning. Explain.
7. The argument shows an inconsistency. Explain.

Rarely will an alert individual find himself completely unprepared for the impromptu situation. Although he cannot prepare specifically for the unexpected occasion, he can equip himself and condition himself for meeting such occasions. (1) He can confirm the habit, which ought to be a normal consequence of his education, of reading, inquiring, conversing, observing, and thinking widely on those general and particular subjects which men in society at all times and at a given time concern themselves with. He will find, what frequent speakers have always found, that within wide limits the same lines of thought, developed in much the same way, will be adaptable to many speaking situations. He will accumulate, therefore, a store of such lines of thought, which he will be able to call to mind and to adapt properly to a variety of circumstances. (2) Like the contestant in an honest quiz show or a student preparing for an examination in special circumstances, he can pay special attention to the basic ideas and information likely to be needed in the situation he is going to face. (3) He can train himself to listen closely, take note of his reactions, and develop the knack of swiftly arranging his remarks. The more speaking experience he gains and the more resources of idea, information, and illustration he accumulates, the more readily will he be able to react. A good impromptu speech, with an idea worth remembering, cannot be made from an empty or lethargic mind.

INQUIRIES

1. A person in the audience of a play or a speech sometimes feels like exclaiming, in reverse of the more usual comment, "Don't *do* something; just *stand* there!" In your experience, what makes gesture and bodily movement in a speaker seem excessive and distracting? the smallness of room or audience? too obvious an excess of descriptiveness? exaggerated emotion? What determines your measure of excess? Analyze your response to the visible aspects of several speakers. Try to generalize your responses.

2. Conversely, what factors make movement and gesture seem too little?

3. Think about the observation that delivery is best when it does not attract attention to itself, favorably or unfavorably? Does your experience confirm that observation? Under all circumstances and for all kinds of speeches? When not?

4. Consider the remark, intended as commendation, "That speaker has an informal, chatty manner" and this one, "He was too chatty; he talked down to us." What conditions and circumstances of speaking might give rise to each of those comments? what particular factors in the delivery would one be responding to?

5. What different demands does the invisibility of the speaker on radio or audio-tape make from those on television or film? Listen to the President of the United States on radio and then on television and compare your impressions of his delivery. Under which conditions does he seem more credible? Why?

FURTHER READING

Baird, A. Craig, Franklin H. Knower, and Samuel L. Becker. *General Speech Communication.* 4th ed. 1971. Chapters 14-16.

Bryant, Donald C. and Karl R. Wallace. *Fundamentals of Public Speaking.* 5th ed. 1976. Chapter 18, which includes a useful section on the causes and treatment of stage fright; and Chapter 19 on voice, pronunciation, and gesture.

Caton, Charles A. (ed.) *Philosophy and Ordinary Language.* 1963. Chapter 8, "The Theory of Meaning," by Gilbert Ryle.

Monroe, Alan H. and Douglas Ehninger. *Principles and Types of Speech Communication.* 7th ed. 1974. Chapters 5 and 6.

Norman, Donald. *Memory and Attention: An Introduction to Human Information Processing.* 1969.

Parrish, W.M. "The Concept of 'Naturalness,' " *Quarterly Journal of Speech,* 40 (December 1951), 448-54.

Reid, Loren. *Speaking Well.* 2nd ed. 1972. Chapters 10-12.

Winans, James A. *Public Speaking.* 1917. Chapter 2, "Conversing with an Audience."

CHAPTER 11

Special Forms, Occasional Speeches, The Public Interview

Most situations call for speeches whose purposes are primarily informative or persuasive. Frequently, however, the *main* purpose is something else—to extend or receive a courtesy or to carry out some other formal duty. When these special purposes prevail, the principles and practices of effective speaking which are the subject of this book are just as important and should be just as carefully applied as in expository and persuasive speeches. That is, these special speeches should be carefully prepared, audience and occasion should be analyzed, clear plans and outlines should be developed, ideas should be developed concretely and vividly, style should be appropriate, delivery should be characterized by conversational quality.

In such speeches, as a matter of fact, certain qualities of content and presentation are even more important than they are in other speeches, because the audience is almost always aware ahead of time what the speaker's purpose is and where his discourse will lead. Neatness and clarity of structure; plentiful and vivid example and concrete detail; ease, audibility, clarity, fluency, and liveliness of utterance; propriety and grace of style—a high premium is to be placed on each of these in speeches of introduction, of presentation of a gift or award, of welcome and response to welcome, and in after-dinner speeches and other speeches of entertainment.

In addition to the heightened value to be placed in such speeches on the qualities just enumerated, the purposes and occasions prescribe for the speaker certain basic and essential requisites of content—certain established formulas, so to speak—within which he must function. His success depends on how well he works out his speech without exceeding his function and without violating the accepted rules of the job he is doing. The rules for each kind of speech are few and should be followed, but the opportunities for individual variation are many. In these speeches, however, as in all others, there can be no adequate substitute for good sense, good will, keenness of mind, and a feeling for the fitting and proper.

SPEECHES OF INTRODUCTION

Speeches of introduction are so common and so frequently bad that everyone should prepare himself for the times when he will make them. Many speakers would much rather not be introduced at all than be subjected to, and be present while the audience is subjected to, the "introductions" which they often encounter. Speakers are usually introduced either by friends and colleagues (who may be very poor speakers) who know them well, or by chairmen who know them only slightly by repute but wish to seem well acquainted, or by individuals or functionaries known to the audience but who do not know the speaker at all. This, alas, is a just statement of a dismal situation, and there is not very much we can do to improve it unless those persons who introduce speakers will undertake to improve themselves.

Speeches of introduction are often inexcusably poor in both delivery and substance. The delivery is likely to be either feeble and indistinct or stiff and self-conscious. Introducers often say too much or too little, and too frequently they lack tact and taste. These faults need not prevail, however, if introducers will understand their functions, be content to serve those functions, and take their tasks seriously.

Purposes

A speech of introduction should accomplish, as far as possible, two purposes; and those two purposes accomplished to the best of his ability, the introducer should do no more. (1) It should place audience and speaker on a footing of mutual acquaintance, confidence, and sympathy. (2) It should promote the purpose of the speech. It is no part of the purpose to display the introducer, *his* relation to the speaker, *his* relation to the audience, *his* relation to the subject. Whatever the introducer says should advance one of these two purposes. He must resist the temptation to turn aside from them.

Materials

The irreducible minimum of content for a speech of introduction, even when the speaker is thoroughly well known to the audience, is the speaker's *name and identity*. Such brevity, however, is ordinarily undesirable, unless the audience has been brought to attention and quiet beforehand, because the introduction, like the first few speeches of the first act of a play, is likely to be lost in the stir of the audience's settling down. Shailer Mathew's famous introduction of President Wilson, which has become the norm for presenting the President, only *identified* but did not name the speaker. His entire introduction consisted of these words:"Ladies and gentlemen: The President of the United States." In further promoting acquaintance and confidence between speaker and audience, the introducer should mention favorably but *moderately* why the speaker is qualified to talk on his subject: his experience, his position, his special capabilities.

In promoting the purpose of the speech, the introducer will not only try to direct favorable attention to the speaker by referring to his qualifications, but he should lead that attention toward the subject. He should remind the audience why the subject is especially important or significant either in general or in relation to the occasion, to recent events, to coming events such as the anniversary of a person or an institution, or to the particular audience. Again the length or detail of such remarks will be measured by the audience's previous acquaintance with the subject and its significance. The introducer should not labor the obvious; he should remember also that the speaker himself may wish to point out the importance and significance of his subject by way of getting his speech under way.

There may be ideas properly suggested to the introducer by the audience itself: compliments which he, rather than the speaker, might pay in the interest of good will. If the audience is large or especially distinguished, the introducer may compliment it for being so. He should not, however, *call* it large or distinguished if it obviusly is not. Such remarks infuse an inappropriate tone of humor, sarcasm, or insincerity into the relation of speaker and audience. If the audience is small, it is well not to mention size or to apologize for a small audience.

Whenever possible, the introducer should consult the speaker beforehand to confirm the accuracy of his information—especially name and titles—and to find out what the speaker wishes to have said and what he wishes not to have said. Then, unless it is utterly impossible, the introducer should respect the *speaker's wishes.*

Warnings about Content and Language

Restraint in both length and content is highly desirable. The introducer is the host or the representative of the host. The audience wants to hear the speaker. It is a safe rule that if the speaker is to talk from *five* to *fifteen* minutes, the introducer should not use more than from *thirty* seconds to *two* minutes, and normally no speech of introduction should last more than *five* minutes.

Tact and Taste. Extravagent praise embarrasses both speaker and audience. It is very easy, if one is not careful, to let a perfectly genuine wish to do justice to a speaker's excellence get out of control and turn into extravagance. One should not dwell on a speaker's exploits, although one ought to mention those which are relevant. Such remarks as, "You will now hear an interesting and inspiring speech," are usually more harmful than helpful to the speaker-audience relation. It is better that the audience should find the speaker exceeding their expectations than failing to approach the quality predicted. Extravagance discredits the introducer and embarrasses speaker and audience.

Though good humor should always pervade a speech of introduction, the use of humor, especially humor involving the speaker or tending to make light of occasion or subject, is questionable. There are some few occasions, however, where the expert use of good-humored humor is proper. See, for instance, Streeter's introduction of Dean Jones of Yale at the inauguration of President Hopkins of Dartmouth in O'Neill's *Models of Speech Competition.*[1] When in doubt, omit humor.

Find fresh, sincere, and plausible substitutes for such trite and hackneyed phrases as "it is an honor and a privilege," "a scholar and a gentleman," "a man who . . ., and a man who . . ., and a man who . . . ."

Arrangement of the Speech

Essential information belongs near the conclusion. Essential information includes the *subject,* and usually, but not always, the speaker's *name.* A sense of anticlimax and impatience to get on with the speech develops in the audience if much is said after the subject is announced. Even when a speech of introduction is very short, the essential information should not come in the first sentence. The audience may not hear or understand, because of the disturbance of getting settled or because of unfamiliarity with the introducer's voice and manner.

Delivery

It is best not to read a speech of introduction. Even at the expense of some possible fumbling and hesitancy, it is better that the audience and the guest should suppose the introducer to be sincerely uttering his own genuine sentiments than that he should appear to be the impersonal mouthpiece of a piece of paper. Know the ideas thoroughly; plan and practice. The speech must move. But do not read. Maintain a lively sense of communication so as not to sound mechanical and perfunctory.

Pause to get attention before beginning; then speak slowly, distinctly, and loudly enough so as to be easily heard and understood by the guest speaker

[1]J. M. O'Neill, *Models of Speech Composition* (New York, 1921), p. 670.

and by *all* of the audience. Introducers often don't, perhaps because they feel close to the speaker, who is at hand, and not to the audience.

PRESENTING A GIFT, AN AWARD, OR A MEMORIAL

This kind of speech is very often needed because of the many occasions when, in all kinds of societies and business, professional, and civic associations, we wish publicly or semipublicly to acknowledge the distinction attained by individuals, groups, or institutions or to commemorate a person or event with some tangible token.

Watches, fountain pens, pocketbooks, or wallets are presented by their fellow workers or by management to faithful employees who have served ten, twenty-five, forty years. We gather at the dinner table publicly to bid good-bye to an associate who is moving on to another and better job and to present him with a briefcase or a set of luggage.

Words must go with the medals, ribbons, plaques, cups, trophies, certificates, prizes, and scholarships we award to individuals or groups who have excelled in athletes, scholarship, business, industry, charity drives, virtue, or good works. On the occasions of most such awards the audience and the individual honored feel let down or cheated unless someone accompanies the presentation with words of praise and appreciation.

Likewise the presentation of a memorial in honor of the dead creates a solemn and dignified occasion that is hollow without proper words of praise and dedication. Whether the university's literary club presents to the library a book fund in memory of a deceased scholar, a gift primarily for *use*; or whether the war veterans present a statue to the city in memory of the honored dead; in all such situations we expect speeches of presentation appropriate to the donor, the donee, the gift, and the person or event being commemorated.

Purposes

The purposes of speeches of presentation are (1) formally and publicly to exhibit the worth of the recipient, (2) to heighten the sense of appreciation or satisfaction felt by the donor, or donors, and (3) usually to represent the gift as a token or symbol rather than remuneration.

Materials

The minimum expectation from a speech of presentation is that the speaker will mention—or at least *name*—the award, the person receiving it, and the donor, and that he will indicate why the presentation is made. In fulfilling these requisites, especially the last, there are several kinds of material the speaker will be more or less expected to use. These requisites will derive from the fitness of the donee to be honored, of the honor as coming from the donor, and the fitness or significance of the gift itself. Briefly stated, the speaker will:

> Magnify, though not exaggerate, the services, deeds, qualities, accomplishments, and excellences of the recipient.
>
> Say something of the considerations that governed the choice of the gift if these considerations are complimentary to this recipient especially.
>
> Minimize, though not depreciate, the intrinsic worth of the gift.
>
> Go beyond the material characteristics of the gift to discover a deeper meaning, perhaps a symbolic significance (the gift is, after all, a token).

If the donee is a person, name and illustrate with reasonable restraint the deeds and qualities that make him worthy of this distinction. If the recipient has been selected as a symbol of a group or as typical of many other persons, dwell not only on his excellences but on the excellences of others like him. If the recipient is an institution or organization, look especially to the principles and qualities it stands for.

Especially when the gift is a memorial, the speaker should describe the qualities of the person being commemorated, look to the reasons for his being especially worthy of memory, and mention the qualities and motives of the donor. This last sometimes involves some history of the donor, especially of his relations to the person or event being remembered, and to the donee.

Concerning the gift itself, the speaker should call attention to any special qualities that make it particularly valuable or significant. If, for example, it shows fine workmanship or if it is a rare gift, the speaker should show pride in these qualities. The qualities it symbolizes or of which it reminds one should be attached complimentarily to the person being honored. If it is intended for use, let the use seem real and appropriate to both donor and donee.

Manner of Presentation

Like the speech of introduction, the speech of presentation should seem to express the genuine sentiments of the speaker and the donor. If possible it should be spoken extemporaneously. It is better if not read from the page. Its special qualities should be clear, simple organization and felicity.

If the occasion permits, the speaker should look with satisfaction at the gift when he is speaking about it; and he should address the recipient directly and should look at him, at least when the actual, physical presentation is being made. Though on many occasions the speaker is presumed to be speaking only to the recipient, the audience is in fact a real part of the function and deserves to hear and understand. The speaker should, therefore, avoid the appearance of carrying on a private conversation with the recipient and a few persons close at hand. He should throughout speak *clearly, distinctly,* and *audibly.*

ACCEPTING A GIFT, AN AWARD, OR A MEMORIAL

In accepting a complimentary honor, a speaker will seldom offer any ideas or information unknown to the audience. He will, however, be expected not only to *feel* but to *show* appreciation. Sometimes, of course, his "speech" may consist of no more than saying "Thank you." Many situations, however, seem to call for a protraction of the process of acceptance and for gracious amplification of the speaker's appreciation so that a dignity may be infused into or maintained in the occasion and so that the audience may have time to take full satisfaction in the recipient's evident pleasure. Thus the speaker will look for proper and gracious ideas through which to convey his thanks. There are, of course, times when a speaker may genuinely exclaim, "I don't know how to thank you. I didn't deserve it." This formula, however, is shopworn and should be used with great caution. Especially should a speaker avoid introducing an obviously planned speech with the statement, "I am speechless; I can't find words with which to thank you."

Materials

On any occasion when more than a mere "Thank you" is in order, the acceptance speaker should include, in felicitous sentences, the following materials:

> Admiration, thanks, and appreciation for the gift or the honor.
> Expression of appreciation for the kindness of friends.
> Minimization, though not depreciation, of his own services or merits.
> Sharing of the honor, where it is possible, with others.

In amplifying these ideas the speaker may remark on his own experience, referring perhaps to his trials and difficulties, if he can do so without self-glorification—without featuring his personal successes. Whenever he refers to successes, he should let them appear to be attributable to the assistance he has had from other people. It is proper for him to pay tribute to others—his friends and associates. In referring to the gift, the speaker will tell what it means to him beyond its intrinsic worth or its practical use, what it inspires him to accomplish in the future, what it symbolizes with respect to his past associations and his future aspirations and ideals.

On some occasions, when the spirit of the scene is genial rather than sober or formal, the speaker may admit pleasant humor and jest into his speech of thanks. The ultimate effect of his humor must never be to depreciate the gift, himself, or the motives of the donor. Never make a jest for the sake of the jest and then try to set things right by saying, "And now to be serious for a moment. . . ." While receiving the gift, look at the person presenting it; in admiring the gift, look at it; in thanking the donor, don't ignore his presence.

Let there be no relaxing in such essential qualitites of all public utterance as *clearness, distinctness,* and *easy audibility.*

WELCOMING AN INDIVIDUAL OR A GROUP

Speeches of welcome put a premium on tact and taste in the choice of material and on grace and felicity of style and delivery.

Purpose

The purpose of a speech of welcome is to extend a sincere greeting to a person or to a group—such a greeting as offers good fellowship and hospitality. It serves the same purpose on a public occasion that a sincere greeting does between individuals, or that the opening of a door does when one is bidding a guest welcome.

Materials

The least a speaker should do in such a speech is:

> Indicate for whom he is speaking.
> Present complimentary facts about the person or group to which the courtesy is being extended.
> Predict pleasant experiences.

In all of this he should take pains to *illustrate,* not to argue.

In elaborating his address of welcome the speaker may have recourse to three general types of materials. First, it is likely that the host thinks favorably of the spirit, purposes, and accomplishments of the guest and the group or organization the guest represents. The speaker may, therefore, undertake to explain or to point up the purpose or spirit of the occasion—to declare graciously why it is appropriate and significant that the host and guest should come together under the present circumstances. This is the sort of thing most mayors try to do when welcoming to their cities the conventions or representatives of prominent organizations. Thus was the United Nations

Conference welcomed to San Francisco in April 1945, and thus was a new president of a metropolitan university welcomed by a spokesman of the Chamber of Commerce.

Secondly, the host may wish to explain or publicly to rehearse the spirit or purpose of the organization or institution extending the welcome. "This is what we are," says the speaker, "and we trust that you will find us good." Thus might the spokesman of a school or college prepare the way for a visitor from another school or college who has come to observe the operation of a well-established system of independent study for undergraduates. The speaker, however, must take care not to seem boastful or to suggest that the visitor is lucky to be allowed to observe the local wonders. If the visitor comes to impart information or to confer some favor upon the hosts, perhaps the welcoming spokesman ought to refer to the visitor's special qualifications and accomplishments. Welcoming a new director for the Boy Scout organization or the artist who is to paint the murals in the new post office might well call for material of this kind.

In the third place, and perhaps most frequently, the speaker will think it fitting to pay a tribute to the person or organization being welcomed. Dawes' tribute to the Jewish Welfare Board[2] was an example of this method. This sort of tribute is often mishandled by thoughtless or ill-prepared speakers with a weakness for generality and extravagance. The speaker should, if possible, praise the guest for specific distinctions rather than general virtues, and he should keep his praise well within the limits of plausibility.

General Characteristics of the Speech

The speech of welcome is well organized. The audience is gratified by form and progress as well as by content, is comfortably aware of where the speaker is going and how he is getting there. There is always a central theme that is serious and complimentary. There is usually a definite approach or introduction that leads gracefully to the suggestion of the main theme, and there is a conclusion, brief and dignified.

The mood of a speech of welcome is more serious and exalted (though, we hope, not more stuffy) than the mood of a speech of introduction, for on these occasions the guest himself and what he represents, rather than his speech, will be the main attraction. The mood is more dignified and more suggestive of formality. There may even be a touch of ritual in it such as the symbolic offering to the guest of the key to the city. And the mood tends to be strongly emotional. The guest expects the language of emotion; the audience demands it. The speaker must, then, get beyond casual coldness, but he must not exceed good sense by extravagance and spoil everything by gushing.

[2]J. M. O'Neill and F. K. Riley, *Contemporary Speeches* (New York, 1930), pp. 13-14.

The speech should exhibit taste and judgment. The manner and the material must fit all elements of the occasion: speaker, audience, guest, time, place, circumstances.

In spite of all the "must's," however—and there are few that good will and good sense will not dictate—there is plenty of room for individuality and originality in the speaker. Newness or freshness (not, however, "smartness") in stating old ideas, or the handling of an old topic in a novel way, provides an adequate challenge to the ingenuity of any speaker.

RESPONDING TO A WELCOME

A speech of response is basically only a speech of welcome or presentation in reverse. Hence the speaker will:

Indicate for whom he is speaking.
Express appreciation of the kindness of friends.
Speak complimentary words about the person or group extending the courtesy.
Minimize his own merits, though not depreciate them.
Anticipate pleasant experiences.

In the speech of response, as in the speech accepting a gift or award, the speaker does not, at first, have the initiative. He is following another speaker who has set the pace, so to speak, and has established the tone of the occasion. Whether the previous speaker has done poorly, has shown bad taste and little judgment, or has kept the occasion on a high level of propriety and dignity, the responding speaker dare not abruptly change the pace or tone.

Circumstances, therefore, make the speech of response often the most difficult of all speeches of courtesy because it is the hardest to prepare for and because, when you have prepared, it is impossible to be reasonably sure that what you thought of saying will fit the circumstances. In the first place, the speech of response must often be impromptu, and therefore one is tempted to be content with muttering a few general inanities and letting it go at that—like the average "thank you" letter after Christmas. Furthermore, the response may have to follow different kinds of leads, which are frequently unpredictable. One may have to respond to the presentation of a gift or token of esteem or of some mark of honor. Or one may be offered a tribute whose content, and hence the resultant position he may find himself in, cannot be foretold. And then one may be tendered a speech of welcome that cuts the bottom out from under most of what he intended to say. One may, for example, have decided to comment on the spirit, purposes, or virtues of the welcoming group, only to find them already displayed beyond his power to magnify. Or one may have elected to characterize the spirit of the occasion, only to hear the preceding speaker steal every last rumble of his thunder. This kind of speech, therefore, must be composed with the utmost sincerity and as much ingenuity as is available.

Purpose

The speech of response to welcome (with or without presentation of a token) has one purpose only, to express *appreciation.* The speaker will do well to let that purpose thoroughly dominate him and to draw his materials according to an understanding of the full implications of what it is to "appreciate." To appreciate is not merely to thank. It is to *value,* to perceive accurately the *whole worth* of a thing, to *understand.* The speaker will ask himself: Why do I value this address of welcome? this gift? this tribute? the people welcoming me? the group I represent? He will then tell his hosts and his audience.

Materials

He will generally evince his appreciation by elaborating one or more of the following themes. He will express appreciation of the significance of the occasion, what it means and will mean to him and to those whom he represents. He will pay tribute to the organization, institution, community, or persons offering the welcome. He will explain the purpose or spirit of the organization for whom he is speaking. He will, as a matter of fact, adapt to his response the same kinds of materials that might have been used in welcoming him.

General Characteristics

In form, the speech of response is much like the speech of welcome. It always has a theme. In praising the sponsoring organization, it is always possible to find some particular excellence. The speech will always have an approach and a conclusion. The special problem of the approach will be the neat and gracious fitting of the speaker's own theme into the situation left by the preceding speaker. This at times may be no small problem! The speaker must avoid the impression of ignoring, either in his manner or in the ideas he uses, the speech with which he was welcomed. Here again words may "fail," but he should not say so unless they really do. The audience expects him to talk. As a matter of fact, a speech of response is usually much longer than a speech of welcome.

It is, perhaps, useless reiteration to say that the speech must *fit* the occasion. The material must be appropriate. More, possibly, than others, this speech puts emphasis on content. Therefore the speaker must know whereof he speaks. Vagueness or plain ignorance will not serve. Blunders in taste and judgment are less likely if one is well equipped with information.

In summary, the speaker has been the recipient of formal courtesy. He must show his *appreciation* of that courtesy.

THE PUBLIC INTERVIEW

Adapting oral communication to the opportunities and demands of changing functions and circumstances and to the resources of new media such as radio, television, and electrical amplification requires some operational adjustment of the basic techniques of good public speaking. In the next chapter we offer an introduction to one of the popular and serviceable processes and forms of the present time, group discussion. Another current popular form of more properly *public* address is the public interview.

We label as *public interview* that sort of speaking situation which includes, for example, the press conference either before a live audience of reporters and observers, or before microphone and TV camera, and hence "public"; the sort of public affairs talk show put on regularly by the television and radio networks (especially on Sunday mornings), such as "Meet the Press," "Face the Nation," and "Issues and Answers"; hearings by city councils and public commissions to assess public reaction and to explain or defend policy through public interchange; and many other question-and-answer situations, from on-camera conversation with victims of flood or high food prices to the Senate committee hearings on a new Justice of the Supreme Court.

These patterns, though varying greatly in length and in other particulars, are generally familiar, perhaps so much so as to be taken for granted. On the regular, more or less formalized programs, persons of current importance or conspicuousness are questioned for half an hour or so by one or more interviewers from the news media. The subject may range widely in any given interview, depending on the matters of public interest with which the guest is known or thought to be related. The business of the interviewers is to elicit or provoke from the guest some information, interpretation, opinion, explanation, argument, defense, or evasion which might attract public interest: the Mayor of New York on revenue sharing, Ralph Nader on appropriations for the Environmental Protection Agency, Bella Abzug on the Equal Rights Amendment.

New Forms of Public Communication

Such programs help to ventilate major public issues of presumed national interest, and usually involve skilled and experienced speakers. After all, these are "award winning" nationwide shows, and the networks cannot afford to exhibit poor talent. In kind, however, they are no more than enlargements and formalizations of speaking situations that are coming to be more and more common in the experience of business and professional people, politicians and bureaucrats, labor leaders, financiers, student organizers, critics, and advocates, and all other citizens who by accident or design maintain a high profile in public. Some writers on public communication, in fact, seem to think of the "speech" as dying out of real public life even as the "oration" died out half a century ago. They seem to find the less formally structured, the more verbally interactive situations characteristic of contemporary America. Now obviously, people still do give "speeches," or at least give prepared talks, very often. We believe, therefore, that the main thrust of this textbook is not anachronistic, a thing of the past. The public "conversation" kind of speaking, what we call here the public interview, has not supplanted the speech in public communication. Obviously, though, it is particularly well suited to television and radio, and therefore much in evidence.

Adapting To The Interview

By no means does it follow that one who has learned to make effective speeches will be a good performer in the public interview—any more than it follows that an accomplished public speaker will be a fine conversationalist. Nor does it follow that for "spontaneous, unrehearsed" performance, instruction is futile, that "some can do it and some can't, and that's that." The particular forms and procedures through which public discourse is carried on vary with circumstances and functions; the principles and foundations of communication do not. Adapting the principles and practices that are the subject of most of this book to the public interview calls for only some small measure of agility and versatility. Are not the audiences before the television tube and the loudspeaker composed of the same more or less rational people who gather in the civic auditorium, the union hall, and the Sunday service? Will not their responses and their decisions be affected by a speaker using basically the same operating practice?

James A. Winans, author of one of the first and best modern textbooks on public speaking, conceived of his subject as enlarged conversation, in which the speaker, despite minimum verbal feedback from his listeners, responds to them and they to him *as if* they were conversing. The public interview very explicitly is an enlarged conversation; it is a literal conversation between interviewer and speaker; it is an enlarged conversation between speaker and audience "out there," and indirectly, between interviewer and that same audience.

Planning

The principal procedural adaptations the speechmaker will need to make for the public interview have to do with organization and delivery. Neither adaptation will be radical. In the interview the speaker is not in primary control of either the overall organization of his talk or the way it develops. To a considerable extent his questioners or interviewers determine what will be talked about and for how long. However, the speaker can determine what his idea-statements will be and how he will enlarge on them; and he can usually determine where the interview will *not* go, though he may not be able to take it where he pleases. In presentation (delivery), the interview seems superficially impromptu (see Chapter 10), as if the speaker were performing without preparation or forethought; at its best, it may show the liveliness of vigorous, unplanned conversation. Under most circumstances, however, it will resemble more clearly the extemporaneous mode of presentation, such as we have emphasized in Chapter 10 and through the rest of the book.

Delivery Is Extemporaneous

The public interview is extemporaneous in that the speaker usually knows—or can guess with reasonable confidence—what he will be expected to talk about. Hence he can prepare as he would for an extemporaneous speech. Actually, he prepares a collection of brief extemporaneous speeches on key questions of the moment. He can recall and review what he already knows and thinks. He can become familiar anew with relevant information, and he can examine positions other than his own that are likely to be explored by the interviewers or that may be preoccupying the audience. He cannot afford to be taken by surprise in a matter with which he should have been familiar.

Advance Preparation Desirable and Possible

He can formulate and organize his ideas and positions in advance so that he will be ready to take advantage of opportunities to develop the ones to his liking without having to force them into unrelated contexts. He can provide himself with a repertory of examples, comparisons, explanations, images, values, motives, and other means of amplification and development to use as the interview moves from one idea to another. He can work out beforehand, as debaters often do, units that he is reasonably sure will fit the probable subjects. Perhaps he will even rehearse these little speeches. In other words, a speaker who expects to appear in a public interview will review his general experience and knowledge as it bears on subjects of current concern, and bring himself up to date on new knowledge that may be useful. On some subjects and in certain circumstances, there may be advance agreement that certain kinds of questions will be asked and not others, certain subjects brought up and not others. After all, while an unrestricted interview may delight both the interviewer and the public, a speaker normally cannot be required to talk on subjects he does not choose to talk on. Ordinarily, and for most persons, of course, it is desirable to be as comprehensive as possible in admitting subjects to discussion.

On the radio especially there are question-and-answer programs in the form of an interview, which are really only prepared dialogue read from a typescript by the questioner and the expert. Some programs in this format may work very well, for both good scripts and poor ones may be written for instructional or dramatic purposes, and performers may be good readers or poor ones. There is much that most of us can do to develop our skill at reading aloud, an important skill for the public speaker. Most students of speaking, whether novices or not, would profit from a course in reading aloud (in the oral interpretation of literature, as the course is usually called), but that is not the *special* skill of presentation the public interview calls for.

Versatility and Adaptability Necessary

Though the mode of presentation in the public interview is, as we have said, basically extemporaneous, it incorporates some of the skills of the impromptu, which it resembles. Though the speaker has prepared himself on the subject and may have worked out answers to anticipated questions, he is unlikely to know just when, how, and in what order the questions will be asked, and what the further lines of pursuit by his questioners may be. In such speaking, therefore, adaptability and versatility in both material and language are at a premium. The student may encourage those qualities in himself by becoming thoroughly at home with useful patterns of thought—those we describe and explain, for example, in Chapter 2—and by building into his or her tactical resources the patterns of response to questions or to statements of position or idea which we listed in discussing impromptu speaking in Chapter 10. Those operational patterns can be useful to anyone involved in the public interview in whatever form, and also in other give-and-take situations requiring adaptability and presenting elements of the unforeseeable. The student would do well to memorize them for ready application. To repeat, however: That speaker will be best able to adapt and adjust to circumstances who has the confidence that comes from thinking through and talking through beforehand most aspects of the problems he will be called on to discuss.

Special Adjustments

The special adjustments, and perhaps the principal adjustments of any kind for the speaker in the public interview are those required by the physical circumstances. If the interview takes place before the television camera, the speaker must realize that his audience "out there" will see him and hear him not so much as if he were in their living room with them but as if he were in closeups on a movie screen. The speaker's facial expression and his eye contact are especially crucial. If he has a faraway look and an expression of blankness, vagueness, and indirectness, the T.V. audience will think of him as having those qualities. That is, the "conversational quality" becomes a matter of the greatest importance, and the speaker should take measures to enhance it. It is possible, obviously, to become so accustomed to the TV situation as to be comfortable and natural-seeming in it, but the inexperienced person would do well to seek suggestions from those with studio experience. If, as is usually true, there is more than one camera in use, the speaker should learn how to tell which "live" camera has him looking directly into the faces of his TV audience. Otherwise, when he should be talking directly to them, he may seem to be avoiding them and looking off into space. Those who manage the production can be very helpful, but the speaker himself must see to it that he has a lively look in his eyes and a lively tone in his voice.

Speaker and Audiences

Adjustment to the realities of multiple simultaneous audiences is a second kind of adjustment required of the good speaker in the public interview. On television the interviewed speaker always has two simultaneous audiences, and sometimes three, as with the William Buckley program. To the speaker the most obvious and pressing audience is the interviewer or interviewers. They create the occasion for his talking; they determine the direction the talk will take; they enter into either the antagonist or collaborator relationship that gives flavor to the program. They are real, and the speaker must behave as if he knew and accepted them as participants in a joint venture.

However visible and audible the questioners may be, however, they make up the secondary, not the primary, audience—the audience for whom the program is produced. If there is a studio audience, it may serve as a live surrogate for the primary TV audience and as a supplementary antagonist to the speaker or interviewers, but usually its chief function is to give the participants in the interview the sense of a real audience, which the camera and microphone cannot.

The speaker's concept of his audience and of his relation to it is always of great importance in public speaking. Toward the primary TV audience the speaker in the public interview may adopt either of two basic concepts. (1)

That the audience is *over*hearing the conversation or interview and is not being addressed in its own person by the speaker. The public interview has various dimensions; and this is the dramatic concept, in which the TV audience is in a position analogous to the audience for Shakespeare's *Julius Caesar.* It hears the public interview as the Shakespeare audience hears Antony address the Roman crowd—as a spectator to the whole transaction, not as a participant in it. (2) That the audience is a direct participant, having questions asked on its behalf, receiving the answers in its own person, and coming to its conclusions as actor, not spectator.

The way the TV cameras are managed will tend to suggest that the audience is either to *hear* or that it is to *over*hear. The speaker, however, is always addressing that audience, and he and they know it. He must always realize that though audiences (or so think the producers) seem to enjoy dramatic conflict between interviewer and "guest" (which some interviewers specialize in cultivating), his success with the audience will depend on how he conducts himself, not on how the interviewer behaves. He must show himself not only as a person in command of his ideas and his information, but one able to generate and maintain an image of fairness, integrity, and public responsibility, frequently in the face of attempts to expose his weaknesses.

The public interview, then, is a special case of the rhetorical situation, the various aspects of which we have examined in detail and in practical operating terms through many chapters of this book. The student should try to frequently observe the transaction we have been discussing. He will see in it adaptations of the basic principles and methods of responsible public discourse, and he will note the particular tactics the medium invites.

The public interview as we now observe it is probably not the ultimate form of serious public communication for the electronic world. There can be little doubt, however, that it will continue to develop, thus making possible the discussion of more and more subjects involving more and more speakers. The educational, public, and civic channels that are regular parts of cable television systems, for example, will invite increasingly broad participation, and that participation is likely to make great use of the talk show. The business of this portion of the book, therefore, is to call attention to this special kind of speaking situation, to sketch its characteristics and some techniques appropriate to it, and to emphasize how important it is for students of speaking to study the public interview and gain experience in it.

INQUIRIES

1. Recall speeches of introduction—of speakers, of visitors to the campus or city or organization, of new members of the club or community—that seemed to you to do the job pleasantly and efficiently, and others that you found inappropriate, perhaps even embarrassing to speaker and audience. Identify and list the qualities or elements that seemed to make the difference in each case.

2. Prepare a one-minute introduction of one of your classmates for his next speech to the class, and a two-minute introduction of that classmate exactly as you would prepare it if he or she were scheduled to speak on the same subject to the local Rotary Club. What important problems would you have in the one situation that would be less important in the other?

3. Observe over a period of three or four weeks one or more of the nationally televised public interview programs. Give special attention to the differing *formats*, to the techniques of *questioning* exhibited, to the presence or absence of *adversary* relationships, to the kinds and methods of *statement* and *support* characteristic of the different speakers, to the role of the television audience as the *hearer* or the *overhearer* and how that relationship seems to be indicated. Report your findings and check them against the findings of others. Make recommendations on how to use and how not to use those programs for models.

4. What elements or qualities in the speaker's presentation in a public interview tend to attract you and hold your attention? Which tend to bore you or to make you discount a speaker's message?

5. Consider the language—the choice of words, grammar, pronunciation, articulation, sentence management—of the ordinary, "educated' participant in public interviews. From your observation, draw up rules or principles of language that could be applied beneficially by your classmates to improve their performance in those situations.

FURTHER READING

Becker, Samuel L. and H. Clay Harshbarger. *Television: Techniques for Planning and Performance.* 1958.

Monroe, Alan H. and Douglas Ehninger. *Principles and Types of Speech Communication,* 7th ed. 1974, chapters 22 and 23. These chapters provide illustrative examples.

Ross, Raymond S. *Speech Communication: Fundamentals and Practice.* 2nd ed. 1970. Chapter 13, "Special Occasion Speaking."

Walters, Barbara. *How to Talk with Practically Anybody about Practically Anything.* 1970.

Wright, S.W. *Better Speech for All Occasions.* 1948.

The inclusion of speeches and portions of speeches in the preceding pages would, no doubt, have some advantages; but it seems doubtful those advantages would justify lengthening the chapter and interrupting the reading of the text. Though speeches for special purposes have certain definable requisites, each such speech is so much a product of the occasion that no one speech is truly illustrative of what another ought to be. We have chosen, therefore, to refer student and teacher to the following collections rather than to furnish a selected anthology in these pages.

Brigance, W.N. *Classified Speech Models.* 1928.
Lindgren, Homer D. *Modern Speeches.* 1926, 1930.
Modern Eloquence. 1929.
O'Neill, J.M. *Models of Speech Composition.* 1921.
————. *Modern Short Speeches.* 1924.
————, and F.K. Riley. *Contemporary Speeches,.* 1930.
Sarret, Lew, and W.T. Foster. *Modern Speeches on Basic Issues.* 1939.

CHAPTER 12

Group Discussion

Group discussion as treated in this chapter is that small-group activity in which individuals come together to talk out a mutual problem and to reach a decision. Each participant functions both as speaker and listener. More formally defined, group discussion is *a cooperative and systematic attempt by several persons through the joint use of oral discourse to reach a decision on a recognized problem, mutually satisfactory to the participants.*

Small-group activity of this sort plays a major role in contemporary society. In business, boards of directors make key decisions. In government, groups are constituted as task forces to study such matters as crime, urban renewal, and drug abuse. The Walden II Commune is governed through small group meetings. This book is probably assigned for the course because a small group was given the task of selecting a textbook.

Though the small, task-oriented group presents special problems because of its ongoing, face-to-face interaction, most of the fundamental skills already examined in this book are essential to its success. The ability to investigate, to organize, to develop and analyze argument is of prime importance. To this sort of ability new skills and concepts may usefully be added.

Group functions are the subject of extensive study in the fields of communication, psychology, and sociology, and many good books of theory and instruction are available on the subject. We list several of them at the end of the chapter. We do not, of course, profess in this chapter to treat the subject

In revising this chapter we have drawn in part upon the new chapter prepared by Vernon E. Cronen for the fifth edition of our *Fundamentals of Public Speaking* (1976).

have not, at least in their minds, defined the important terms in the same way. In many discussions of education, for example, few persons attach precise meanings to terms like *intellectual* and *cultural.* These require special definition.

Quibbling over precise definitions, however, can be deadly boring and time-consuming. Participants, particularly the leader, must decide when the group is confused because of ambiguity in terms or when further refinement of definitions is not of sufficient value to justify taking an additional amount of the total time available.

Although the normal order is from 1 to 4 through Dewey's steps, discussion members may feel the need of redefinition at any step. Discussion of possible solutions (step 4) often makes for a new awareness of some phase of the problem (step 2). Sometimes a group can give only a limited time to a particular subject and may agree to omit one or more of the steps.

Preparation for Discussion

The outline

Few people would be so naive as to expect a systematic development of any program without planning for it. The chairman or certain of the members should prepare in advance an outline that anticipates the sort of questions to be answered during the discussion.

The items should be stated as impartial questions. They should never constitute a rigid guide, but should simply suggest the type of questions to which answers are sought. Members are expected to modify, add, or eliminate items during the actual discussion if the need arises.

Each participant should receive the outline long enough in advance that he can do whatever investigation and advance thinking may be necessary for him to be a *responsible, well-informed member.* The following outline indicates the sort of planning that should be done.

Should the Federal government establish uniform driver's license requirements for all United States citizens?

CHAIRMAN'S INTRODUCTION (2-3 MINUTES)

DISCUSSION PROPER

I. What conditions involved in the licensing of drivers cause some people to believe there is a problem?
   A. How serious is the problem of highway accidents in the United States today?
      1. How many people are killed and injured each year?
      2. What is the economic cost to the nation of automobile accidents?
      3. Does the situation seem to be improving?

B. How nearly uniform are requirements for drivers' licenses throughout the nation?
   1. What are the specific requirements in certain of the states?
   2. How widely do the requirements vary?
      a. What is the earliest age at which one may receive a driver's license anywhere in the U.S.?
      b. What is the oldest any state demands that a person be before he can qualify for a driver's license?
      c. What variation is there in such other matters as the nature of written tests required, requirements to pass vision tests, requirements to pass driving tests, amount of license fee, etc.
C. Are there good reasons to believe that driving license requirements are too lax in some states?
   1. Is the number of accidents related to the laxity of driving examinations?
   2. What justifications (if any) are there for the belief that stricter licensing laws would decrease accidents?
      a. What does one's common sense decree?
      b. What do authorities say?
      c. What do available statistics reveal?
D. Are there valid reasons to believe that *uniformity* in examinations would decrease accidents?
   1. Do accidents occur because of discrepancies or variations between the regulations of various states?
   2. Are drivers confused and less efficient because of the present situation?

II. What solutions might handle present problems?
A. Would greater efforts to educate drivers be a feasible solution?
   1. Through what agencies should (could) education be given?
   2. What subjects or areas might be stressed in such a program?
B. Would a Federal law establishing minimum requirements (but not maximum) be of help?
   1. Which items might be covered by such a law?
   2. Would such a law be consistent with present relations between the Federal and State governments?
C. Could legislation be enacted that would take the power of licensing drivers from the various states and give it to the Federal government?
   1. What possible forms might this action take?
      (Congressional enactment, Constitutional amendment, etc.?)
   2. Would such a law be consistent with present relations between the Federal and State governments?
D. Can the problem be ignored or left to resolve itself?
E. What other solutions seem possible?

III. Which solution is most feasible?
A. Which solution would most effectively erase the problems previously discussed?
B. Would the solution favored create significant problems that need to be considered before the solution is approved?
C. Would the favored solution receive the support of the public and of officials?

CHAIRMAN'S (OR RECORDER'S) CONCLUDING SUMMARY

Note the form of this outline. Items are stated as complete questions. Although the approach obviously rests on Dewey's four steps, it does not follow them exactly. In this discussion, the answers to Part I would probably lead through both *awareness of the problem* (Dewey's first step) and the precise *nature of the problem* (his second step), but this order need not and should not always be followed meticulously. In the actual discussion consideration of possible solutions may at the same time determine the best solution. Other variations are frequently desirable. *The group should never feel obligated to follow the exact order, to confine itself only to items listed, or to include all matters that were thought important in the planning.* To be guided by such an outline would permit orderly procedures. Probably no important information or ideas would be overlooked.

The Chairman (Task Leader)

The successful accomplishment of a group task in discussion will depend in large measure on an effective task leader. In the first place, the emergence of a leader seems to bring increased group efficiency. Groups with leaders are likely to spend significantly more time discussing the substance of their topics and less on procedures and irrelevancies than groups without leaders, and they seem to be able to hold to particular themes longer. Leadership thus tends to extend the group's attention span.

Responsibilities

Obtaining background information on the subject. This will enable him to understand the significance and implications of contributions so that he can steer the discussion within profitable channels.

Planning the discussion outline or the agenda. The chairman may do this entirely unaided; he may share the responsibility with certain group members; or the group may hold a preliminary session simply to develop agenda. In any event, the chairman should see that an outline proposing an order of discussion is prepared and is made available to the group in advance.

Introducing the subject. This responsibility is met through the techniques set forth in Chapter 7. The chairman should get attention and orient participants and audience (if any). The suggestions offered for getting attention in the introduction to a speech apply also to a chairman's opening remarks. The orientation normally takes longer in the introduction to a discussion than it does in a speech.

Inexperienced chairmen frequently fail to realize the importance of the introduction. Certainly one would not give a thirty-minute or an hour talk without a skillful, complete introduction. The introduction to an hour of discussion should, if anything, be planned even more carefully than the opening remarks to an hour lecture. The group must be ready to start thinking.

Guiding the discussion. The chairman strives to keep the group from heading off on tangents. Whenever remarks seem to be irrelevant or off the point, he should encourage the speaker to explain how they relate to the matter of the moment. He can say tactfully, "Mr. X, will you explain how your remark relates to so-and-so?" or "Mr. X, we are considering such-and such a point. What light does your statement throw on it?"

He seeks also to keep his associates moving forward through the agenda. He is alert to opportunities to crystallize and summarize their contributions, agreements, and points of conflict so that their deliberations will be as efficient as possible.

He seeks to consolidate opinion toward a consensus to which the participants will commit themselves. When it appears that the group favors a particular proposal or decision, he may try phrasing it and ask whether there is general agreement. When it appears that agreement is not possible on a single proposal and a majority and minority division seems inevitable, he may ask a representative of each group to phrase its proposal. In terminating discussion, it is essential to crystallize opinion so that all can recognize a concrete result which no one person has provided, but in which each has had a hand.

He must meet all of his responsibilities with tact and good humor. Each participant should feel that he is important to the discussion. The chairman can encourage this feeling; at least he should do nothing to destroy it.

Maintaining his own impartiality. The leader should not take sides when differences develop among the participants. He should not take a definite stand on a controversial issue that may differ from the position taken by some participants in the group. Yet if he becomes aware of a matter that ought not be ignored, he may say, for example, "Do any of you care to express the point of view which I have sometimes heard that . . . ?" or "Jack has expressed himself very strongly. Do any of you care to take a different stand?"

Only if the chairman remains neutral will the group freely express its ideas. He must encourage participation. To do that he should remain the impartial moderator, a person willing and eager to have all views aired. It is possible, of course, that a chairman may find himself in a dilemma: if he remains impartial, the wrong decision may be made by the group; if he takes sides, he cannot remain impartial. The way out of the dilemma depends on the chairman's evaluation of the situation. Perhaps the decision to be made is sufficiently important for him to sacrifice himself as group chairman and exert his influence on the side he considers right. Only in rare circumstances, however, will he find it necessary or advisable to give up his role as the unbiased group leader.

Summarizing the collective opinion or decisions of the group. In some discussions, the chairman (or the recorder) can make a major contribution with brief summaries that pull together what has been done and said so that the group is ready to move forward in common understanding. This is an extremely important duty of the chairman, for when a group loses its way and begins to wallow, confusion and a sense of futility set in. Undirected and unguided discussions, too often the rule, are to a large extent responsible for the feeling that discussion gets nowhere. Furthermore, random discussion makes a true consensus difficult, if not impossible.

The ability to summarize concisely and accurately is not easily acquired, but it can be learned through practice. Where and when to summarize, it is impossible to say; the leader must listen attentively to the discussion and exercise his best judgment. As a rule, however, summaries should at least be employed at each of the major stages of discussion.

> It seems evident, then, that the conditions giving rise to our problem are so-and-so, so-and-so, etc. Are we ready now to see exactly what our problem is?
>
> Do we agree that our problem can be defined as so-and-so?
>
> For such-and-such a proposal, we have heard the following reasons . . . . Does anyone wish to comment further on them?
>
> Such-and-such proposals have been made. Does one of them seem to be superior? Which one is most desirable? Most practical?
>
> Such-and-such weaknesses have been urged against such-and-such a proposal. Shall we reject it?
>
> Mr. X interprets the evidence of such-and-such an argument in this way; Mr. Y in this way. Which interpretation shall we accept?
>
> We agree on these points . . . ; we seem to differ on these . . . . Can we resolve the disagreement?

The chairman (or the recorder, if one has been designated) should also summarize at the conclusion of the conference. The temptation to omit such a summary is often great. The chairman may think that anything he says will be so obvious to all as to be a waste of time; he may feel incapable of stating the exact results of the meeting; since the group has disagreed upon what he considers to be the most vital issues, he may reason that there is nothing to summarize. Yet, *in all cases a final summary should be made.* The final statements may simply list the areas upon which there has been agreement and those where the group has failed to agree, but an impartial restatement of conclusions or final convictions (or perhaps a brief review) should be considered an indispensable part of any discussion.

Because interim summaries and the final summation are essential but frequently difficult to make, and because a chairman often finds all his mental faculties needed simply to guide the discussion, the use of a *recorder* is becoming increasingly popular. The *recorder's* one responsibility is to keep a record of what has happened and to be ready at any time upon request of the chairman or the group to summarize part or all of the preceding discussion.

This eases the burden of the chairman, of course. It also provides a slightly different type of summary. *Good* chairmen assume greater prerogatives for interpreting and synthesizing in their summaries than do good recorders. The recorder is expected only to report back what the group has done.

The chairman-leader in action

The good leader respects the opinion of others and lets the participants do most of the talking. He listens closely with the attitude that the other person may well be sensible and right, may have something valuable to contribute. He enters the conversation no more than is absolutely necessary.

The leader is sensitive to the reactions and attitudes of the participants, and is well aware of both advantageous and disadvantageous group tendencies. He knows, for example, that the group situation increases the uniformity of individual judgments and tends to produce unanimous decisions. Against this tendency, a strong leader can function to protect minority opinions, and thus protect the group from jumping to hasty and unprofitable decisions. He can shield the minority from majority pressure. Sometimes a group with a pressing problem will want to rush through to a decision that seems almost self-evident at the outset of a discussion.

> The fraternity rushing rules have broken down because fraternities jump the gun by starting before the date agreed upon. Obviously we could suspend or fine the offending fraternities.

Thus might an interfraternity council conclude after ten or fifteen minutes of discussion. In such cases, a chairman might delay formal approval of the easy and obvious decision by encouraging examination of the possible weaknesses of the solution. He might say:

> We apparently approve of such-and-such a decision. But before we act finally, should we not look to the possible outcome of our decision? What are its weaknesses?

If he is fairly skillful he might lead the group to consider the weaknesses at a subsequent meeting and might even get one or two speakers to present the possible arguments against the decision. Such a procedure sometimes leads back to a reconsideration of the entire problem and to other solutions. It is the only means of testing a decision carefully before it meets the ultimate test of actual experience.

The good chairman does his best to encourage everyone to participate without penalizing those who have more to say than others. The better informed and more alert participant has more to contribute than the ill-formed and the dull individual; some know more about some aspects of a question than they do about other phases of the problem, and it is unfair to them and the group to curb them unduly. Only when all the participants are eager to speak is it wise to adopt the rule that no person may speak a second time until all have had a chance to chime in. In encouraging participation, a chairman will often encounter two extreme types of difficult members who will need special handling:

> *The long-winded speechmaker.* With him the chairman may be forced to assert his authority. He can say. "Will the speaker please conclude his remarks?" or "We have time now for only a concluding sentence from you; will you summarize briefly?"

> *The silent, reluctant soul.* He is somewhat more of a problem than the loquacious person. Sometimes he can be drawn out by a skillful question, but care must be taken not to embarrass him unduly. It is probably wise to avoid questions calling for specific information and definite knowledge, such as, "Can you supply further information on this point, Mr. *X*?" or "Does your experience suggest an illustration on this point?" He may not have the information and can only say no. Rather, prefer questions that call for his response to what has already been said, such as, "Will Mr. *Y*'s proposal accomplish the goal (or one of the goals) we have agreed upon?"

Another way the effective leader can contribute is by helping the group take advantage of what we may call *productive conflict.* Such an idea may seem to run counter to the common notion of discussion as the antithesis of debate. Yet as we have observed, one of the frequent obstacles to effective group discussion is the tendency of the more aggressive members to push for rapid consensus. Less aggressive, less powerful individuals do not speak up, though they might be able to contribute significantly if they did. Such people withdraw and give in, especially to those they see as more powerful than themselves. This tendency toward acquiescence and unanimity is especially distressing because there seems to be little or no relation between the ability of the group to reach a rapid consensus and the effectiveness of its decision. A good leader, therefore, should do more than defend the minority position from premature disposal. He should realize that conflict of ideas can be constructive. It can produce more creative solutions than comparable discussions with less conflict. Such conflict, of course, should be based on the substance of the topic and not on emotional relationships among group members. Conflict focusing on substance is one mark of a successful group conference; emotional conflict typifies the unsuccessful conference. If properly handled the exploitation of conflict will not upset the emotional state of the group. When differences are resolved in a way that yields a creative and successful solution, members find the experience more satisfying.

In order to encourage creative conflict and to use the abilities and resources of the whole group, the task leader, as we have said, should ask questions that cause the group either to reconsider its current direction or to broaden its outlook. In most situations the danger lies in the rush to consensus, not in substantive conflict. The following are kinds of remarks that prompt fruitful conflict.

> Mr. Smith has stated a possible course of action which I sense as very different from Mr. Jones's. Mr. Jones, where do yours and Mr. Smith's stands differ?

> I think the last two statements we have heard show very different conceptions of the problem. Shouldn't we try to specify and record precisely what the differences are and then speak to each of those differences?

> We have all been acknowledging the need to resolve the problem of water pollution, but I suspect from your comments that some of you regard the problem as highly pressing and others do not see the problem as so large or of such immediate impact. Let's talk about the scope and immediacy of the problem.

> [After a period of silence] Miss Simpson has stated her opinion quite clearly: that high medical costs are the result of doctors' greed. Before we pass on to another point, let's survey some other possible causes and see what information can be marshalled for alternative explanations as well as for Miss Simpson's.

The chairman is in a good position to draw out less dominant persons who may have much to offer. Thus some opinions do get stated that otherwise might not, opinions that facilitate group functioning. But reluctance to offer one's own opinions deprives the group of potentially valuable ideas.

In short, the chairman or task leader should keep the discussion as rational, informative, and productive as possible. He must train a sharp eye on argument and evidence. When the participants themselves overlook what seem to be poor reasoning and unsound evidence, the chairman should tactfully enter the discussion, not as an advocate with an axe to grind, but as a friendly critic. The student chairman in particular would do well to learn—if necessary, to memorize—the chief rules that make for sound evidence and good reasoning (see Chapters 3 and 8). He can then frame typical questions that will allow him indirectly but positively to guide the group in weighing and considering evidence and argument.

When evidence is lacking, he can say:

> You have heard Mr. X's point. Can anyone supply information (an example, data, authoritative opinion) at this point?

> Mr. X, why do you hold that view? Can you give us the reason for your statement?

That kind of question is perhaps the most valuable single query a leader can make, because it leads discussion onward and gives others a chance to criticize and evaluate.

When evidence and reasoning seem weak, the leader might ask any one of these questions:

Mr. *X* has offered a broad generalization. Do you think it is well founded?

Mr. *X* cited Professor *Y* in support of his point. How much reliance should we place on Professor *Y*'s opinion (or data)?

Mr. *X* has drawn an analogy between so-and-so and so-and-so. Do you accept the analogy as sound?

One cause giving rise to the problem before us has been stated. Are there other causes? Mr. *X* has suggested in his argument that *A* causes *B*. Is the connection sufficiently clear and direct?

Observe that in the examples above, each question is prefaced by a direct reference to what has been said, and in actual discussion the reference should specifically mention the evidence or reasoning to be evaluated. This practice contributes immeasurably to the *clarity* of discussion. The only exception to this practice of direct reference comes when a participant's remarks have been so brief or so pointed and clear that direct reference is obviously superfluous. Then the chairman can use a question alone, such as, "Is Mr. *X*'s example typical?"

Unless he has the ability to plan a discussion outline, to summarize accurately, and to sense at once whether a comment applies to the subject at hand or will lead the group onto some tangent, a person cannot fulfill his responsibilities as a chairman. Unquestionably, the abilities and the work of the group leader are tremendously important to the success of the discussion. Certainly, not everyone has sufficient inherent ability to do the task as well as it should be done. If an intelligent person is unsuccessful, however, the chances are not that he lacks the mental capacity, but rather that he is making insufficient use of his abilities.

Such capacities and qualities as we have explored perhaps suggest that the ideal discussion leader is the embodiment of the most of the social virtues —tact, fairness, tolerance, patience, broadmindedness, courtesy, a sense of humor, and quickness of wit. Unquestionably an effective discussion leader should reveal these qualities, but the student eager to learn how to participate effectively in discussion need not despair if at first he falls short of the ideal. Such qualities, like most excellences of personality, can be fostered, and practice in discussion can help to develop them.

The Participant

Most of the suggestions that we have made to guide the chairman apply with equal force to an intelligent participant in discussion. Indeed, he can sometimes come to the aid of an inexpert chairman by tactful questions such as, "Mr. Chairman, are we ready to have an expression of opinion on such-and-such a proposal?" "Can we say that our principal goal is this: . . . ?" "Is this a fair definition of our problem? . . ." He may even summarize occasionally and thus aid in unifying discussion.

In order to function with the greatest efficiency, each member of a discussion group should try to act in the following ways:

Listen attentively. As in the impromptu speech, it is what others say that stimulates a member's thought and prompts him to speak. He must be willing to listen and give others a chance to make their contributions.

Enter the discussion whenever he has a relevant remark to make or a question to ask. Any member should follow the impulse to speak when an idea prompts him. If he hesitates and leans back, he will soon find that he is willing to do nothing but listen, and the chairman, if discussion is lively, may not try to draw him out. He then becomes a liability to the group rather than an asset. He should be *alert and active.*

Make a deliberate and persistent attempt always to relate his remarks to what has been said. He should open his contribution with specific reference to the point or argument or idea he wants to explain further, add to, criticize, question, or refute. This practice gives clarity to discussion. Examples of what he might say are:

> Mr. *X* has said so-and-so. Another illustration of the same point is. . . . As to Mr. *X*'s point that . . ., Senator Fulbright said. . . . What is the meaning of so-and-so? I don't understand. (This is better than, "I don't understand that," or "What do you mean?" Neither *what* nor *that* is sufficiently specific.)

> The argument that foreign aid cements friendship seems doubtful, because. . . . (This is preferable to "That argument seems doubtful." Again the word *that* may not carry a specific reference to the hearers.)

> I agree (or cannot agree) with Mr. *X*'s statement that so-and-so is true. (This is better than "I cannot agree with Mr. *X*.")

> We have said so-and-so and so-and-so. Now I'd like to raise a different question. (This is better than "I'd like to raise a different question.")

This habit of specifically relating what one has to say to what has gone before is invaluable.

Develop the ability to organize his remarks. The suggestions we have offered earlier (pages 186-87) for the patterning of impromptu speeches are as useful for discussion and conversation as for the impromptu speech. Discussion is marked by little speeches as well as by questions and one-sentence answers.

Avoid statements and references that cause clashes of personality and that provoke stubborn, uncooperative attitudes. Members must avoid name-calling and uncomplimentary references. If you tell someone he sounds like a reactionary, a radical, a Red, a stubborn fool, a liar, an ignoramus, or a hypocrite, he is likely to resent the label. He feels he must defend *himself* with a sharp rejoinder. When this happens, discussion is diverted from the critical examination of information, arguments, and evidence and descends to personalities. A red herring is drawn across the path of discussion; such remarks provoke antagonistic attitudes, setting a tone that increases the difficulty of reaching a decision acceptable to all. The profitable use of productive conflict is impossible.

Admit the truth of well-founded criticism. This is not easy for a young, sensitive person, for once he has publicly committed himself to a position or an argument, his tendency is to defend it. Pride rushes forward saying, "This is *my* argument and if I abandon it, I shall lose face."

Develop the willingness to see a good idea, originally his, become the property of some other person or of the group. He should not insist upon everyone's acknowledging his "copyright," nor should he insist that an idea, just because it is his, must be kept constantly before the group. There is no place for strong pride of paternity in *group* discussion.

Be willing to compromise but not eager to. When participants learn that a spirit of cooperation is necessary to successful discussion, they are often too quick to compromise when they face the need of making a final decision on a proposal. The too-ready compromiser weakens the quality and progress of cooperative thinking just as surely as the diehard. As we all know, it is easier to say "yes" than "no." The antidote to hasty compromise appears to be this: Let a member stick to his proposal or his argument until others present evidence and argument that lead him to abandon or modify it. If he believes his position is well grounded, then others can be led to accept it or will be stimulated to point out weaknesses he will admit. He might say something like this:

> Mr. Chairman, I cannot agree to the proposal before us until we have further examined such-and-such a point. It seems to me, as I have previously stated, that such-and-such is sound. Am I mistaken?

By preserving the integrity of his own convictions, a participant leads—even *forces*—a group to do a better job of thinking than if he acquiesces too readily in the belief that unanimity must be secured at all costs. Sincere belief in a rational position should not be confused with obstinacy.

Conclusion

No group can solve a problem if it lacks the resources. A well-led group of six individuals with adequate preparation and background can evolve a unique integration of resources that none would have evolved on his own. A group of six *uninformed* individuals on the other hand, will simply have no resources to integrate. Early critics of group discussion referred to it contemptuously as "pooled ignorance," and with some justification, for the notion that a committee, just because it is several people instead of one, will come up with a better solution than the individual, is preposterous.

Problems also occur in groups when one member or more fails to become sufficiently well informed. When a member's performance is parasitic, when he is manifestly dependent on the information and behavior of others, the result is more conflict within the group and less constructive, task-oriented activity. Each individual, obviously, has a major obligation to be thoroughly prepared. Failure in this respect deprives the group of some of its potential resources and exposes it the possibility of disruption. Only when they include informed participants who understand the processes of group interaction can groups be significant contributors to the solution of social problems.

INQUIRIES

1. In this chapter we have been concerned with that kind of small-group communication in which the purpose is to arrive at consensus (not majority opinion or compromise) in the solution of social problems. What other functions or purposes have you observed, or can you envision, for the small-group oral interchange? How do they differ from what we have been considering? Consider, for example, the study group, the round table, the panel discussion, the bull session.

2. Formulate topics for present discussion that are worthy of the group's time. As we have said, they should be controversial, stated impartially as questions, and be capable of being profitably explored in the time available. Compare your topics with those of classmates, or try them out on your associates. Do you and others seem to agree more than you disagree on what are the important contemporary problems? What do you make of your observation?

3. Divide your class into groups and hold discussion sessions on some of the questions you have arrived at. Do not pick leaders at first, but rather let leadership emerge. Try to define the qualities and characteristics that seem to make leaders. Have the class as a whole rate the solutions agreed on by the several groups on the basis of probable effectiveness, practicability, and ingenuity.

4. Consider the current concepts of interpersonal communication, small-group (or group) communication, public (or mass) communication. Do the labels refer to essentially the same processes except for the numbers of people involved, or are there other important grounds of difference? If so, what? Do you find the concepts and distinctions useful in identifying real differences in the kinds of communication you encounter?

FURTHER READING

Abramson, Mark. *Interpersonal Accommodation.* 1966.

Bormann, Ernest G. and Nancy C. *Effective Small Group Communication.* 1972.

Brandenburg, Earnest S. and Waldo W. Braden. *Oral Decision-Making.* 1955.

Cathcart, Robert S. and Larry A. Samovar, eds. *Small Group Communication: a Reader.* 1970.

Davis, James H. *Group Performance.* 1969.

Gulley, Halbert E. *Discussion, Conference, and Group Process.* 1960.

Jacobson, Wally D. *Power and Interpersonal Relations.* 1972.

Shepherd, Clovis R. *Small Groups: Some Sociological Perspectives.* 1964.

Speeches for Analysis and Discussion

Study of the speeches collected in this chapter should serve student and instructor in at least two important ways. It should help to interest the student and in a measure to involve him or her in some of the problems and issues agitated and examined through public discussion in our times and in comparable times. It should serve also, not, of course, to provide "models" of speech composition, but to furnish practical evidence of many of the techniques, methods, and materials that competent speakers use and have used as they go about the complex business of adjusting ideas to people and people to ideas in the public arena. Not only may the student find in these speeches, ready to hand, much that he will want to try out in his own speaking, and some tactics and materials he will think it desirable to avoid; he may also, through these speeches and others, which he will study similarly, see into speechmaking as a source of historical record and as one of the significant factors in the dynamics of his society. So far as time permits, there will arise much profit from the serious application to these and comparable speeches of such methods and processes of analysis as we presented in the previous chapters.

In selecting speeches to be included in this small collection we offer only a sampling of what students may profitably study. The book market, especially the paperback market, is liberally stocked with collections of speeches and controversial materials on almost any subject of current concern. We mention a few such collections below, which are readily available to classes in public speaking. What we have attempted is to represent conveniently for classroom study kinds of speaking occasions, types of subjects, and themes and forms of speaking that an educated citizen is likely to be involved with in either his own speaking experience, his role as member of audience and responder to speaking, or his exploration as student of social-political processes. We intend this appendix, therefore, as a source of useful illustrative materials for the student speaker, and as a collection of stimulating readings.

Besides such well-known sources of speech texts as *The New York Times* and the metropolitan press in other parts of the country, the semimonthly *Vital Speeches of the Day,* the *Congressional Record,* and the comparable British *Hansard,* a good source for contemporary American speeches is the annual volume of *Representative American Speeches* in the "Reference Shelf" series of the H. W. Wilson Company of New York, collected and edited since 1971 by Waldo W. Braden.

Students interested in speeches of earlier times will find the following especially useful:

Aly, Bower and Lucile Aly (eds.) *Speeches in English.* 1968.

Bryant, Donald C., *et al.* (eds.) *An Historical Anthology of Select British Speeches.* 1967.

Graham, John (ed.) *Great American Speeches: 1898-1963.* 1970.

McBath, James and Walter Fisher (eds.) *British Public Addresses: 1828-1960.* 1971.

Parrish, Wayland M. and Marie Hochmuth [Nichols]. *American Speeches.* 1954.

Characteristic of contemporary paperback collections are:

Devlin, L. Patrick (ed.) *Contemporary Political Speaking.* 1971.

Linkugel, Wil A., R. R. Allen, and Richard L. Johannsen (eds.) *Contemporary American Speeches: A Sourcebook of Speech Forms and Principles.* 1965.

Scott, Robert L. and Wayne Brockriede (eds.) *The Rhetoric of Black Power.* 1969.

Smith, Arthur L. (ed.) *Rhetoric of Black Revolution.* 1969.

Tanner, Leslie B. (ed.) *Voices from Women's Liberation.* 1970.

Bruce Barton

Which Knew Not Joseph

Bruce Barton, when he died in 1967, was Honorary Chairman of the Board of the advertising agency Batten, Barton, Durstine and Osborn, with which he had been associated for many years. He had been an editor of two magazines and was an author of a number of books. For four years [1937-1941] he was Republican member of Congress from

By permission of the author. The text followed is that in *Modern Speeches,* rev. ed., comp. by Homer D. Lindgren (New York, 1930), pp. 358-364.

*the Seventeenth New York District. Bruce Barton is regarded as one of
the ablest business and political speakers of the 1920's and 1930's.
This speech was delivered to the Public Relations Section of the
National Electric Light Association at New York in 1923. The controlling idea of the speech may be phrased as "You must advertise persis-
tently and wisely." To the audience this message was not exactly news.
Accordingly, the speaker's task was to present the old idea in a fresh
manner and to impart new life and strength to a credo his hearers
already regarded with favor. The student should note the methods of
arousing and sustaining interest employed and should observe how
Mr. Barton handled his partisan audience.*

There are two stories—and neither of them is new—which I desire to tell you,
because they have a direct application to everyone's business. The first
concerns a member of my profession, an advertising man, who was in the
employ of a circus. It was his function to precede the circus into various
communities, distribute tickets to the editor, put up on the barns pictures of
the bearded lady and the man-eating snakes, and finally to get in touch with
the proprietor of some store and persuade him to purchase the space on
either side of the elephant for his advertisement in the parade.

Coming one day to a crossroads town our friend found that there was only
one store. The proprietor did not receive him enthusiastically. "Why should I
advertise?" he demanded. "I have been here for twenty years. There isn't a
man, woman or child around these parts that doesn't know where I am and
what I sell." The advertising man answered very promptly (because in our
business if we hesitate we are lost), and he said to the proprietor, pointing
across the street, "What is that building over there?" The proprietor
answered, "That is the Methodist Episcopal Church." The advertising man
said, "How long has that been there?" The proprietor said, "Oh, I don't
know; seventy-five years probably." "And yet," exclaimed the advertising
man, "they ring the church bell every Sunday morning."

My second story has also a religious flavor. It relates to a gentleman
named Joseph, who is now deceased.

Those of you who were brought up on the Bible may have found there
some account of his very remarkable business career. Those of you who have
not read that book may have heard of Joseph through the works of Rudyard
Kipling.

Said Mr. Kipling:

> Who shall doubt the secret hid
> Under Cheops' pyramid
> Was that the contractor did
> Cheops out of several millions.
> And that Joseph's sudden rise

To comptroller of supplies
Was a graft of monstrous size
Worked on Pharoah's swart civilians.

The account of Joseph in the Old Testament is much more complete and to his credit. It tells how he left his country under difficulties and, coming into a strange country, he arose, through his diligence, to become the principal person in the state, second only to the King. Now, gentlemen, the Biblical narrative brings us to that point—the point where Joseph had public relations with all the best paying jobs—it brings us up to the climax of his career and then it hands us an awful jolt. Without any words of preparation or explanation, it says bluntly:

And Joseph died, and there arose a new king in Egypt which knew not Joseph.

I submit, gentlemen, that this is one of the most staggering lines which has ever been written in a business biography. Here was a man so famous that everybody knew him and presto, a few people die, a few new ones are born, and *nobody* knows him. The tide of human life has moved on; the king who exalted the friends of Joseph is followed by a king who makes them slaves; all the advertising that the name "Joseph" had enjoyed in one generation is futile and of no avail, because that generation has gone.

Now what has all that to do with you? Very much indeed. When we gathered in this room this afternoon, there were in this country, in bed, sick, several thousand old men. It perhaps is indelicate for me to refer to that fact, but it is a fact, and we are grown up and we have to face these things. On those old men you gentlemen collectively have spent a considerable amount of time and a considerable amount of money. It is to be supposed that you have made some impression upon them regarding your service and your purposes and your necessities. But in this interval, while we have been sitting here, those old men have died and all your time and all your money and whatever you have built up in the way of good will in their minds—*all* your labor and investment have passed out with them.

In the same brief interval, there have been born in this country several thousand lusty boys and girls to whom you gentlemen mean no more than the Einstein theory. They do not know the difference between a Mazda lamp and a stick of Wrigley's chewing gum. Nobody has ever told them that Ivory Soap floats or that children cry for Castoria, or what sort of soap you ought to use if you want to have a skin that people would like to touch. The whole job of giving them the information they are going to need in order to form an intelligent public opinion and to exercise an intelligent influence in the community has to be started from the beginning and done over again.

So the first very simple thing that I would say to you (and it is so simple that it seems to me it ought to be said at every convention of this kind) is that this business of public relations is a very constant business, that the fact that you told your story yesterday should not lead you into the delusion of supposing that you have ever told it. There is probably no fact in the United States that is easier to impress upon people's minds than that Ivory Soap floats, and yet the manufacturers of Ivory Soap think it is not inconsistent or wasteful to spend more than a million dollars a year in repeating that truth over and over again.

Cultivating good will is a day by day and hour by hour business, gentlemen. Every day and every hour the "king" dies and there arises a new "king" to whom you and all your works mean absolutely nothing.

Now the second very simple thing which I might say to you is that in your dealings with the public, in what you write and say, you must be genuine.

When I came to New York a great many years ago I had a lot of trouble with banks. It was very hard to find any bank that would be willing to accept the very paltry weekly deposit that I wanted to make. Finally I discovered one which was not as closely guarded as the others, and I succeeded for a period of three years in being insulted by the teller every Saturday. At the end of three years when I came to draw out my money I had an audience with the vice-president who wanted personally to insult me. I said to myself, if I live and grow old in this town, some day I think I would like to take a crack at this situation.

And so as the years passed (as they have the habit of doing), and I lived and grew old, one day a bank official came in to us and said he would like to have us do some advertising for him. I said to this banker, "Now you go back to your office and shave off all the side-whiskers that there are in your bank and you take all the high hats and carry them out into the back yard of the bank and put them in a pile and light a match to the pile and burn them up, because I am going to advertise to people that you're human, and it may be a shock to have them come in and find you as you are.

So he went back to his bank and I wrote an advertisement which said:

> There is a young man in this town who is looking for a friendly bank; a bank where the officers will remember his name and where some interest will be shown when he comes in, etc.

It was very successful. It was too successful. It was so successful that we could not control it, and all over the country there broke out a perfect epidemic, a kind of measles, of "friendly banks." Bankers who had not smiled since infancy and who never had or needed an electric fan in their offices suddenly sat up and said, "Why, we are friendly."

Well, our bank dropped out. The competition was too keen. But it culminated, I think, in a letter which I saw and which was mailed by the president of a really very important bank in a large city. I won't attempt to quote it verbatim, but it was to this effect:

Dear Customer: As I sit here all alone in my office on Christmas Eve thinking of you and how much we love you, I really wish that you and every other customer could come in here personally so I could give you a good sound kiss.

Well, that is a trifle exaggerated, but the fact is this—if you don't feel these things you can't make other people feel them. Emerson said, as you will remember, "What you are thunders so loud I cannot hear what you say." Unless there is back of this desire for better public relations a real conviction, a real genuine feeling that you are in business as a matter of service, not merely as a matter of advertising service—unless there is that, then it is very dangerous, indeed, to attempt to talk to the public. For as sure as you live the public will find you out.

The third very simple thing, and the last thing that I suggest, is this: in dealing with the public the great thing is to deal with them simply, briefly, and in language that they can understand.

Two men delivered speeches about sixty years ago at Gettysburg. One man was the greatest orator of his day, and he spoke for two hours and a half, and probably nobody in the room can remember a single word that he said. The other man spoke for considerably less than five minutes, and every school child has at some time learned Lincoln's Gettysburg Address, and remembers it more or less all his life. Many prayers have been uttered in the world—many long, fine-sounding prayers—but the only prayer that any large majority of people have ever learned is the Lord's Prayer, and it is less than two hundred words long. The same thing is true of the Twenty-third Psalm, and there is hardly a Latin word in it. They are short, simple, easily understood words.

You electric light people have one difficulty. I was in Europe this spring, and I rode a great deal in taxicabs. In England I sat in a taxicab and watched the little clock go around in terms of shillings. Then I flew over to Amsterdam and watched it go around in terms of guilders. Then I went down to Brussels and it went around in terms of francs. Then I went to France and it went around in terms of francs of a different value.

I would sit there trying to divide fifteen into one hundred and multiply it by seven, and wonder just where I was getting off, and I have no doubt now that really I was transported in Europe at a very reasonable cost, but because those meters talked to me in terms that were unfamiliar I never stepped out of a taxicab without having a haunting suspicion that probably I had been "gypped."

In a degree you suffer like those taxicab men. You come to Mrs. Barton and you say, "Buy this washing machine and it will do your washing for just a few cents an hour." She says, "Isn't that wonderful!" She buys it, and at the end of the month she sits with your bill in her hands and she says, "We have runs this five hours and that will probably be so and so." Then she opens the bill and finds that she has not run it five hours; that she has run it 41 kws.

and 11 amp. and 32 volts, and that the amount is not so-and-so but it is $2.67.

Well, that is a matter that I suppose you will eventually straighten out.

Asking an advertising man to talk about advertising at a convention like this is a good deal like asking the doctor to talk about health. I have listened to many such addresses and they are all about the same. The eminent physician says, "Drink plenty of water. Stay outdoors as much as you can. Eat good food. Don't worry. Get eight hours' sleep. And if you have anything the matter with you, call a doctor."

So I say to you that there is a certain technique about this matter of dealing with the public, and if you have anything seriously the matter with you—whether it be a big advertising problem or merely a bad letterhead (and some of you have wretched letterheads)—there probably is some advertising doctor in your town who has made a business of the thing, and it may be worth your while to call him in. But in the meantime, and in this very informal and necessarily general talk, I say to you, "Be genuine, be simple, be brief; talk to people in language that they understand; and finally and most of all, be persistent." You can't expect to advertise in flush times and live on the memory of it when you are hard up. You can't expect to advertise when you are in trouble, or about to be in trouble, and expect to get anything in that direction. It is a day-by-day and hour-by-hour business. If the money that has been thrown away by people who advertised spasmodically was all gathered together it would found and endow the most wonderful home in the world for aged advertising men and their widows. Don't throw any more of that money away. If advertising is worth doing at all, it is worth doing all the time. For every day, gentlemen, the "king" dies, and there arises a new "king" who knows not Joseph.

John F. Kennedy

Inaugural Address, January 20, 1961

The late President John F. Kennedy's Inaugural Address, January 20, 1961, is one of the distinguished speeches of our time. "Its impact on Americans of both parties," wrote Life *magazine, "and on people everywhere in the world was immediate and impressive." The* New Yorker *called it such a speech as an Athenian or a Roman of the great ages of Demosthenes and Cicero could not have listened to unmoved.*

Although the Inaugural ceremony provides a formal occasion on which the American people expect the new President to set the tone for

Reprinted by permission of the White House.

the incoming Administration, no fixed pattern for the Inaugural Address has emerged over the years. Some Presidents have undertaken in considerable detail and at length to outline programs and to elaborate positions to which they wished to commit themselves and their parties. Others, like Lincoln in his Second Inaugural, have sought primarily and briefly to enunciate ideals for the country and to move their fellow citizens to renewed commitment to worthy principles and courageous action. President Kennedy's address belongs among the latter. Its appropriateness to the temper of its time and to the mood and condition of the country and of the world can hardly be in doubt.

For these reasons the address is eminently worth study. We would direct the student's attention especially to the style—to the selection and management of the language. We recommend that he study it carefully for the qualities of clarity, simplicity, appropriateness, and impressiveness which we have discussed in Chapter 9. Detailed analyses of it may be found in Chapter 23 of our Fundamentals of Public Speaking, *5th edition, 1976.*

My fellow citizens:

We observe today not a victory of party but a celebration of freedom—symbolizing an end as well as a beginning—signifying renewal as well as change. For I have sworn before you and Almighty God the same solemn oath our forebears prescribed nearly a century and three-quarters ago.

The world is very different now. For man holds in his mortal hands the power to abolish all form of human poverty and all form of human life. And yet the same revolutionary beliefs for which our forebears fought are still at issue around the globe—the belief that the rights of man come not from the generosity of the state but from the hand of God.

We dare not forget today that we are the heirs of that first revolution. Let the word go forth from this time and place, to friend and foe alike, that the torch has been passed to a new generation of Americans—born in this century, tempered by war, disciplined by a hard and bitter peace, proud of our ancient heritage—and unwilling to witness or permit the slow undoing of those human rights to which this nation has always been committed, and to which we are committed today—at home and around the world.

Let every nation know, whether it wishes us well or ill, that we shall pay any price, bear any burden, meet any hardship, support any friend, oppose any foe to assure the survival and success of liberty.

This much we pledge—and more.

To those old allies whose cultural and spiritual origins we share, we pledge the loyalty of faithful friends. United, there is little we cannot do in a host of new co-operative ventures. Divided, there is little we can do—for we dare not meet a powerful challenge at odds and split asunder.

To those new states whom we welcome to the ranks of the free, we pledge our word that one form of colonial control shall not have passed away merely to be replaced by a far more iron tyranny. We shall not always expect to find them strongly supporting our view. But we shall always hope to find them strongly supporting their own freedom—and to remember that, in the past, those who foolishly sought power by riding the back of the tiger ended up inside.

To those people in the huts and villages of half the globe struggling to break the bonds of mass misery, we pledge our best efforts to help them help themselves, for whatever period is required—not because the Communists may be doing it, not because we seek their votes, but because it is right. If a free society cannot help the many who are poor, it cannot save the few who are rich.

To our sister republics south of our border, we offer a special pledge—to convert our good words into good deeds—in a new alliance for progress—to assist free men and free governments in casting off the chains of poverty. But this peaceful revolution of hope cannot become the prey of hostile powers. Let all our neighbors know that we shall join with them to oppose aggression or subversion anywhere in the Americas. And let every other power know that this hemisphere intends to remain the master of its own house.

To that world assembly of sovereign states, the United Nations, our last best hope in an age where the instruments of war have far outpaced the instruments of peace, we renew our pledge of support—to prevent it from becoming merely a forum of invective—to strengthen its shield of the new and the weak—and to enlarge the area in which its writ may run.

Finally, to those nations who would make themselves our adversary, we offer not a pledge but a request: that both sides begin anew the quest for peace, before the dark powers of destruction unleashed by science engulf all humanity in planned or accidental self-destruction.

We dare not tempt them with weakness. For only when our arms are sufficient beyond doubt can we be certain beyond doubt that they will never be employed.

But neither can two great and powerful groups of nations take comfort from our present course—both sides overburdened by the cost of modern weapons, both rightly alarmed by the steady spread of the deadly atom, yet both racing to alter that uncertain balance of terror that stays the hand of mankind's final war.

So let us begin anew—remembering on both sides that civility is not a sign of weakness, and sincerity is always subject to proof. Let us never negotiate out of fear. But let us never fear to negotiate.

Let both sides explore what problems unite us instead of belaboring those problems which divide us.

Let both sides, for the first time, formulate serious and precise proposals for the inspection and control of arms—and bring the absolute power to destroy other nations under the absolute control of all nations..

Let both sides seek to invoke the wonders of science instead of its terrors. Together let us explore the stars, conquer the deserts, eradicate disease, tap the ocean depths and encourage the arts and commerce.

Let both sides unite to heed in all corners of the earth the command of Isaiah—to "undo the heavy burdens . . . [and] let the oppressed go free."

And if a beachhead of a co-operation may push back the jungles of suspicion, let both sides join in the next task: creating, not a new balance of power, but a new world of law, where the strong are just and the weak secure and the peace preserved.

All this will not be finished in the first one hundred days. Nor will it be finished in the first one thousand days, nor in the life of this Administration, nor even perhaps in our lifetime on this planet. But let us begin.

In your hands, my fellow citizens, more than mine, will rest the final success or failure of our course. Since this country was founded, each generation of Americans has been summoned to give testimony to its national loyalty. The graves of young Americans who answered the call to service surround the globe.

Now the trumpet summons us again—not as a call to bear arms, though arms we need—not as a call to battle, though embattled we are—but a call to bear the burden of a long twilight struggle, year in and year out, "rejoicing in hope, patient in tribulation"—a struggle against the common enemies of man: tyranny, poverty, disease, and war itself.

Can we forge against these enemies a grand global alliance, north and south, east and west, that can assure a more fruitful life for all mankind? Will you join in that historic effort?

In the long history of the world, only a few generations have been granted the role of defending freedom in its hour of maximum danger. I do not shrink from this responsibility—I welcome it. I do not believe that any of us would exchange places with any other people or any other generation. The energy, the faith, the devotion which we bring to this endeavor will light our country and all who serve it—and the glow from that fire can truly light the world.

And so, my fellow Americans: Ask not what your country can do for you— ask what you can do for your country.

My fellow citizens of the world: Ask not what America will do for you, but what together we can do for the freedom of man.

Finally, whether you are citizens of America or citizens of the world, ask of us here the same high standards of strength and sacrifice which we ask of you. With a good conscience our only sure reward, with history the final judge of our deeds, let us go forth to lead the land we love, asking His blessing and His help, but knowing that here on earth God's work must truly be our own.

Spiro T. Agnew

THOUGHTS ON BROADCAST JOURNALISM

Within a year of the beginning of his first term as Vice President, Mr. Agnew emerged as the most interesting, rhetorically the most distinctive and ingenious, and the most overtly abrasive of the spokesmen of the Nixon Administration. He undertook to ally the Nixon outlook on foreign and domestic affairs with the preferences and prejudices, the sources of confidence and those of suspicion, of the "silent majority" of "mid-Americans." A successful politician of foreign ancestry, and an Eastener (Baltimore) himself, he played effectively nevertheless upon the latent distrust or envy which much of the United States felt for the Eastern "establishment." In October 1969 he had castigated "an effete corps of impudent snobs who characterize themselves as intellectuals." In spite of indignant response from many commentators, who could see themselves being caricatured, much of Agnew's national audience might very well have responded, "I wouldn't have known how to say it, but he's right."

When, therefore, the network news analysis of the President's Vietnamization speech displeased an Administration already at odds with some elements of the press, the Vice President, before an essentially friendly and therefore appreciative audience, brought his verbal ingenuity and his acid to bear upon the networks. His Thoughts on Broadcast Journalism *constituted his address to the Midwest Republican Committee in Des Moines, Iowa, November 13, 1969. The national response was something of an uproar, "censorship" being called from one side, "irresponsibility" from the other.*

Interesting analyses of this speech may be found (1) by Martin Mayer, "The Brilliance of Spiro Agnew, in Esquire *for May 1970; and (2) by Karlyn Kohrs Campbell in her* Critiques *of Contemporary* Rhetoric, *1972.*

Tonight I want to discuss the importance of the television news medium to the American people. No nation depends more on the intelligent judgment of its citizens. No medium has a more profound influence over public opinion. Nowhere in our system are there fewer checks on vast power. So, nowhere should there be more conscientious responsibility exercised than by the news media. The question is . . . are we demanding enough of our television news presentations? . . . And, are the men of this medium demanding enough of themselves?

The text is that included in *Representative American Speeches: 1969-1970,* edited by Lester Thonssen ("The Reference Shelf Volume 42, Number 4"; 1970), pp. 60-70, where it is reprinted with permission of Mr. Agnew.

Monday night, a week ago, President Nixon delivered the most important address of his Administration, one of the most important in our decade. His subject was Vietnam. His hope was to rally the American people to see the conflict through to a lasting and just peace in the Pacific. For thirty-two minutes, he reasoned with a nation that has suffered almost a third of a million casualties in the longest war in its history.

When the President completed his address—an address that he spent weeks in preparing—his words and policies were subjected to instant analysis and querulous criticism. The audience of seventy million Americans—gathered to hear the President of the United States—was inherited by a small band of network commentators and self-appointed analysts, the *majority* of whom expressed, in one way or another, their hostility to what he had to say.

It was obvious that their minds were made up in advance. Those who recall the fumbling and groping that followed President Johnson's dramatic disclosure of his intention not to seek reelection have seen these men in a genuine state of nonpreparedness. This was not it.

One commentator twice contradicted the President's statement about the exchange of correspondence with Ho Chi Minh. Another challenged the President's abilities as a politician. A third asserted that the President was now "following the Pentagon line." Others, by the expressions on their faces, the tone of their questions, and the sarcasm of their responses, made clear their sharp disapproval.

To guarantee in advance that the President's plea for national unity would be challenged, one network trotted out Averell Harriman for the occasion. Throughout the President's address he waited in the wings. When the President concluded, Mr. Harriman recited perfectly. He attacked the Thieu government as unrepresentative; he criticized the President's speech for various deficiencies; he twice issued a call to the Senate Foreign Relations Committee to debate Vietnam once again; he stated his belief that the Vietcong or North Vietnamese did not really want a military take-over of South Vietnam; he told a little anecdote about a "very, very responsible" fellow he had met in the North Vietnamese delegation.

All in all, Mr. Harriman offered a broad range of gratuitous advice—challenging and contradicting the policies outlined by the President of the United States. Where the President had issued a call for unity, Mr. Harriman was encouraging the country not to listen to him.

A word about Mr. Harriman. For ten months he was America's chief negotiator at the Paris peace talks—a period in which the United States swapped some of the greatest military concessions in the history of warfare for an enemy agreement on the shape of a bargaining table. Like Coleridge's Ancient Mariner, Mr. Harrimen seems to be under some heavy compulsion to justify his failures to anyone who will listen. The networks have shown themselves willing to give him all the air time he desires.

Every American has a right to disagree with the President of the United States, and to express publicly that disagreement.

But the President of the United States has a right to communicate directly with the people who elected him, and the people of this country have the right to make up their own minds and form their own opinions about a presidential address without having the President's words and thoughts characterized through the prejudices of hostile critics before they can even be digested.

When Winston Churchill rallied public opinion to stay the course against Hitler's Germany, he did not have to contend with a gaggle of commentators raising doubts about whether he was reading public opinion right, or whether Britain had the stamina to see the war through. When President Kennedy rallied the nation in the Cuban missile crisis, his address to the people was not chewed over by a roundtable of critics who disparaged the course of action he had asked America to follow.

The purpose of my remarks tonight is to focus your attention on this little group of men who not only enjoy a right of instant rebuttal to every presidential address, but more importantly, wield a free hand in selecting, presenting and interpreting the great issues of our nation.

First, let us define that power. At least forty million Americans each night, it is estimated, watch the network news. Seven million of them view ABC; the remainder being divided between NBC and CBS. According to Harris polls and other studies, for millions of Americans the networks are the sole source of national and world news.

In Will Rogers' observation, what you knew was what you read in the newspaper. Today, for growing millions of Americans, it is what they see and hear on their television sets.

How is this network news determined? A small group of men, numbering perhaps no more than a dozen "anchormen," commentators and executive producers, settle upon the 20 minutes or so of film and commentary that is to reach the public. This selection is made from the 90 to 180 minutes that may be available. Their powers of choice are broad. They decide what forty to fifty million Americans will learn of the day's events in the nation and the world.

We cannot measure this power and influence by traditional democratic standards for these men can create national issues overnight. They can make or break—by their coverage and commentary—a moratorium on the war. They can elevate men from local obscurity to national prominence within a week. They can reward some politicians with national exposure and ignore others. For millions of Americans, the network reporter who covers a continuing issue, like ABM or Civil Rights, becomes in effect, the presiding judge in a national trial by jury.

It must be recognized that the networks have made important contributions to the national knowledge. Through news, documentaries and specials, they have often used their power constructively and creatively to awaken the public conscience to critical problems.

The networks made hunger and black lung disease national issues overnight. The TV networks have done what no other medium could have done in terms of dramatizing the horrors of war. The networks have tackled our most difficult social problems with a directness and immediacy that is the gift of their medium. They have focused the nation's attention on its environmental abuses . . . on pollution in the Great Lakes and the threatened ecology of the Everglades.

But it was also the networks that elevated Stokely Carmichael and George Lincoln Rockwell from obscurity to national prominence. Nor is their power confined to the substantive.

A raised eyebrow, an inflection of the voice, a caustic remak dropped in the middle of a broadcast can raise doubts in a million minds about the veracity of a public official or the wisdom of a Government policy.

One Federal Communications Commissioner considers the power of the networks to equal that of local, state and Federal governments combined. Certainly, it represents a concentration of power over American public opinion unknown in history.

What do Americans know of the men who wield this power? Of the men who produce and direct the network news—the nation knows practically nothing. Of the commentators, most Americans know little, other than that they reflect an urbane and assured presence, seemingly well informed on every important matter.

We do know that, to a man, these commentators and producers live and work in the geographical and intellectual confines of Washington, D.C., or New York City—the latter of which James Reston terms the "most unrepresentative community in the entire United States." Both communities bask in their own provincialism, their own parochialism. We can deduce that these men thus read the same newspapers, and draw their political and social views from the same sources. Worse, they talk constantly to one another, thereby providing artificial reinforcement to their shared viewpoints.

Do they allow their biases to influence the selection and presentation of the news? David Brinkley states, "objectivity is impossible to normal human behavior." Rather, he says, we should strive for "fairness."

Another anchorman on a network news show contends: "You can't expunge all your private convictions just because you sit in a seat like this and a camera starts to stare at you. . . . . I think your program has to reflect what your basic feelings are. I'll plead guilty to that."

Less than a week before the 1968 election, this same commentator charged that President Nixon's campaign commitments were no more durable than campaign balloons. He claimed that, were it not for fear of a hostile reaction, Richard Nixon would be giving into, and I quote the commentator, "his natural instinct to smash the enemy with a club or go after him with a meat ax."

Had this slander been made by one political candidate about another, it would have been dismissed by most commentators as a partisan assault. But this attack emanated from the privileged sanctuary of a network studio and therefore had the apparent dignity of an objective statement.

The American people would rightly not tolerate this kind of concentration of power in Government. Is it not fair and relevant to question its concentration in the hands of a tiny and closed fraternity of privileged men, elected by no one, and enjoying a monopoly sanctioned and licensed by Government?

The views of this fraternity do *not* represent the views of America. That is why such a great gulf existed between how the nation received the President's address—and how the networks reviewed it.

As with other American institutions, perhaps it is time that the networks were made more responsive to the views of the nation and more responsible to the people they serve.

I am not asking for government censorship or any other kind of censorship. I am asking whether a form of censorship already exists when the news that forty million Americans receive each night is determined by a handful of men responsible only to their corporate employers and filtered through a handful of commentators who admit to their own set of biases.

The questions I am raising here tonight should have been raised by others long ago. They should have been raised by those Americans who have traditionally considered the preservation of freedom of speech and freedom of the press their special provinces of responsibility and concern. They should have been raised by those Americans who share the view of the late Justice Learned Hand that "right conclusions are more likely to be gathered out of a multitude of tongues than through any kind of authoritative selection."

Advocates for the networks have claimed a first amendment right to the same unlimited freedoms held by the great newspapers of America.

The situations are not identical. Where the New York *Times* reaches 800,000 people, NBC reaches twenty times that number with its evening news. Nor can the tremendous impact of seeing television film and hearing commentary be compared with reading the printed page.

A decade ago, before the network news acquired such dominance over public opinion, Walter Lippmann spoke to the issue:

> There is an essential and radical difference [he stated] between television and printing . . . the three or four competing television stations control virtually all that can be received over the air by ordinary television sets. But, besides the mass circulation dailies, there are the weeklies, the monthlies, the out-of-town newspapers, and books. If a man does not like his newspaper, he can read another from out of town, or wait for a weekly news magazine. It is not ideal. But it is infinitely better than the situation in television. There, if a man does not like what the networks offer him, all he can do is turn them off, and listen to a phonograph.

"Networks," he stated, "which are few in number, have a virtual monopoly of a whole medium of communication." The newspapers of mass circulation have no monopoly of the medium of print.

"A virtual monopoly of a whole medium of communication" is not something a democratic people should blithely ignore.

And we are not going to cut off our television sets and listen to the phonograph because the air waves do not belong to the networks; they belong to the people.

As Justice Byron White wrote in his landmark opinion six months ago, "It is the right of the viewers and listeners, not the right of the broadcasters, which is paramount."

It is argued that this power presents no danger in the hands of those who have used it responsibly.

But as to whether or not the networks have abused the power they enjoy, let us call as our first witnesses, former Vice President Humphrey and the city of Chicago.

According to Theodore H. White, television's intercutting of the film from the streets of Chicago with the "current proceedings on the floor of the convention created the most striking and *false* political picture of 1968—the nomination of a man for the American presidency by the brutality and violence of merciless police."

If we are to believe a recent report of the House Commerce Committee, then television's presentation of the violence in the streets worked an injustice on the reputation of the Chicago police.

According to the Committee findings, one network in particular presented "a one-sided picture which in large measure exonerates the demonstrators and protesters." Film of provocations of police that was available never saw the light of the day, while the film of the police response which the protesters provoked was shown to millions.

Another network showed virtually the same scene of violence—from three separate angles—without making clear it was the same scene.

While the full report is reticent in drawing conclusions, it is not a document to inspire confidence in the fairness of the network news.

Our knowledge of the impact of network news on the national mind is far from complete. But some early returns are available. Again, we have enough information to raise serious questions about its effect on a democratic society.

Several years ago, Fred Friendly, one of the pioneers of network news, wrote that its missing ingredients were "conviction, controversy and a point of view." The networks have compensated with a vengeance.

And in the networks' endless pursuit of controversy, we should ask what is the end value . . . to enlighten or to profit? What is the end result . . . to inform or to confuse? How does the on-going exploration for more action, more excitement, more drama, serve our national search for internal peace and stability?

Gresham's law seems to be operating in the network news.

Bad news drives out good news. The irrational is more controversial than the rational. Concurrence can no longer compete with dissent. One minute of

Eldridge Cleaver is worth ten minutes of Roy Wilkins. The labor crisis settled at the negotiating table is nothing compared to the confrontation that results in a strike—or, better yet, violence along the picket line. Normality has become the nemesis of the evening news.

The upshot of all this controversy is that a narrow and distorted picture of America often emerges from the televised news. A single dramatic piece of the mosaic becomes, in the minds of millions, the whole picture. The American who relies upon television for his news might conclude that the majority of American students are embittered radicals, that the majority of black Americans feel no regard for their country; that violence and lawlessness are the rule rather than the exception, on the American campus. None of these conclusions is true.

Television may have destroyed the old stereotypes—but has it not created new ones in their place?

What has this passionate pursuit of "controversy" done to the politics of progress through logical compromise, essential to the functioning of a democratic society?

The members of Congress or the Senate who follow their principles and philosophy quietly in a spirit of compromise are unknown to many Americans—while the loudest and most extreme dissenters on every issue are known to every man in the street.

How many marches and demonstrations would we have if the marchers did not know that the ever-faithful TV cameras would be there to record their antics for the next news show.

We have heard demands that senators and congressmen and judges make known all their financial connections—so that the public will know who and what influences their decisions or votes. Strong arguments can be made for that view. But when a single commentator or producer, night after night, determines for millions of people how much of each side of a great issue they are going to see and hear; should he not first disclose his personal views on the issue as well?

In this search for excitement and controversy, has more than equal time gone to that minority of Americans who specialize in attacking the United States, its institutions and its citizens?

Tonight, I have raised questions. I have made no attempt to suggest answers. These answers must come from the media men. They are challenged to turn their critical powers on themselves. They are challenged to direct their energy, talent and conviction toward improving the quality and objectivity of news presentation. They are challenged to structure their own civic ethics to relate their great freedom with their great responsibility.

And the people of America are challenged too . . . challenged to press for responsible news presentations. The people can let the networks know that they want their news straight and objective. The people can register their complaints on bias through mail to the networks and phone calls to local stations. This is one case where the people must defend themselves . . . where the citizen—not Government—must be the reformer . . . where the consumer can be the most effective crusader.

By way of conclusion, let me say that every elected leader in the United States depends on these men of the media. Whether what I have said to you tonight will be heard and seen at all by the nation is not *my* decision; it is not *your* decision; it is *their* decision.

In tomorrow's edition of the Des Moines *Register* you will be able to read a news story detailing what I said tonight; editorial comment will be reserved for the editorial page, where it belongs. Should not the same wall of separation exist between news and comment on the nation's network?

We would never trust such power over public opinion in the hands of an elected government—it is time we questioned it in the hands of a small and unelected elite. The great networks have dominated America's airwaves for decades; the people are entitled to a full accounting of their stewardship.

Dora E. Damrin

The James Scholars and the University

Educated at Ohio Wesleyan (B.A.) and at the University of Illinois (Ph.D.), Dora E. Damrin spent five years with the Educational Testing Service at Princeton, New Jersey, where she was instrumental in developing the Medical Aptitude Test, now in wide use. For five years until her death she was Assistant Director of the James Scholar Program for superior students at Illinois. A vivid, dynamic person, she was deeply interested in education and in all kinds of students, those of normal intellect as well as those with superior abilities.

After a comforting luncheon in the University of Illinois Union Building, December 4, 1964, Dr. Damrin addressed about three hundred high school principals, teachers, university faculty and administrators who gather annually to confer on their common problem, the education of young men and women. How fared the high school student who went on to the university? Past occasions of this kind were usually marked by school and college teachers generously congratulating each other on their successes and admitting their shortcomings, if at all, in private conversations later. So there was immediate attention and some astonishment when Professor Damrin announced clearly and firmly that she proposed to concentrate on "our failures." The speech is im-

Printed by permission of Professor Robert E. Johnson, first Director of the James Scholar Program.

pressive, marked by the use of essential and telling facts, refutation of the stock excuses for poor student performance in college, specific illustration and clear characterization of the types of student failures, and a pointed plea for the kind of academic freedom she thinks talented, high-minded students want and deserve. Readers should take note of the dominant tone—intellectual and factual—and the clear undertone of accusation and indignation.

In previous talks which I have prepared for these articulation conferences I have spoken at length about the success of the James Scholar Program and its participants. Today I wish to present the other side of the coin and talk about our failures.

A strange phenomenon has been occurring since the start of the James Program in 1959. Each year we have raised and tightened our standards for admitting high school students to the Program, and each year—with only one minor exception—the percent of students who are dropped at the end of their freshman year for their failure to achieve good grades has steadily increased. Let me give you some specific data. In 1959 we admitted 137 students. This group had a mean high school rank of 93.8. By the end of their freshman year 36 percent or one out of every three students had been dropped. Last year, September 1963, we admitted 289 students. The mean high school rank for this group hit an all time high of 94.7. By the end of their freshman year 49 percent—or one out of every *two* students—had been dropped. This fall our new class of freshman numbered 473 students. The mean high school rank for *this* group was a fantastic 96.2. One out of every four of these Scholars was the valedictorian or salutatorian of his high school. One out of every two Scholars had received a letter of commendation or a finalist rating on the National Merit Scholarship Tests. Without even looking at these students' mid-semester grades I can predict with unhappy certainty that one out of three will be dropped at the end of this, their first semester, and that by the end of next semester the attrition rate will approach the 50 percent level.

From 1959 through 1961 the attrition rate for the 284 valedictorians and salutatorians in the Program was 16 percent. For the 1963 class the rate for valedictorians and salutatorians had jumped to 39 percent. These same findings hold true for Illinois State Scholarship winners, National Merit finalists, and National Merit Scholars. And so we must ask the question, "What is happening to these eminently capable and highly qualified students?" "Why is it that they are not achieving grades commensurate with their developed abilities?" As most of you know, the James Scholar needs to maintain only a B average to remain in the program—and certainly these students are *more than* qualified to do this.

When I present these data to my colleagues at the University the typical reaction is, "The kids come from small high schools." There is absolutely no evidence that this is true. The correlation of size of high school with James Scholar grades is *zero*. The University's first Rhodes Scholar in many years was a James Scholar who graduated in a class of 64 students. One of the most brilliant young women we have ever had in the program—a student who graduated as a valedictorian at the University—came from a high school class of 34 students. The pat answer of "the small high school" simply is not true.

When I present these data to high school teachers and counselors the typical reaction is, "The University grades too hard—*especially* in the honors classes which all James Scholars are required to take." This is equally untrue. Our research shows that James Scholars in good standing, as well as James Scholars who have been dropped from the honors programs for low grades, obtain significantly *higher* grades in their honors courses than they do in the regular courses taken by the average University student. The rumor that "honors courses are graded on the curve" is sheer myth.

Still another hypothesis that we have tested concerns the students' preparation for college honors work. We compared the records of Scholars who reported that they had participated in honors courses in high school with the records of Scholars who said they had *no* honors work in high school. There was no significant difference in the drop-out rate for the two groups.

In due time we turned our attention to students' attitudes and values in regard to their high school work. Many of you have participated in this research—as you will recognize when I mention the Student Record Form. This is a short, 20 item questionnaire which a teacher who is selected by the student in question completes and sends to us. Those of you who are familiar with this Form have perhaps recognized the many revisions it has undergone. This instrument presently has been developed to the point where it is more predictive of students' success in the James Scholar program than are high school rank and standardized test scores. As such it has provided us with some interesting clues about why so many of our eminently qualified high school valedictorians, salutatorians, National Merit winners, and others drop out of the program. The answer is not a very happy one—for either high school teachers or, and most especially, for University faculty members.

James scholars who make high scores on the Student Record Form are more successful than those who make low scores. What is the high-scoring student like? He is a veritable paragon of academic virtue. He is conscientious, interested, docile, well-adjusted, well-mannered. He studies hard—*regardless* of the assignment and *regardless* of his interest in it. His papers are neat and handed in on time. He thoroughly enjoys his high school work. He participates heavily in the extracurricular program of the school. In short, he is a joy to his high school teachers and later will become a joy to his college professors. He has accepted and internalized *our* values and *our* standards—

he performs as *we* wish him to perform—and from us he receives our accolade of merit, the golden A. It is practically impossible for this student to fail.

What about the students who make low scores on the Student Record Form? These students are not such paragons. In high school they subject themselves to the rules of grade-getting, they play the game, but they do this primarily for the sake of getting into the University where—they believe— they will find the freedom to develop along lines which are of interest to *them.* At the University they will be able to express themselves, they will be able to pursue fascinating subjects taught by masters, they will meet other students as enamored of "real" learning as they themselves are, in short— they will have arrived, at long last, at a place where they can be themselves.

It is precisely at this point that their academic downfall begins, because the University—like the high school—rewards only those students who conform to its rules. Disillusionment comes quickly. Having spent four years in high school conforming—consciously or unconsciously—to a set of alien values for the sake of obtaining the grades necessary for college admission, these students literally "give up" when they discover that the University—in the words of one of our drop-outs— "is nothing more than a warmed-over high school." For some students, on the order of 10 percent of each entering class, the shock is so great and the disappointment so bitter that they quit altogether, leaving the campus to take menial jobs in business and industry. The common complaint of these students is that they "can't find themselves" and our common diagnosis of their trouble is that they are "maladjusted."

The majority of the honors program drop-outs, however, remain in school and graduate often with close to the minimum grade average required, and frequently having been placed on academic probation for one or more semesters.

You will notice that the University says that "they" the students are maladjusted; it takes no part of the blame itself. Perhaps it should. You must keep clearly in mind that I am talking about a group of students who are among the brightest and most competent young people in the nation—half of whom fail to achieve at capacity level. Are all of these young people "maladjusted" or are they registering their protest against an environment which forces them, in Paul Goodman's terms, to "grow up absurd"?

This is not to say that there are no instances of severe psychological maladjustment among James Scholars, because there are. I am saying, however, that by rewarding conformity and punishing all forms of erratic behavior the University is doing nothing to mitigate these students' problems and everything to compound them. I am suggesting that the University—despite the administrative headaches it will cause—should relax some of its academic rules and should permit these students greater freedom in the pursuit of the things that interest them.

In talking and working with honors students over the past five years I have come to recognize three rather distinct types. Not all drop-outs fit into one of these categories, but enough do to make some consideration of them worthwhile. I shall describe them in turn.

First is the student I refer to as the intellectual rebel. This student has the audacity to believe that he knows more than we do about what a good education consists of. Let me give you a few cases in point.

At present I am involved in what I believe will prove to be a futile attempt to get a National Merit Scholar re-admitted to the University. As a sophomore this student was doing A and B work in college courses designed for advanced undergraduates and graduates. Even so, he found the majority of his classes boring, irrelevant, and lacking in the kind of intellectual challenge he was seeking. One day he received a B+ on a mid-semester examination for which he had not opened a book. This did it. He cut classes for the remainder of the semester, appeared for none of his final examinations, and deliberately failed himself out of the University. Now he has reached the point where he thinks he can stand us again—especially if we will let him do a lot of independent study. In his petition for re-admission he wrote, "Society requires this silly piece of paper called a diploma and I have found that I need it for what I want to do with my life." Such a statement is not one to endear this young man to the faculty. Unless he recants I doubt that he will be admitted. Honesty—for these students at least—is *never* a good policy.

Another example is a brilliant young science major who will not graduate because of his refusal to take some required laboratory courses in his curriculum. He refuses on the grounds that the courses are a waste of his time and he has too many other important things to do. He says—and truthfully— that he could gain proficiency in the courses by spending a couple of nights reading the book and that if he ever needs the lab technique he can pick it up in a week—although in his field of interest he won't ever need it anyway—so why should he bother?

Then there is the young woman who came to my office in a rage over not being permitted to take the unheard of conglomeration of courses which interested her. She said she had no intention of getting a *degree,* she wanted only an *education,* and that she was a much better judge of her needs and interests than anyone else. She said she planned to marry in two years, but that if she changed her mind she could always go back and pick up the requirements. A college dean informed her in no uncertain terms that her schedule would *not* be approved for the rather strange reason that—quote— "the University is interested only in students who really want to learn something." She conformed for one semester, then quit.

A second type of James Scholar drop-out is the social reformer. These students, when not in jail for violating the draft laws or for participating in civil rights demonstrations, give first place to "the cause" and study only when they have the time and energy. Their transcripts show a weird assortment of A's and E's, and of A's and "Absents"—indicating that on more than one occasion they did not bother to appear for a final examination. Unlike the intellectual rebel who insults and angers us, the social reformer tends to be a gentle and reasonable young person over whom we weep because of what we regard as the waste of his or her talents. But these students, convinced of the rightness of their belief, pity *us* for our ignorance and lack of social conscience. There is little communication between them and the faculty; there is a great deal between them and the administration; and administrators are notoriously unsympathetic toward such students.

The third, and perhaps most tragic, type of academic failure is the one I have termed the socially-conditioned misfit. This is the talented student who tries to break free of the social conditioning he has been subjected to during the years prior to his enrollment in the University. He is the son of a doctor who doesn't want to *become* a doctor, the daughter of a family who insists that her education must be "useful" yet who doesn't want to become a public school teacher, or the bright young man of artistic bent who has for years been conditioned to the idea that the only worthwhile career today is the career of the scientist or engineer. These students find themselves in University curricula which are anathema to them. Their lack of genuine interest in a field subtly chosen for them by others leads to mediocre or failing grades, loss of their scholarships, severe harassment from their families, and bitter disappointment in themselves.

These are the students with whom the University has the least patience. It just doesn't make sense for a boy with a college board math score in the 700's to make C's and D's in the calculus and in elementary science courses. Transferring out of the hated curriculum rarely proves to be a satisfactory solution because the student seldom has any clear idea of what he wants to do. He lacks the strength of the intellectual rebel and possesses none of the dedication of the social reformer. He is trapped in a morass of self doubt which destroys his chance for academic success in *any* field.

Now what is it that I would have the University do for the rebels, the reformers, and the misfits? It seems that we as a University should have greater faith in these, our most capable students. Give the rebels freedom, let them pursue independent work with the best teachers on the campus, forget our sacred course, curriculum, and degree requirements. Give the reformers greater support and deeper understanding—our rebuff merely drives them deeper into themselves and farther out of contact with the mature intellectual world. Have patience with the misfits, give them time to re-orient and re-establish themselves, let them keep their scholarships, bear with them during the painful process of change. Most important of all, I believe, is for us to adopt the attitude that when a James Scholar fails the fault may lie not in *his* stars but in ourselves.

Alfred E. Smith

The Cooing Dove

This speech was given by the Governor of New York in Albany on October 23, 1926, in his fourth successful campaign for the office. His Republican opponent was Ogden Mills, a man of wealth who was then Congressman from New York. Governor Smith [1873-1944], a son of "the sidewalks of New York," had held public office almost since the beginning of the century in New York City and New York State. He was distinguished by great energy, unsurpassed knowledge of the business of the state, the ability to select excellent advisors, and great skill as a popular speaker. One of his favorite expressions was "Let's look at the record," and he knew the record. What distinguishes this from the usual campaign speech, in which one deplores one's opponent's record and praises one's own, is perhaps Governor Smith's abundant and specific evidence enlivened by the deft use of a catch refrain, taken from his opponent, to give emphasis and structure to the speech.

I will take for my text tonight an extract from a speech recently made by Congressman Mills in which he said, "If I am elected Governor, I will get along with the Legislature like a cooing dove."

Let us look back a little into the history of the State and see how many Governors played the part of a cooing dove in their dealings with the Legislature; see what happened to the State when they did and when they did not.

Theodore Roosevelt did not play the part of the cooing dove. He played the part of the chief executive of the State. He laid his requests before the Legislature and backed them up with all the force and power that he could bring to his command. Had he been the cooing dove, the legislative leaders would have forced upon him the appointment of incompetent people. Had he played the part of the cooing dove, he would have sat quietly by and permitted the Legislature to defeat his proposal for the taxation of special franchises. His fight with the Legislature on that subject is a matter of State history.

Let us look into the administration of Governor Hughes. Surely, the Congressman would not hold that Governor Hughes played the part of a cooing dove. If he had, there would have been no legislation setting up the Public Service Commission and, consequently, no control over the public-utility corporations. It is a matter of history that Governor Hughes, far from playing the part of the cooing dove, went around the State and appealed to the

The text is from *Progressive Democracy*, Henry Moskowitz, ed. (New York, Harcourt, Brace and Company, 1928). Reprinted by permission of Harcourt Brace Jovanovich, Inc.

people to sustain him in his argument with the Legislature for the suppression of gambling and called extraordinary sessions of the Legislature for the purpose of compelling the Legislature to act upon his suggestion. He was not playing the part of the cooing dove when he bitterly fought both houses of the Legislature, under the control of his own party, in the interest of primary ballot reform and short ballot. He was not playing the part of the cooing dove when he called on the Senate for the removal of a man whom he deemed to be unfitted for the post of superintendent of insurance, only to be defeated by a Senate, the majority of which belonged to his own party. It was because he did not play the part of the cooing dove that the people of this State in 1910 were so thoroughly disgusted with Republican misrule in the Legislature that the State went overwhelmingly Democratic, electing not only a Democratic Governor but a Democratic Legislature in both branches.

Governor Whitman did not always play the part of the cooing dove. He did not play it when he sought to eliminate useless patronage in the various taxing departments of the State and to consolidate them into one. In this attempted reform he was defeated by the Legislature of his own party, who desired to keep the patronage in the hands of the comptroller. However, when he did play the part of the cooing dove, think of what happened to the State. While in that role, the Legislature put over the direct-settlement clause in the Compensation Law, which gave the insurance companies the power to deal directly with injured men and women; and Congressman Mills himself was the great driving force behind that amendment in the State Senate. While playing the role of the cooing dove, the Legislature succeeded in ripping and tearing apart all the great departments of the State government for patronage purposes and, not content with that, created numerous new boards and commissions for the same purpose. While Governor Whitman acted the role of the cooing dove, the Legislature destroyed the Hughes Water Power Act and made it ineffective for the purposes for which it was originally designed.

In 1919 and 1920, I was Governor. It is a matter of history that I did not play the part of a cooing dove. If I had, there would have been no amendment to the Constitution for the reorganization of the government. There would have been no rent laws for the protection of tenants threatened with dispossession during the housing shortage throughout the State. There would have been no repeal of the direct settlement clause in the Workmen's Compensation Act that was defrauding injured men and women out of half a million dollars a year, according to the report of a special commissioner appointed to investigate the whole question. Had I gotten along with the Legislature like a cooing dove, I would have written my name on the infamous Lusk Laws that questioned the devotion to this country of our great army of school teachers, and subjected our private schools to examinations for license before they could operate. Had I played the role of the cooing dove, I would have agreed to the repeal of the Direct Primary Law and I would have signed, instead of vetoing, millions of dollars of local appropriations not made in the interest of, for the benefit of, the State but made for the benefit of prominent legislators, in the localities from which they came.

Governor Miller arrived in the Capital city in 1921. He played the role of the cooing dove, and the infamous Lusk bills became law. The Labor Department was again thrown into chaos by a ripper bill intended to secure for the Republican organization the patronage of that great department. The Public Service Commission Law was amended so as to take away from localities all control over their own contracts with their public-service corporations. Governor Miller got along with the Legislature like a cooing dove, and certain members of the Legislature received large fees as a result of selling to the State the Black Lake Bridge in St. Lawrence County for $68,000, when the supervisors of the county ten years before had refused to give $18,000 for it and were sustained in the decision by the Court of Appeals. Governor Miller played the role of the cooing dove when he let the Assemblyman from Wayne County dip into the highway maintenance funds for the construction of a bridge over Great Sodus Bay against the policy of the State as defined by law. The cooing dove act was played overtime when the superintendent of public works let a contract for the construction of the power houses on the canal on a cost-plus basis, which meant that the contractor could not lose.

The Governor and the Legislature were like cooing doves in their desire to get political credit for a low appropriation bill, although to accomplish it they were compelled to neglect the known wants of the State. They neglected to make any appropriation whatever in 1922 for indemnities to the owners of slaughtered tuberculosis cattle. They made inadequate appropriation for the repair and maintenance of existing improved highways. In the interest of a so-called economy, they continued paying rental of $45,000 a year for the State Police Barracks which could have been purchased, and were afterwards, for $480,000. They purchased a piece of land adjoining the State camp at Peekskill on the installment plan, and, spread over a period of years, they were to pay $44,000 more than the land could have been purchased for in cash. They neglected to the tune of more than half a million dollars to make adequate appropriation for the repair and maintenance of the State's equipment on the canal system. They crippled the Labor Department by cutting its appropriations in half. They neglected to the sum of $710,000 to make adequate appropriation for the construction of the hydroelectric plants at Crescent Dam and Visscher's Ferry. They made absolutely no appropriation for grade-crossing removal but did, contrary to accepted custom, appropriate $175,000 for a special grade-crossing elimination in the city of Jamestown. It is impossible to escape the conclusion that this was done as a matter of local favor.

As a result of the cooing-dove performance, the hospitals of the State were neglected to such an extent that two of the hospital commissioners were compelled to resign because according to their statement, the amount of money appropriated for the care, comfort, and cure of the unfortunate insane was totally inadequate. As a result of the cooing dove performance, the appropriation for the Soldier's Memorial Hospital at Kings Park was transferred and the Memorial Hospital delayed until I returned to Albany in 1923. Had I played the role of the cooing dove for the last four years in Albany, what would have happened? There would have been no reorganization of the State government brought to a successful conclusion, after the Legislature and its Republican leaders did every human thing they could to stop it. Had I gotten along with the Legislature like a cooing dove, there would have been no rehabilitation of the Workmen's Compensation Commission and the Department of Labor. There would have been no amendments to the Medical Practice Act in the interest of the public health, because I had to fight for them for four years before they were finally written into the statute books in 1926. There would be less generous support for the public school system of the State were it not for my fight with the Legislature on the Rural School Bill, which brought about the recommendation of the legislative committee for larger quotas to the school districts of the State to provide better salaries for school teachers. If I had pursued the cooing-dove policy, nothing would have happened in the housing situation. Had I gotten along with the Legislature like a cooing dove, the Adirondack power grab would in all human probability have become law. Had I gotten along with the Legislature like a cooing dove, there would have been no automobile regulation. The Republican Assembly defeated it in 1923 and under the force of strong public opinion was compelled to enact it in 1924, but they left the State without its protection for a full year.

When the Legislature convened on the first Wednesday in January 1925, it was made apparent to the people all over the State that the leaders intended to fight. They regarded my election in the fall of 1924 by an overwhelming plurality as something of an accident. It must be fresh in the minds of the people that the Lieutenant Governor himself made the statement that I dared not leave the State. They started in before the Legislature convened in a spirit of open hostility to the executive and continued that hostility in spite of my public invitation to them to co-operate with me in the interest of the great reforms in the government for which I was fighting. Had I been a cooing dove, there would have been no tax reduction, although the platform adopted by the Republican Party at Rochester in 1924 specifically promised it. It must be fresh in the minds of everybody that the Republican leaders on Capitol Hill in the spring of 1925 fought to the death to prevent tax reduction and did it upon the senseless ground that they did not desire a Democratic Governor to have the credit for carrying out their own platform pledge.

Were it not for my vigorous stand, there would be no provision for grade-crossing elimination looking to a speedy elimination of death traps throughout the State. There would be no provision for bond issue to complete uncompleted construction and to give the State the necessary funds to rehabilitate the State hospitals and charitable institutions. This was fought, even after it passed the Legislature under the fire of well-directed public opinion, by the leaders of the Republican party throughout the State. In every Republican county it was overwhelmingly defeated. Congressman Mills and former Governor Miller, challenging me to debate it in New York and Buffalo, turned all the strength of the Republican machine against it.

Had I gotten along with the Legislature like a cooing dove, the State would have no office building and would have to wait years and years for the completion of the Teachers' College and the State Laboratory. Had I gotten along like a cooing dove in 1924, the government of this State would have cost the people upwards of eleven million dollars more as a result of pork-barrel bills passed by the Republican Assembly tending to extend the influence of the party in various sections of the State.

In 1925 we would have lost $10,826,781.04 by the same process. What has Congressman Mills to say about these figures? This is not the first time I have given them out since the campaign opened. He is strangely silent about them. All over the State he is talking the economy of the Republican party and the extravagance of Governor Smith. How does he get away from the clear fact, the figures of which can be found in the office of the comptroller, that had it not been for me in one year alone the Republican majority in the Legislature would have increased the cost of this government by more than ten million dollars, all for purposes not needed for the actual operation of the government? Until he makes some definite explanation of what I here set forth, he ought to stop talking about Republican economy. There is no such thing. They do not know what it means—and those that have any knowledge of it hate it.

One of the greatest reforms in the government of this State now pending is the executive budget. I had to fight the Republican Legislature to the death for that reform. The legislative leaders followed me all over the State making misstatements and false representations. There was no cooing-dove performance about that—if there had been, the people of the State would be denied indefinitely the benefits that will flow from its enactment into constitutional law.

In order to provide proper nursing service and number of attendants in the State hospitals, I had to use all the force that I could bring to my command to put into action the report that came from Dr. Pierce Bailey and Dr. Biggs, who said among other things that the ward-service shortage in the State hospitals was due in great part to the low wages paid by the State; and both of these eminent authorities said that if the State is to give the service it should to the unfortunate wards of the State, the salaries of the nurses and attendants should be made adequate. The work of caring for the insane requires such patience and skill that it should be sufficiently paid for. Carrying out that recommendation cost the State $1,120,000. Had I got along with the Legislature like a cooing dove, the right kind of nurses and attendants for the proper care of the unfortunate insane would not be forthcoming.

It is a matter of history, because I spoke of it at great length over the radio from the Assembly chamber, that had it not been for the vigorous fight that I put up the State of New York would be deprived of some very advantageous spots for parks and parkways. Had I pursued the role of the cooing dove, the owners of the wealthy estates on Long Island would have driven what they call the rabble of New York into the middle of the island and deprived them of the advantage to get near the water. As matters stand, they succeeded with the help of the Republican leaders in delaying, at great cost and inconvenience to the State, the fulfillment of the park program by one full year, thereby defeating the will of the people expressed by over a million majority when they voted the bonds for park purposes.

Had I played the role of the cooing dove there would have been no statutory consolidation of the scattered activities of the State pending the submission of the constitutional amendment. As it was, the Republican leaders by the brute strength of majority control in the Assembly in 1923 and 1924 and in both houses in 1925 and 1926 defeated, as they said they would, every proposal to consolidate departments when it interfered with Republican patronage.

It is known to everybody in the State of New York from Montauk Point to Niagara Falls that I am no cooing dove, and what is more I never will be. Everything I ever got in this world I had to fight for. I did not have it handed to me on a gold platter. Congressman Mills' Campaign Committee classed me with the great majority of the people in the State who had to either work or starve. The same advertisement says that Mills did not have to work. He can essay the cooing-dove role if he likes; I an unable to do it. While I am at the head of the government in this State, I will continue to fight for what I think will be in the best interests of the State and all of her people. I fought with the Congressman a year ago and licked him and all those he was able to muster to aid in his campaign. I think I am entirely within the truth when I say that it is because I have vigorously fought for the betterment of the State government, for the protection of our wards, and for the benefit of all our people that I have spent more years in the executive office than any Governor since the days of Dewitt Clinton. The people of the State of New York want clear-headed, strong-minded fighting men at the head of the government and not doves. Let the doves roost in the eaves of the Capitol—not in the Executive Chamber. So much for the doves, let us pass them up.

Booker T. Washington

Atlanta Address

Booker T. Washington, principal of the Tuskeegee Normal and Industrial Institute, Alabama, from 1881 until his death in 1915, was born a

> *Negro slave and became the leading spokesman of the Negro cause in America. Because of his position and his high reputation, he was invited to speak at the Cotton States Exposition at Atlanta, September 18, 1895. His speech on that occasion is a distinguished example of successful adaptation to a very ticklish situation. He had to gain or hold the respect of the white men and avoid offending their prejudices at the same time that he asserted the dignity and humanity of the Negro. The speech is firm but not belligerent, self-respecting but not aggressive, modest but not fawning, warning but not threatening, fair alike to the white and the Negro. The structure is marked by a refrain drawn from a highly effective but brief story. The student might consider what in the speech would be more appropriate or less appropriate today, and what in it might be received well or ill today by blacks or by whites.*

One-third of the population of the South is of the Negro race. No enterprise seeking the material, civil, or moral welfare of this section can disregard this element of our population and reach the highest success. I but convey to you, Mr. President and Directors, the sentiment of the masses of my race when I say that in no way have the value and manhood of the American Negro been more fittingly and generously recognized than by the managers of this magnificent Exposition at every stage of its progress. It is a recognition that will do more to cement the friendship of the two races than any occurrence since the dawn of our freedom.

Not only this, but the opportunity here afforded will awaken among us a new era of industrial progress. Ignorant and inexperienced, it is not strange that in the first years of our new life we began at the top instead of at the bottom; that a seat in Congress or the state legislature was more sought than real estate or industrial skill; that the political convention or stump speaking had more attractions than starting a dairy farm or truck garden.

A ship lost at sea for many days suddenly sighted a friendly vessel. From the mast of the unfortunate vessel was seen a signal. "Water, water; we die of thirst!" The answer from the friendly vessel at once came back, "Cast down your bucket where you are." A second time the signal, "Water, water; send us water!" ran up from the distressed vessel, and was answered, "Cast down your bucket where you are." And a third and fourth signal for water was answered, "Cast down your bucket where you are." The captain of the distressed vessel, at last heeding the injunction, cast down his bucket, and it came up full of fresh, sparkling water from the mouth of the Amazon River. To those of my race who depend on bettering their condition in a foreign land or who underestimate the importance of cultivating friendly relations with the Southern white man, who is their next-door neighbour, I would say:

The text is from *The Negro and the Exposition,* by Alice M. Bacon, Occasional Papers of the Trustees of the John F. Slater Fund, No. 7 (Baltimore, 1896).

"Cast down your bucket where you are"—cast it down in making friends in every manly way of the people of all races by whom we are surrounded. Cast it down in agriculture, mechanics, in commerce, in domestic service, and in the professions. And in this connection it is well to bear in mind that whatever other sins the South may be called to bear, when it comes to business, pure and simple, it is in the South that the Negro is given a man's chance in the commercial world, and in nothing is this Exposition more eloquent than in emphasizing this chance. Our greatest danger is that in the great leap from slavery to freedom we may overlook the fact that the masses of us are to live by the productions of our hands, and fail to keep in mind that we shall prosper in proportion as we learn to dignify and glorify common labour and put brains and skill into the common occupations of life; shall prosper in proportion as we learn to draw the line between the superficial and the substantial, the ornamental gewgaws of life and the useful. No race can prosper till it learns that there is as much dignity in tilling a field as in writing a poem. It is at the bottom of life we must begin, and not at the top. Nor should we permit our grievances to overshadow our opportunities.

To those of the white race who look to the incoming of those of foreign birth and strange tongue and habits for the prosperity of the South, were I permitted, I would repeat what I say to my own race, "Cast down your bucket where you are." Cast it down among the eight millions of Negroes whose habits you know, whose fidelity and love you have tested in days when to have proved treacherous meant the ruin of your firesides. Cast down your bucket among these people who have, without strikes and labour wars, tilled your fields, cleared your forests, builded your railroads and cities, brought forth treasures from the bowels of the earth, and helped make possible this magnificant representation of the progress of the South. Casting down your bucket among my people, helping and encouraging them as you are doing on these grounds, and to education of head, hand, and heart, you will find that they will buy your surplus land, make blossom the waste places in your fields, and run your factories. While doing this, you can be sure in the future, as in the past, that you and your families will be surrounded by the most patient, faithful, law-abiding, and unresentful people that the world has seen. As we have proved our loyalty to you in the past, in nursing your children, watching by the sick-bed of your mothers and fathers, and often following them with tear-dimmed eyes to their graves, so in the future, in our humble way, we shall stand by you with a devotion that no foreigner can approach, ready to lay down our lives, if need be, in defence of yours, interlacing our industrial, commercial, civil, and religious life with yours in a way that shall make the interests of both races one. In all things that are purely social we can be as separate as the fingers, yet one as the hand in all things essential to mutual progress.

There is no defence or security for any of us except in the highest intelligence and development of all. If anywhere there are efforts tending to curtail the fullest growth of the Negro, let these efforts be turned into stimulating, encouraging, and making him the most useful intelligent citizen. Effort or means so invested will pay a thousand per cent interest. These efforts will be twice blessed—"blessing him that gives and him that takes."

There is no escape, through law of man or God, from the inevitable:

> The laws of changeless justice bind
> Oppressor with oppressed;
> And close as sin and suffering joined
> We march to fate abreast.

Nearly sixteen millions of hands will aid you in pulling the load upward, or they will pull against you the load downward. We shall constitute one-third and more of the ignorance and crime of the South, or one-third its intelligence and progress; we shall contribute one-third to the business and industrial prosperity of the South, or we shall prove a veritable body of death, stagnating, depressing, retarding every effort to advance the body politic.

Gentlemen of the Exposition: As we present to you our humble effort at an exhibition of our progress, you must not expect overmuch. Starting thirty years ago with ownership here and there in a few quilts and pumpkins and chickens (gathered from miscellaneous sources), remember the path that has led from these to the inventions and production of agricultural implements, buggies, steam-engines, newspapers, books, statuary, carving, paintings, the management of drug stores and banks, has not been trodden without contact with thorns and thistles. While we take pride in what we exhibit as a result of our independent efforts, we do not for a moment forget that our part in this exhibition would fall far short of your expectations but for the constant help that has come to our educational life, not only from the Southern states, but especially from Northern philanthropists who have made their gifts a constant stream of blessing and encouragement.

The wisest among my race understand that the agitation of questions of social equality is the extremest folly, and that progress in the enjoyment of all the privileges that will come to us must be the result of severe and constant struggle rather than of artificial forcing. No race that has anything to contribute to the markets of the world is long in any degree ostracized. It is important and right that all privileges of the law be ours, but it is vastly more important that we be prepared for the exercises of these privileges. The opportunity to earn a dollar in a factory just now is worth infinitely more than the opportunity to spend a dollar in an opera house.

In conclusion, may I repeat that nothing in thirty years has given us more hope and encouragement, and drawn us so near to you of the white race, as the opportunity offered by this Exposition; and here bending, as it were, over the altar that represents the results of the struggles of your race and mine, both starting practically empty handed three decades ago, I pledge that, in your effort to work out the great and intricate problem which God has laid at the doors of the South, you shall have at all times the patient, sympathetic help of my race. Only let this be constantly in mind, that while, from representations in these buildings of the product of field, of forest, of mine, of factory, letters, and art, much good will come—yet, far above and beyond material benefits will be that higher good, that let us pray God will come, in a blotting out of sectional differences and racial animosities and suspicions, in a determination, even in the remotest corner, to administer absolute justice; in a willing obedience among all classes to the mandates of law, and in a spirit that will tolerate nothing but the highest equity in the enforcement of law. This, this, coupled with our material prosperity, will bring into our beloved South a new heaven and a new earth.

Index

A

Acceptance speeches, gift and award, 195-96
Accuracy in reading, 45
Acknowledgments, phrasing of, 59-60
Action response of audience, 6
Action words, selection of, 160-61
Actions, how to secure, 142-45
Activity language, 168
Adaptability required in public interviews, 203
Advance preparation for public interviews, 202-3; *see also* Planning
Adverbs, use of conjunctive, to keep subheads distinct, 120
Aesop, 73
Agnew, Spiro T., 236-43
Agreement, understanding vs., in group discussions, 210
Alarm
  controlling, in impromptu speeches, 185
  stage fright and, 23-26
Allen, R. R., 227
Aly, Bower, 227
Aly, Lucile, 227
American Men of Science: Physical and Biological Sciences; Social and Behavioral Sciences, 52

American Speeches (Parrish and Hochmuth), 227
Amplification, *see* Development
Analogical arguments, 150-51
Analogies, 72-73
Analysis, speeches for, 226-58
Analytical knowledge of subject matters, as material of persuasion, 129-30
Antithesis, use of, 17
Applied Science and Technology Index, 52
Appreciation expressed in response speeches, 199, 200
Appropriateness
  of examples, 70-71
  of language, 161-66
  of purpose, 102
  of subjects to speakers and audience, 33-39
Arguments, forms of, 147-54
Aristotle, 2, 15, 162, 171
Arrangement of speeches of introduction, 192
Art Index, 52
Articles, as materials resources, 49-52
Artistry in visual materials, 96
"Atlanta Address" (Washington), 160, 254-58
Attention materials used in introductions, 112-16

Index

269